P9-DEC-650

Theory in the Classroom

Theory in
the Classroom

Edited by
Cary Nelson

LIBRARY

University of Illinois Press
Urbana and Chicago

for Aaron Nelson

© 1986 by the Board of Trustees of the University of Illinois
Manufactured in the United States of America
C   5   4   3   2   1

This book is printed on acid-free paper.

Library of Congress Cataloging-in-Publication Data

Main entry under title:

Theory in the classroom.

   1. College teaching—Addresses, essays, lectures.
2. Education, Humanistic—Addresses, essays, lectures.
3. Social sciences—Study and teaching (Higher)—
Addresses, essays, lectures. I. Nelson, Cary.
LB2331.T44   1986   378′.125   85–16531
ISBN 0–252–01265–8 (alk. paper)

LB
2331
.T44
1986

Contents

Preface

Theory in the Classroom is a collection of new essays. Several of the contributors—Grossberg, Penley, Schroeder, Treichler, and I—held joint appointments in the University of Illinois's Unit for Criticism and Interpretive Theory at the time these essays were written. We have all participated in the unit's jointly taught graduate seminars in theory and in a biweekly faculty seminar in theory that has met continuously since 1977. This has produced an unusually heterogeneous and collaborative setting for teaching that is reflected in a number of the essays.

Several people made suggestions that were very helpful in revising the book. I want in particular to thank Lawrence Grossberg, Wallace Martin, Andrew Ross, Paula Treichler, and Richard Wheeler.

Some of the work in this collection grew out of a 1983 summer institute and conference organized by the Unit for Criticism and Interpretive Theory. Support for this project was provided by the National Endowment for the Humanities and by a number of campus units, including the School of Humanities, the College of Liberal Arts and Sciences, the George A. Miller Committee, the Research Board, the College of Communications, International Programs and Services, Women's Resources and Services, the School of Social Sciences, and a large number of academic departments.

Finally, I should explain that all the essays are documented in footnotes except for Treichler's, where we felt the large number of references would be more accessible (and more useful to writers and teachers) in the form of an alphabetical list.

CARY NELSON

Introduction

Viewed from an uneasy distance—perhaps with fear and loathing, since indifference may now be impossible to sustain—the rapid theorizing of the humanities and social sciences in the last twenty years may seem a single, unified, almost willed event. Indeed the essays included in this collection, emphasizing the humanities but with implications for interpretive writing and teaching in the social sciences as well, do reveal common concerns and a related commitment to self-scrutiny. Yet the essays are diverse and even at odds in their viewpoints. They are all devoted to rethinking their theoretical assumptions and the nature of interpretation, to making scholarly and pedagogical practices reflective and self-critical, but they are also devoted to very different notions of what self-consciousness and interpretation are. In their similarities and differences they create a map of the current critical scene, tracking, with unusual specificity, its place and reception in the classroom.

Although the individual writers did not, for the most part, aim for this effect, the essays here may be taken as implicitly commenting on one another's positions. In part this reflects their temporal proximity and their involvement in related problems, but it also points to a unique feature of current critical theory—its grounding in internal debate and the marking of multiple differences. It may help give us a sense of what these essays aim to accomplish if we take note of how interpretive practice has changed since the 1960s. Fifteen years ago an essay like A. D. Hutter's "Literature, Writing, and Psychoanalysis: A Reciprocity of Influence" would have been grounded almost exclusively in an opposition to antipsychoanalytic positions and by a defense of its own potential. Now differences within psychoanalysis and between different pedagogical contexts are given equal emphasis. Constance Penley's "Teaching in Your Sleep: Feminism and Psychoanalysis" could not have assumed that readers would even consider the relations between feminism and psychoanalysis a useful subject. Paula A. Treichler's "Teaching Feminist Theory" would have been devoted to defending a feminist practice, asserting its theoretical and pedagogical unity, and marking feminism's others. Now the multiple discourses of feminism both within and outside the classroom can be demarcated, alongside feminism's relations to more traditional scholarship. Vincent B. Leitch's "Deconstruction and Pedagogy" would either have defended its place within a humanistic tradition or claimed a decisive difference from it; now its claim is for a difference only by way of its reflections on its own implication in classroom structures and institutional power. S. P. Mohanty's "Radical Teaching, Radical Theory: The Ambiguous Politics of Meaning" would have been secure in its liberation from mere textuality; now it seeks to incorporate into its own practice the tradition of skeptical close textual analysis whose limitations it describes. Susan Wells's "Jürgen Habermas, Communicative Competence, and the Teaching of Technical Discourse" and Lawrence Grossberg's "Teaching the Popular" would have been constructed as arguments for the right of their respective objects of interpretation to exist within serious fields of study; now they offer their own domains as revisions of the theories they draw on and criticize. Finally, William Schroeder's "A Teachable Theory of Interpretation" would have offered itself as the unfolding of a secure consensus, rejecting only the sort of complacently positivist historicism that imagines its analyses transcend the problematics of interpretation. Of course all these essays are still partly constituted by naming a rejected other (Hutter's, for example, differentiates acceptable and unacceptable versions of psychoanalysis by way of their respective commitments to testing theory against therapeutic practice), but they are also equally involved in many more complex differentiations—variously deferential, collaborative, corrective, debunking, and coopting. It is here that they comment implicitly on each others' enterprises.

The opening essay, by Schroeder, takes what may seem, in part, a fairly traditional position—that textual meaning is decidable and that interpretive disagreements are generally adjudicable. Yet the essay gets its sense of necessity from what is actually an utterly heterodox position—that we have very few examples of full interpretations available to us. Since many of us can feel almost suffocated by the history of interpretation surrounding certain texts, this will be a surprising claim. It leads Schroeder to map out a detailed system not only for evaluating interpretation but also for doing and teaching interpretation, a system radically at odds with both poststructuralism and liberal pluralism, at odds as well with many of the other essays in this collection. Schroeder presents a communal, collaborative pedagogy, in which students and teacher together critique and modify an evolving model. From the perspective of Penley's essay, however, Schroeder's classroom may seem instead to be a discipline demanding complete identification with the instructor's superego.

At the other end of the spectrum from Schroeder, but with some points of political connection with Penley, Leitch argues that meaning is not only inherently or textually determined but is also controlled and delimited by interpretive practices. He urges that we become conscious of the politics of the production of meaning and recommends the liberating virtue of maintaining multiple meanings in conflict with one another, rather than seeking the authority of a single reading. Mohanty would agree that interpretation is always political, never innocent, never purely textual, but he would argue the need to specify political effects and to choose among political strategies; diversity for him would not in itself be a virtue. Grossberg takes a complex and rather different position, arguing that meaning is established by particular audiences, who use texts according to their needs and social positioning. Meaning for Grossberg becomes radically contingent; in effect, it can be evoked but never decisively established. In implicit opposition to Schroeder, he describes his method as "unteachable," which is not actually to say that he cannot teach his method but rather that the method needs to be constructed anew for different contexts and that the interpretive process can never be completed or fully mastered. For Schoeder, a text can have a meaning which, though difficult to come by, might finally be established for all time. For Grossberg, texts can always be given new meanings by new groups. Such a collective process of rereading culture from a different perspective and giving texts meanings they have been prevented from having in the past is one way of describing Treichler's project in "Teaching Feminist Theory." If Treichler is recounting the ambitious rereading and reterritorializing of all texts, Wells is trying for the first time to treat as communicatively and intersubjectively meaningful texts that have hitherto been considered purely instrumental.

As these comments suggest, the declared subject matter of each of these essays is in many ways an occasion for taking a general position on the nature of theory, interpretation, and pedagogy. Though all the essays claim their application is limited to specific fields, readers will note that each has much wider implications. The gentle mutual clarification and progressive correction demonstrated in Hutter's description of the interchanges between the literary study of narrative and the study of narrativity in clinical settings serves also as a brief for the much wider adoption of his humanistic pedagogical model. Similarly, but with less idealistic aims, Penley's effort to bring psychoanalysis and feminism into a mutually critical dialectic suggests that all theory should be taught that way. Treichler's detailed analysis of the aims and difficulties of feminist pedagogy serves equally as a challenge to all university teaching. Grossberg's analysis of popular culture implicitly argues that the meaning of the most treasured aesthetic texts is also altogether a construction of its particular audiences. Wells by extension attacks the attribution of simple instrumentality in any cultural field. Schroeder's construction of the underlying logical structure of interpretive evidence can, for the most part, be applied far beyond the narrative arts to which he limits himself. The critiques of the politics of knowledge mounted by Leitch and Mohanty would have their equivalents in every part of the university curriculum.

Somewhat surprisingly, until very recently there has been very little writing devoted to the relations between recent theory and pedagogical practice. Recent books by Gregory Ulmer and Robert Scholes, along with the present collection, suggest increasing need to consider the connections and implicit tensions between theoretical and pedagogical practices. Nonetheless, the relative silence through much of the 1970s and 1980s on these issues needs some comment. If the need were merely for advice about how to teach difficult theoretical positions, it would not be surprising that people involved in articulating theory have not chosen to write about teaching. Yet, as these essays demonstrate, the relations are considerably more complex than that. Are some theoretical positions at odds with conventional teaching practices? What role do students have in articulating theory? Does the classroom exert a significant pressure toward changing theoretical positions? What happens to an interpretive practice in making it teachable? What is the relationship between a class devoted to studying theory and the rest of a student's training in a discipline?

These questions are not necessitated by the prevalence of theory alone. The theoretical activity in American humanities disciplines in the 1960s did not, for the most part, force this more charged relation between theory and pedagogy. Negotiations between theory and teaching were then more often mutually supportive and even symbiotic. Students proved willing to adopt codified modes of analysis that gave them relative power within an easily accessible discursive space; without much special historical knowledge they could speak and write about texts and social practices, thereby obtaining mastery over the objects of interpretation and rough equality with their instructors. Faculty members, on the other hand, could depend on a productive interchange between teaching and research; classroom analyses could be revised and expanded for publication. On a deeper level, students and teachers found it possible simultaneously to intensify and contain their experience of complex objects and practices. In the process, the "application" of theory to specific objects could serve, synecdochically, as a secure way of structuring and producing the significance of the whole phenomenal world.

So long as different bodies of theory remained self-contained and relatively unreflective about their assumptions and practices, this pattern could persist. But with the move from structuralism and semiotics to poststructuralism and deconstruction, with the rise of a self-critical Marxism in direct dialogue with other bodies of theory, and with the extraordinary growth of feminist theories in contest with traditional disciplines, the relation between theory and classroom practice changed radically. For these newer theories are not constituted as a series of interpretive vocabularies that can easily be detached from their discursive contexts and applied to other texts. Theoretical work often undermines the very categories it offers for our consideration. Its commitment is not to the technology of interpretation but to various forms of writing, not to schematic and easily teachable methodologies but to complex discursive practices. Moreover, much recent theory is concerned with the political effect of its writing practices. That is not to say that one cannot find useful interpretive strategies in the newer theory but rather to say that such an effort, if it is an exclusive one, is appropriately located within the discursive space of a disciplinary pedagogy, within its reactive territoriality, rather than within theory itself.

The classroom had been one of the major sites that disciplines used to naturalize difference and otherness, to domesticate theory and assimilate its questions to practical considerations about the production of disciplinary discourse. Now the classroom was becoming, on the one hand, a site from which to challenge the untheorized reaches of traditional disciplines, and, on the other hand, an embarrassment to theory. The latter point has several explanations. First, the classroom itself was largely an untheorized site, except by way of the 1960s politics that could not be sustained without an overriding sense of historical crisis and opportunity. Second, the newer textually based theory was notoriously difficult to teach, since it resists summary, translation, and codification. Teaching it could often seem a form of comic betrayal. Pedagogy, in this context, seemed better left unthought. Yet we were faced with the possibility that teaching and professional writing would be two unrelated or even antagonistic activities, with an outmoded certainty reigning in the classroom and doubt and intellectual play reigning in our writing. Writing would be aimed, in effect, at challenging the very values and ideology the classroom continued to serve.

Given the ideological and economic pressure placed on the classroom both by academic disciplines and by the society at large, it is perhaps not surprising that it has remained largely untheorized. Indeed, pedagogical writing is rife with the most grandiose species of idealization. I would not want to claim that these essays (or, for that matter, any essays) lack their own constitutive idealizations. Yet there is a recurrent will to self-reflection here, one that, however discontinuous and precoded, makes these essays a significant advance over most of what is available elsewhere. Moreover, their differences, which evoke not a happy pluralism but the competitive stresses in contemporary theory, help to highlight each other's limitations.

Both directly and indirectly these questions receive a good deal of attention here. The results, I believe, prove both challenging and original. It is often claimed, for example, that students lead teachers to reevaluate their positions. Most often, however, teachers have a relatively trivial kind of change in mind, such as a class discussion that leads to a new reading of a poem or the acceptance of a new motivation for social behavior; that hardly represents a significant change in a teacher's basic assumptions. The changes at work in these essays are rather more dramatic; their relation to the classroom, however, varies considerably. Several people in the collection have worked to theorize their students' needs and have altered their own practices as a result; others feel compelled to resist their students' assumptions, but as a result their theoretical positions are grounded in a counterreaction.

Grossberg develops his interpretive theory in response to student resistance to his readings of popular culture. Schroeder develops a position demanding a level of precision and a sequential, logical presentation of evidence that extends pedagogical clarity to the entire practice of interpretation. After analyzing the resistances to knowledge structured both into institutionalized American psychoanalysis and into a feminism that rejects psychoanalytic categories—resistances that students often come to her classes to confirm—Penley recommends that psychoanalysis and feminism urge each other toward a more fully critical self-awareness. Treichler reinforces the current plurality of feminisms by describing the needs and positions of very different student populations; the feminist theory classroom becomes a microcosm of the hopes and stresses of feminist theory as a whole. Partly as a result, she is led to make a radical demand of feminist theory—that it must be articulated to the needs and interests of different populations of women—that most bodies of theory would find incomprehensible or intolerable. Wells uses recent theory to challenge the typically unreflective, intellectually-debased pedagogy of a whole field. Yet despite her sharp critique of the ideology of technical writing, she remains sensitive to her students' needs and tries to answer them with a self-reflective technical discourse. Finally, in different ways, most of these essays are concerned with the institutional constitution of pedagogical practices.

We all know, I believe, that it is important to teach recent theory, but we also know that it is often nearly impossible to do so. These essays will be of considerable help there, in part because they often give theoretical weight to pedagogical conflicts, a more realistic and intellectually productive approach than the blatant idealization more typical of pedagogical writing. Indeed, I expect that many readers will want to distribute them to their classes. With that end in mind, the authors have all made a special effort to write clearly, thereby overturning one habitual distinction between the discourses of theory and pedagogy. This collection, however, takes a significant further step: it suggests that the scene of pedagogy is a necessary part of theoretical rigor.

Theory in the Classroom

CARY NELSON

Problematizing Interpretation: Some Opening Questions

1. What is an interpretation? What are its material and argumentative limits? What are the aims of interpretation?

2. Why do we interpret? Can we speak of a will to interpret, a need to interpret, a desire to interpret, a fear of interpreting?

3. Do interpreters seek power over the objects they interpret? Over other interpreters?

4. To what extent do texts themselves control, solicit, and limit our interpretations?

5. Does interpretive writing differ from the kind of interpretation we do continually in the rest of our lives?

6. Are the objects or social practices we interpret themselves interpretations of other, prior objects and social practices? Of life? What is the relation between our interpretations and the interpreting they do?

7. Are some interpretations better than others? How do we decide? Can interpretations be adjudicated? Is it a matter of taste? A matter of politics?

8. What leads you to change your interpretation of a work? Can you describe the experience?

9. What is involved in negotiating your way through a variety of interpretive positions so as to define and establish your own?

10. Do deliberate or unintended misinterpretations have value? Are interpretations typically overstated?

11. How do you describe what an interpretation does?

12. Can interpretations be summarized, translated?

13. Are interpretations themselves like translations?

14. Can a theory of interpretation be summarized?

15. Does an individual's subjectivity determine how or what he or she interprets? In what way? To what degree? Does the act of interpretation itself determine subjectivity?

16. Is it possible to read a text or experience an object without interpreting it?

17. How might we describe or understand the relationship between the initial perception and experience of an object and a written interpretation?

18. How does our understanding of a text or object change as we write a full interpretation of it?

19. Are some things more worthy of interpretation than others?

20. Can *anything* be interpreted?

21. Can one account for the experience of a text or object that seems uninterpretable?

22. Can one define the general nature of all objects of interpretation? Is there a single unified theory that can account, simultaneously, for texts, objects, events, and actions?

23. Is interpretation a methodological question or a question of human nature?

24. Should anything be ruled out of particular kinds of interpretation?

25. Can a full and complete interpretation deal with more than one text, one historical event, or one social practice? Can an interpretation of one Dickens novel, one Balinese cockfight, fully account for another?

26. Can an entire genre be interpreted?

27. Can there be a general theory of interpretation or only regional theories—that is, for cinema, narrative, specific societies?

28. We often argue that a text or a culture needs in part to be described, analyzed, or evaluated in its own terms. To what degree is it desirable to enter into a dialogue with an interpretation on *its* own terms?

29. Does it matter that the author of a text, the participants in a social practice, might be quite unable to comprehend the terms in which we describe and analyze their work?

30. How is difference (sexual, racial, class, national identity) inscribed in interpretation?

31. Does evidence exist within interpretation? In what sense can interpretations be proven?

32. Is there such a thing as a complete interpretation? How would you know? What would the criteria for completeness be?

33. Is any genuine communication possible between an interpreter and an artist or a society distant in time?

34. How long do interpretations continue to have influence? Does it matter?

35. Should interpretations be believing or sceptical in their attitudes toward the objects they interpret?

36. How does a hermeneutics of faith deal with a text it finds abhorrent?

37. Is interpretation better focussed on the observable facts of texts or social practices—their surfaces, as some would argue—or on their deeper meaning? How do we move between these levels? Is this model useful?

38. Can interpretation plausibly focus on what is not present in or what is excluded from a text or social practice? Can such absences be considered structural or determining? Is this still interpretation?

39. Are there hierarchical relationships between different modes of interpretation—description, explanation, understanding, evaluation? Can these moments be differentiated?

40. Is evaluation of or commentary on an interpretation anything more than another interpretation?

41. Is all writing interpretation?

42. Can an interpretation ever overcome the distance between itself and the object it interprets?

43. Does true interpretation depend on an emptying out or negation of the self?

44. Is interpretation bound to identify with, adopt, or defend a text's ideology?

45. To what degree do interpretive communities, disciplinary conventions, control the nature of interpretations?

46. Is interpretation in any sense economically motivated or determined?

47. Are interpretive positions and conclusions historically and culturally specific? Are they historically, sociologically, and politically determined?

48. Can we specify the conditions that make possible the emergence of a particular interpretation?

49. How do interpretations that claim to limit themselves to aesthetic or historical issues also communicate and advocate specific value systems?

50. How are theory and practice related in interpretive writing? Are they separable?

51. Do interpretations speak differently to (and establish different kinds of relationships with) the texts they interpret and other interpretations?

52. Does an interpreter communicate to us as an individual in interpretive writing? Do interpretations have a "voice"?

53. Do we interpret so as to gain an understanding of an author's intention? Do we treat the aims or accomplishments of artistic works as the intentions of individuals even when we do not intend to do so?

54. If a work exists in more than one version, does any version typically have priority? The first? The last? The best? Do the same answers apply to interpretations existing in more than one version?

55. Can a work be perceived in such a way that it is free of, independent of, all interpretation?

56. Are some interpretations more theoretical than others? More philosophical? More self-reflexive? More political? Are there any interpretations that cannot be analyzed in these terms?

57. Is evaluation necessarily a part of interpretation?

58. Do interpretations have aesthetic qualities of their own?

59. In what sense can interpretations be original?

60. Is there a decisive difference, any difference, between interpretation and creation?

61. To what extent is the practice of interpretation mimetic?

62. Are interpretations performances?

63. Do interpretations always have political consequences?

64. Is the history of interpretation progressive? Are our interpretations better than those of earlier periods?

65. What is the use, appeal, or intrinsic worth of an interpretation with which you disagree?

66. Does (should?) interpretation follow a certain logical sequence? Explicitly? Implicitly?

67. Is interpretation preeminently a form of knowledge?

68. Do interpretations aim to communicate?

69. Do interpretations assume that texts aim to communicate?

70. Do interpretations implicitly posit a concrete audience for a text?

71. Could a history of interpretation be written? What should its object and focus be? Who should write it? How long might it last?

72. Can you formulate a psychology of interpretation? An ethics? A theology? A politics?

73. Does this list (or any of the questions) have an implicit ethics, theology, or politics?

74. What role does the classroom, teaching, play in the development and writing of interpretations?

75. What libidinal investments are involved in interpreting a text, negotiating a theoretical position?

76. How would you change these questions?

77. Reread this list of questions, applying them specifically to the scene of pedagogy. Do your answers change?

78. Would this list of questions have any use in the classroom?

79. What sort of text is this list? Obsessional? Playful? What is its structure? Linear? Circular? Metonymic?

WILLIAM R. SCHROEDER

A Teachable Theory
of Interpretation

To fully understand a theory, one must grasp the problem it seeks to solve. The traditional problem to which theories of interpretation have sought to respond is the plurality of interpretations. One school seeks to transcend this plurality by using the author's intention to establish the correct interpretation.[1] Another contends that this plurality is unavoidable because the historical situation limits the perspective of any interpreter.[2] Instead of eliminating the plurality, this school seeks to explain it.[3] Although the theory presented here can be located within these traditional disputes, it is better understood as addressing a different problem and thus pursuing a new goal.[4] The paucity, not the plurality, of bona fide interpretations is its guiding problem; its goal is effective strategies for producing genuine interpretations. To some the fields of criticism may seem overrun by interpretations, but to me instances of genuine interpretation seem all too rare. Though contemporary critics are prolific, engaged in many different, important projects, and more widely cognizant of other disciplines relevant to criticism, they rarely attempt genuine interpretations—full syntheses of the elements of texts and careful formulations of their implications. Instead of a gourmet's feast, we have only a beggar's breakfast.

Two aims can function as standards with which to evaluate the present theory. First, it seeks to elucidate some of our shared intuitions about interpretation; this is its *descriptive* component. Second, it seeks to defend a new ideal of criticism; this is its *prescriptive* component. Thus, though this theory builds on our current intuitions, it aspires toward something richer and more ambitious. Although other critical projects are important, I shall

9

show that interpretation (as I construe it) has a special claim on our attention and that the defensiveness imposed on interpreters by the current critical ambiance is unwarranted.

My theory is a local rather than a global theory; it seeks principles and evaluative criteria relevant to the interpretation of a restricted set of objects (narrative literature and film and drama) rather than general guidelines for interpreting any object.[5] Its principles may not apply to the interpretation of collective actions, historical eras, or other arts; those regions may require different treatment. In addition, the primary target of this theory is *individual works*, not larger literary unities (genres, oeuvres) or trends. Local theories are more useful than global ones, in my opinion, for two reasons. First, global theories are often extremely abstract and therefore less helpful in concrete interpretive work. Furthermore, a global theory is only as good as the local theories it implies. Hence, I prefer to develop strong local theories and work gradually toward a global position. Second, local theories can be more effectively tested against experience. Their flaws are more readily identified, and refinements suggested by interpretive experience are more easily incorporated into them.

Because I seek to create a new interpretive community, teaching the theory effectively is important. One supporting argument for my approach is that it engenders a distinctive attitude in students; it awakens dormant interests and invites serious collective work. It also engenders a respect for the text, an openness to criticism, and a sense of responsibility for offering criticism. In the second part of this essay, I shall elaborate these remarks and indicate some teaching strategies designed to help students master this interpretive approach. The theory itself is presented in three sections: first, the nature of interpretation is examined; then, the process of interpretation is explained; finally, some evaluative criteria are discussed.

I. A Theory of Interpretation

The Nature of Interpretation

An interpretation of a narrative text is a series of hypotheses that coherently explain the organization and elements of the text and that thereby elucidate the text's thematic implications.[6] The 'elements' which these hypotheses must explain range from character selection and development to experienced effects, from imagery to allusions and external horizons, from the functions of the narrative viewpoint to the world constituted by the text, and from asserted statements to the shape, motivation, and outcomes of the plot. The 'hypotheses' are interwoven statements of various degrees of generality which explicate the implicit significance of the text by synthesizing the complex relations among these elements. Many such explanations are possible, but few will capture the full range of sensitive readers' responses. Better hypotheses satisfy formal criteria (e.g., consistency and completeness) as well as articulate and enrich the reading or viewing experience.

By using words like *hypothesis* and *explain* in this definition, I underline some important affinities between doing science and constructing interpretations. First, both activities are governed by methodological and substantive paradigms. Scientists are guided by standard modes of experimentation and existing theories; interpreters are guided by prevailing procedures of analysis and larger discursive unities like genres and oeuvres.[7] Second, data and theory are partially interdependent in both forms of inquiry. New readings (like new theories) can uncover new textual elements (data), and recalcitrant elements (data) demand and suggest revised readings (theories). Third, good work in both areas combines sensitivity to the phenomena and imaginative theoretical leaps; insightful interpreters (theorists) master the tensions between these opposing demands.[8] Fourth, though tradition guides both activities, new developments in other fields may stimulate new readings (theories). New hypotheses rarely emerge accidentally; they often arise as responses to problems discovered in previous readings (theories) or to new perspectives developed in other fields of research. Fifth, commitment to a reading (theory) is provisional and depends on many factors, e.g., the degree of integration it achieves, the problems it resolves, its formal elegance, and its capacity to illuminate experience. Finally, both forms of inquiry appeal to the confirmation of other serious investigators. Though powerful readings (like good theories) do not always win immediate adherence, sustained indifference to them by those familiar with the text (area) is often tantamount to their rejection.

Yet science and the interpretation of narrative texts also exhibit important differences. One concerns the range of data that the respective "explanations" must cover. A scientific theory which

11

explained data from only one experiment would be unhelpful, and an interpretation which applied to many different texts would be too abstract.[9] While an interpretation is meant to account only for the particular elements of the text it addresses, a scientific theory must account for a variety of data in many contexts—past, present, and future. The scientist seeks a general theory that will cover many phenomena, but an interpreter seeks to account for only one text. Thus, the specific elements of a text generally are far more important to the interpreter than the particular details of situations typically are to the scientist. Also, the elements to be 'explained' in a narrative work are finite (though, in practice, difficult to completely enumerate), whereas in science the events to be explained are infinite.

A second difference concerns the relationship of the explanation to the investigator's antecedent intuitions. Interpretation is partially guided by an inarticulate experience of the text to which it gives form. One test of a reading is whether it has rendered these intuitions perspicuously. The data observed by the scientist contain fewer intrinsic clues to the theory which might account for them. Though the scientist is guided by expectations concerning the type of theory likely to be appropriate (usually on the basis of theoretical work in adjacent areas), the data are far less suggestive in themselves. Thus, while the experience of theorizing in science is frequently one of imposing a structure on diffuse data, the experience of interpretation often involves articulating something already implicitly intuited.[10]

Interpretation can also be distinguished from three other activities commonly applied to literature, drama, and narrative film: description, evaluation, and analysis. *Descriptions* of narrative texts often recapitulate the story; this is a standard practice of reviewers. Descriptions may also attempt to clarify the precise aesthetic qualities of the text. In either case, no effort is made to synthesize the text's elements or to establish their significance. At best, descriptions yield data for which interpretations must account. *Evaluations* assess the quality of a text along some dimension, e.g., cognitive, moral, political, aesthetic. One can interpret a text without evaluating it, and one can evaluate a text without doing a full interpretation of it. To interpret is to determine the text's *meaning;* to evaluate, its *values.*[11] Though they are different procedures, interpretation and evaluation can have pragmatic relationships. For example, interpreting a text is a necessary condition for determining its *cognitive* value, and few people would voluntarily interpret a text which they did not appreciate. Despite these relations, the procedures are distinct, and a theory of interpretation need not say anything at all about the evaluation of texts.[12] An *analysis* clarifies the various elements of a text, but it neither determines their significance nor integrates them into a coherent account. The latter processes constitute interpretation per se. Interpretation does, however, require an insightful analysis on which to build. Analysis is thus the first step toward interpretation, but not a sufficient condition for it. In the next section analysis will be examined in greater detail.

This theory of interpretation offers an intermediate position between two extreme hermeneutic schools: the authorial intention theory and radical pluralism. The authorial intention theory holds that the text has a single, determinate meaning, viz., the author's intention in writing the words. The primary motivation for this position is to provide a definitive criterion for validating interpretations: an interpretation is correct if and only if it accords with the author's intended meaning.[13] Radical pluralism asserts that any reader's response to a text is a legitimate interpretation of it. It extends the intuition that texts may have more than one plausible reading to its logical extreme. By accepting the validity of all interpretations, it eliminates the possibility of misinterpretation. My position generates criteria for validating interpretations without appealing to the author's intention. It privileges neither the author's actual intention nor his own statement or knowledge of his intention. It allows that several readings could satisfy the criteria equally well; in such circumstances there would be several legitimate readings. Nevertheless, the stringency of the criteria insures that many readings will fail to pass muster; these are rejected as inadequate. My theory promulgates an attitude toward confirming interpretations that resembles the one scientists adopt toward confirming their theories. Though there are cases in which two theories are equally adequate accounts of the data or in which some considerations support one theory while others support another, often there will be one theory that seems to be the most promising account at a given time. But the presumption is that it may at any point be superseded.

Most critics do not take radical pluralism seriously largely because it denies the possibility of misreading. Some critics embrace a less extreme version of pluralism; they adopt a playful approach to the text, explicating its diverse effects and celebrating the manifold ways in which it might be read.[14] No doubt this approach is a healthy antidote to the monomania of the authorial intention theory, and no doubt it provides a broad sense of the possible directions to pursue while interpreting. Yet this position neglects integration and vitiates the importance of testing interpretations against an experience of the text as a whole. Though it suggests possible interpretive hypotheses and encourages appreciation of individual elements, it refuses to provide a coherent, integrative reading and thus avoids the risks of disconfirmation. The ultimate issue between this kind of pluralist and me concerns the value of interpretation as I construe it, and this issue will be further examined below.

The authorial intention theory seems to be gaining currency again; hence it may be worth restating the central objections to it.[15] First, the author's intention may be inadequately realized, and even if it is perfectly realized, his own knowledge of it may be inadequate. The actual meaning of the text may thus differ from the intended meaning or from the author's statement of it. Hence, in order to comprehend the actual meaning, thorough examination of the text will be necessary even if one knows the author's intention. The author's diaries and interviews, notoriously unreliable in any case, will be at best of secondary importance.

Second, this theory treats a narrative text like an utterance in a specific context, like a message communicated from one person to another. But literature requires a seriousness and care that is not usually afforded in everyday speech situations: its meanings are richer and less explicit; its effects are more powerful and less direct; and the kind of interpretation it demands is more reflective and systematic than that required by everyday utterances. Moreover, even if the author has a specific purpose in writing (e.g., to seduce someone), the text's meaning may far exceed the limits of these purposes. To treat a text like an utterance is to restrict its significance too severely.[16]

Third, the experience of writing suggests that texts have some degree of autonomy. That authors must abide by the text's demands—despite their current or original intentions—suggests that often textual meaning is not wholly a function of their desires and plans. Texts have their own logic to which authors must conform. Even if they initiate the original patterns, these often develop in unexpected ways and limit plausible options; they also may carry meanings unforeseen by their authors. Moreover, authors often discover the text's implications only in the process of writing. Their comprehension of the text is not unlike the reader's; they discover new connections while writing (and rewriting) just as the reader discovers them while reading (and rereading). The author's conception of the text may change as often as the reader's preliminary interpretation.

Fourth, many critics believe that studying the author's variants of a text will help clarify the text's meaning. But the significant variants of a text are *different* texts and thus have different meanings. Insofar as envisioning alternatives to a text facilitates understanding its specific meanings, then many variants (including the author's) should be canvassed, and the meanings of each should be distinguished from the text at hand.[17] The author's variants have no special value in this process.

Finally, the text's actual meaning may differ markedly from the author's professed *beliefs* because he may be exploring alternatives to his beliefs when writing a particular text. There is thus no reason to privilege the author's actual beliefs or his statements of intention when interpreting his text. His reading will be the most adequate one only if it best satisfies the criteria any serious reading must satisfy.

These arguments show that the author's intended meaning—supposing one can discover it—is not necessarily the best interpretation of the text, the best elucidation of the text's meaning. But they do not show that seeking the author's meaning is a fruitless or unintelligible enterprise. Indeed, there may be reasons for concentrating on the author's meaning rather than on textual meaning, e.g., when one's primary task is reconstructing the author's psychology or his intellectual or artistic development. Knowing the author's intention may also be useful in evaluating the text. Uncovering it will require extensive research into the author's journals, correspondence, private papers, and interviews and possibly into the recollections of friends and confidants. The thrust of my arguments is that such secondary research will not necessarily facilitate one's comprehension of the meaning of the text. The time spent on such research will be better spent on the processes of interpretation if one seeks the fullest comprehension of the text.[18]

Someone might claim that my position postulates an omniscient author; i.e., that it interprets a text *as if* all of its elements were intended by such an author.[19] Partisans of the authorial intention theory might then try to reduce my position to a variation of theirs.[20] This attempt would fail. Though I acknowledge the fact of authorship, my theory does not depend on an appeal to the author.[21] The importance of consistency, coherence, completeness, etc., derives as much from the nature of literature and interpretation as from the organizing operations of the author. Incoherent or otherwise disconnected texts may not warrant interpretation even if they are meticulously authored. Critical approaches that seek neither coherence nor completeness, valuable and legitimate though they may be, simply differ from interpretation. If one is not guided by such criteria, one is not doing interpretation. To be sure, the fact that texts are authored can support such criteria, but *if* one were to *interpret* phenomena that lacked determinate authorship, the same rules would apply.[22] So an appeal to the author is not essential. This theory of interpretation is an alternative to, not a variation of, the authorial intention theory. The author's intended meaning is neither the *only* legitimate meaning nor always even *a* legitimate meaning of the text.

Interpretation has now been defined and distinguished from other forms of inquiry, and my theory has been contrasted with some alternatives.[23] Before examining the criteria for evaluating interpretations, I shall examine the process of producing them.

The Process of Interpretation

Interpretation requires two skills: analysis and synthesis. The analysis must be insightful and complete, and the synthesis must be effective and illuminating. In practice the two processes interweave: analysis is guided by a preliminary integrative vision, which is modified and concretized as the analysis proceeds; and new features uncovered by analysis will often suggest alternative integrative visions, which must then be thoroughly tested. Analysis typically will reveal the text's important *themes*. But many levels of synthesis are required to articulate the text's *theses*, the implicit assertions it makes about those themes.[24] The need to determine theses makes interpretation a challenging enterprise.

Formulating regional theses is one useful tool for fashioning interpretations. A 'region' is a distinct thematic area. Isolating and integrating all the data relevant to one region allows one to generate possible regional theses more easily and then to determine the most promising formulation more effectively. Once some plausible regional theses have been established, the terms and outlines of a full interpretation can be created. The interpretation's organizing principles are related to regional theses as regional theses are related to the elements of the text. The same integrative thinking produces regional theses and organizing principles. Regional theses relate the details of a text to the more abstract organizing principles that summarize the interpretation. This intermediate level facilitates both the testing of broad hypotheses through deduction and the gradual integration of diverse elements through comparison and generalization. There can sometimes be several levels of regional theses in a single interpretation.

To determine a regional thesis, one must first assemble the textual elements relevant to a particular theme and then discern the patterns that inform these elements. A full analysis of a text explicates at least eight general types of elements.[25] I will describe each briefly and indicate its use in formulating regional theses.

1. *Explicit Statements.* Statements uttered by characters or narrators that have overtones which transcend the context of utterance are *explicit statements*. Their synoptic character often compels special attention. They must nevertheless be considered carefully when one interprets. The context of utterance, the outcome of the plot, and the relation of other textual elements to them affect their significance. Explicit statements are not always *asserted* by the text. Often they are qualified, questioned, or transformed by it. Only if the entire text supports an explicit statement can one accept it as an asserted statement. Asserted statements often constitute regional theses.

2. *Imagery.* An image is an object, setting, or trait which gains special significance through repetition or by occupying a pivotal role in the narrative. The various occurrences of an image as well as its inherent properties must be studied before a reason-

able hypothesis about its significance can be formulated. Once a plausible reading of an image is discovered, it can be conjoined with other elements to yield regional hypotheses.

3. *Narrative Point of View.* Novels are always narrated by someone, and the film camera sometimes functions like a narrator.[26] To understand the implications of the narrator's viewpoint, one must answer questions like: How often and under what conditions does the narrator submerge into a character? What is the spatio-temporal relation between the narrator and the events recounted? How reliable is the narrator and on what sorts of qualities does he focus? These questions provide clues to the position that the narrator creates for the reader. They may also indicate important qualifications of the status of particular characters and events.

4. *Plot/Action.* The plot or action is the structure which organizes the story's episodes. An episode is a set of events closely related in time and place. (Sometimes the external structure of a text—chapters, scenes, or sequences—will divide the plot into its relevant episodes.) Episodes of a story can be organized in different ways (e.g., progressive, alternating, interwoven, layered asides), and they can have different degrees of autonomy. The meaning of the text is often integrally related to the shape of the plot. For example, whether the events are comic or tragic often depends on the outcome of the plot, and the significance of any single action is often related to that of parallel actions with which it can be compared.

5. *Characters.* Characters perform the actions or undergo the events which constitute the plot. A full analysis of the characters should consider character selection and contrast, development and universalization, and the degrees and kind of influence they have on the action. A text may elaborate a psychology or an anthropology through its presentation of the characters, or it may suggest a theory of history by relating them to social contexts in a distinctive fashion. It may also offer a theory of discourse through the characters' speeches or explore the relation between ideals and action through their responses to events. All the aspects of the treatment of the characters must be weighed carefully before deciding that a text is actually addressing one of these areas.

6. *Notable Effects.* Texts influence readers in many ways—emotional, volitional, attitudinal, and intellectual. Analysis seeks

18

to specify the effects which would be experienced by any sensitive reader. These effects often provide clues to the text's themes. For example, a text which continuously violates the reader's sensibility may be about such violation, or a text which induces laughter may address the conditions of the comic. Such effects may also underline other elements of a text (a speech, a character, an action, an image), and they can carry important independent significance.

7. *Horizons.* Horizons are contexts which may clarify the significance of particular textual elements or events. Horizons may be internal or external: they are internal if they are directly suggested by the text (e.g., allusions), and external if imposed by the interpreter. When classical symbols, myths, names, works of art, or texts are mentioned in the text, then these references may suggest additional, implicit meanings when compared with the text at hand. External horizons situate the text in a relevant series, e.g., a genre or an oeuvre. The series may suggest implicit preoccupations or questions underlying the text being analyzed. Horizons can be immensely helpful, but the interpreter must be familiar with the background reference or context in order to construe its relation to the text being interpreted properly.

8. *World.* Texts create worlds.[27] Their syntax, phrasing, vocabulary, and rhetoric can function as principles of representation. Relations among components of sentences can establish relations among the entities described, and the kinds of components stressed in the sentences can be the predominant kinds of objects in the text's world. The structures of the text's world may contrast with those embedded in everyday perception and thereby illuminate them. The mood and setting of the text can provide this world its color. Stylistic nuances and narrative transitions can elaborate it. The relation of the text's world to the everyday world may suggest regional hypotheses, and this world may condition the meaning of the other elements.

These elements will have different degrees of importance in different texts. The precise significance of any given element can be determined by considering other ways that element could have been handled. The art of interpretation requires a sensitivity to these different degrees of importance, an ability to determine these precise meanings, a sense of how related elements interact, and a capacity to synthesize these factors.

Determining the most promising formulation of a regional thesis may require considerable experiment and revision, but once the relevant data are assembled, the task becomes manageable. Data from all eight types of elements may be relevant to a particular regional theme, but often data from only some of them will be essential. Also, the significance of one element may be related to more than one regional theme. Disagreements about the regional theses may be resolved either by appealing to textual evidence or by evaluating the organizing principles they require. Sometimes one needs to examine the entire interpretation to appreciate the value of its parts.

To create organizing principles is a difficult task. Different kinds of texts require different procedures. Organizing principles can have various kinds of relations to regional theses. Regional theses may be different applications of one general formula, or they may offer qualifications of an abstract intuition, or the organizing principle may be a dialectical synthesis of various theses and antitheses among the regions, or it might function like the conclusion of an argument, the premises of which are regional theses. No single structural model can exhaust the possible ways in which organizing principles can integrate regional theses. Typically some preliminary intuition about the central theme of the text guides both the analysis and the formulation of regional theses. This intuition becomes gradually more refined and explicit as it is tested against the text's details. Stating organizing principles and relating them to regional themes can be as creative as original authorship. Interpretation is also an art.

Among the many motives for interpreting a text are the experiences of being overwhelmed by it, of being called to respond to it, and of being impelled to explore it with the same degree of acumen and power that one experiences through it. One's interpretation should not belie this motivation; one must do justice to the text and respond to it with all one's resources. Far from pacifying texts, interpretation is a kind of reciprocal response, which seeks to trigger a similar response in others; it deepens the text's impact. Successful interpretations make the text "sing" in a new way (like a musician transforms a score). Genuine interpretations avoid reductiveness, simplicity, and insensitivity. Interpreters seek to articulate fully their experience of the text and to inform that experience with repeated reflection on its various elements. Instead of adopting a position of judgment, the interpreter is more often judged by the text. His task is to be equal to its demands.

Interpretation and Evaluation

Under this heading I shall discuss two topics: evaluating specific interpretations and assessing the enterprise of interpretation itself.

Establishing conditions for a truly impressive reading may seem a quixotic task, yet a theory of interpretation which did not generate some evaluative criteria could not be tested and improved, so I shall make an attempt. My theory seeks both a new interpretive ideal and a summary of our intuitions about genuinely powerful readings. It suggests at least seven criteria of evaluation: consistency, proportionateness, adequacy, completeness, depth, sensitivity, and integratedness. Since texts present different kinds of challenges, some of these criteria may have greater weight in some cases. In addition, these criteria are scalar; that is, they admit of degrees. Better interpretations will usually result when more of the criteria are better satisfied. The difficult cases to adjudicate occur when two interpretations of the same text both are strong on some (but different) dimensions and weak on other (but different) ones. I shall clarify each criterion and demonstrate its plausibility.

An interpretation is *consistent* when it assigns similar meanings to similar textual elements unless some change is suggested by the text. If a symbol is read one way in one context and another way in a different context, the reading is inconsistent unless the shift is warranted by a change in the symbol's presentation. This type of consistency does not require that the reading itself be internally consistent, for if the text exhibits tensions and oppositions, these must be registered in the interpretation. The basis of this criterion is the expectation that particular elements have determinate (even if plural) meanings and that changes in meaning are typically signalled. If an element's significance is ambiguous, then the ambiguity should function in every occurrence. Just as language would become incoherent if any word meant anything, so too texts would become incoherent if elements lacked determinate meaning. The difference between interpreting texts and understanding ordinary language is that a narrative text often creates a new vocabulary, syntax, and semantics with its elements while an ordinary utterance usually relies on existing linguistic codes. Often an interpreter wants to assign a new meaning to an element in a new context because the meaning so far assigned is nonsensical or weak in that context. Simply introducing a new meaning in such cases is analogous to a scientist's relying on ad hoc hypotheses to escape objections or anomalies. This criterion insists that an interpretation's many hypotheses about the meanings of the text's elements should consistently apply to the instances of the elements they allegedly explain.

An interpretation is *proportionate* when the relative importance it assigns to elements and thematic regions expresses the relative importance they have in the text. Readings that draw large conclusions from minor elements violate this criterion. Sometimes the relative importance of an element can be revealed by an insightful interpretation, but there are various ways in which it can be indicated formally: the plot may turn on a particular crux; a character may be universalized; an event may be heavily underlined with emotion; an image may be frequently repeated or omnipresent; the world of the work may have a distinctive, much emphasized structure; or an explicit statement may effectively summarize the entire action of the narrative. Interpretations which are indifferent to these foregrounding procedures are disproportionate. The intuition underlying this criterion is that the central concerns of a text will be manifest in its dominant features.

Adequacy, completeness, and depth are closely related; so they need to be carefully distinguished. An interpretation is *adequate* when its regional theses explain all the elements relevant to them. An interpretation is *complete* when all the elements of the text are incorporated in a nonarbitrary fashion. An interpretation is *deep* when all the implicit resonances and layers of meaning in the text are uncovered and explicated. These criteria each describe a kind of exhaustiveness, but the type and range of exhaustiveness differs. A reading can legitimately be faulted if important elements are not explained (incompleteness), if many nuances or an entire dimension of significance is missed (shallowness), or if some regional theses neglect elements that bear on them directly (inadequacy). The basis of these criteria is the presumption that an hypothesis should incorporate all relevant data. Depth often facilitates comparative evaluation; the reading that elucidates more of the text's dimensions of significance is usually superior. Any of these conditions can occur without the other two; they are thus logically independent of one another. Though these criteria are rarely fully realized, the quality of a reading increases according to the degree to which they are satisfied.

An interpretation is *sensitive* when it uncovers implicit relations, functions, and meanings which are not evident even on an attentive first reading. Readings that synthesize what one already intuits are valuable, but those that reveal new, unseen dimensions of the text are more compelling. This criterion requires insightfulness rather than exhaustiveness. As readers become more accomplished, its demands increase because more is required to educate and illuminate the typical reader. Sensitive readings more fully comprehend the text. By instructing and animating the experience of the reader, they contribute to the text's power and conviction.

An interpretation is *integrated* when the regional theses are coherently synthesized. An integrated interpretation is like a powerful scientific theory. Just as a set of concatenated true statements does not produce a theory, so too a set of conjoined regional theses does not produce an interpretation. Integration can be achieved in many ways (e.g., deduction, abstraction, dialectical transformation). The plausibility of a particular type of integration will depend on the particular text. This criterion is justified by the unity and harmony literature typically embodies, but it should be minimized when a particular text lacks the requisite organicity.

Indeed, this last qualification applies to each of these criteria, and it suggests that a fuller clarification of their status is needed. The purposes of interpretation are to enrich our comprehension and appreciation of texts and to realize their fullest possibilities. These criteria are proposed as plausible conditions under which this 'enriching' and 'realizing' occurs. If other criteria contribute to these results, they should be added. If, on occasion, one of these criteria fails to facilitate this result, it should be minimized. If one of them *typically* prevents this result, it should be abandoned. Attentive, sympathetic readers have inarticulate intuitions about the power and range of particular texts, and an interpretation carries conviction when it gives expression to these intuitions in addition to challenging and informing them.

These criteria jointly establish a mode of evaluation that should produce improved readings. The contributions of different interpreters can be clarified, their weaknesses identified, and tasks for further research defined. Thus, they provide adequate foundations for an ongoing discipline of interpretive inquiry. Yet they are neither overly rigid nor unconnected to the outcomes of interpretive experience. The criteria have a built-in self-correction procedure, and they allow interpretive understanding of particular texts to improve itself.

I shall now defend the value of the interpretive enterprise itself, which recently has been criticized on various grounds. Some characteristic objections maintain that interpretation (1) pacifies, assimilates, or consumes a text instead of allowing it to remain alien and disturbing;[28] (2) offers only a mediated form of knowledge, one inferior to a more primordial sensuous experience of the text's form;[29] (3) at best offers only a translation of a text into alternative language and frequently ignores the text's wealth of detail;[30] (4) attempts to dominate or end discussion about the text by offering an irresistible reading that overshadows it.[31] I shall show that these objections are misguided and that in each case the truth typically lies in the opposite direction.[32]

Interpretation, at least as I have described it, neither pacifies nor assimilates the text, but deepens its force and sharpens one's grasp of both its underlying structure and its surface effects. Interpretation makes the meanings of a text explicit and thus memorable. To neglect to interpret a text is to risk losing it, to remain content with general impressions. Not to interpret a text is like not asking someone what they meant when one has not heard or does not fully understand: one may vaguely sense the importance of the statement, but one will not really comprehend it, and one will thus be unable to rethink one's own beliefs in relation to it. One may be moved and challenged by a text one has simply read, but interpreting it animates this challenge and clarifies its full implications.

The assumption underlying this objection is that interpreting a text imposes one's own beliefs on it. But the experience of interpretation does not confirm this. Typically one's own beliefs are suspended when one tries to determine the text's significance. One is absorbed by it and forgets oneself. One seeks *its* structure and coherence, and reformulates one's reading to express it. Only after one interprets it can one compare its assertions with one's own beliefs because only then are its actual implications and complexities evident. In addition, the objection assumes that casting an experience into language mollifies it. But the truth is just the opposite: to fail to articulate and comprehend a strange experience is to consign it to insignificance—either to forget it altogether or to keep it detached from the rest of one's experience. When the text's implications are explicit, it can fully interact with one's beliefs, attitudes, ideals, and world view. It is less easily forgotten or ignored. Without interpretation, one may be enchanted, but the daily grind will soon obliterate the fascination.

Though a sensuous appreciation of a text—as opposed to a cognitive-linguistic comprehension of it—is not impossible, it is not "primordial"; it is inferior when taken by itself; and any good interpretation will include it. One aim of my theory is to overcome the outworn intellect/sensibility and content/form distinctions by revealing their necessary relationships and by suggesting that each side is qualitatively enriched by attention to the other side. Full sensuous appreciation of form is a precondition for insightful interpretations, and full elucidation of form requires accurate statement of the text's subject. Taken by itself, sensuous description is as barren as an interpretation that incorporates only one of the eight elements of a text. Also, such descriptions are neither unmediated nor primordial. They too must be cast into language, however creatively, just like one's intuitions about the text's meaning. There is nothing nearer or more basic about sensibility. It can be mute and uninformative or powerful and rich. Unverbalized sensuous appreciation is analogous to mute implicit interpretation. Each gains power and concreteness through felicitous expression. Unverbalized sensuous or cognitive intuition is simply immune to testing and refinement. Even one's own comprehension of these intuitions is fumbling and inchoate. Moreover, perceiving form is no less complex than apprehending meaning, and each is so interlaced with the other that separating them in practice is extremely difficult.

A strong interpretation neither avoids textual details nor simply translates the text into other terms. Texts can, of course, exist and be appreciated without interpretations, and interpretations are couched in different terms than the texts themselves. But texts become richer when they are illuminated by strong interpretations. Just as people radiate greater energy in the presence of appropriate partners, so too do texts become more complete when given powerful readings. The text challenges the interpreter to do it justice, and an interpretation that rises to the occasion becomes an essential moment in the life of the text. Text and interpretations animate each other. In addition, though interpretation is only one among many useful critical projects, it does make a powerful contribution to understanding the text. The kind of synoptic vision an interpretation provides does not reduce or simplify a text; it sharpens one's grasp of its elements and reveals their relations more perspicuously. Like a master teacher who lives on in his students, the text is renewed and becomes concrete and explicit through its powerful readings. Until it is interpreted, the text is inadequately comprehended. Though it may have an impact on readers, it has not yet sufficiently challenged them to comprehend their experience of it. First, faltering attempts at interpretation may do injustice to the text, but only when some initial efforts are made can they be improved. Gradually the powerful readings which realize the text will emerge. "Translation" and "violation" are then quite inappropriate metaphors for interpretation.

The final objection concerns the effect of powerful interpretations on readers of the text. Instead of dominating them and ending discussion, strong interpretations often challenge them to produce better ones and enliven their experience and understanding of the text. Strong interpretations presuppose insightful analyses, and these reveal patterns and effects often missed on initial readings. Even if a reader does not himself offer a complete alternative reading, he may more readily elucidate his own insights about the text when he has an insightful interpretation to use as a point of departure. Strong interpretations make serious discussions of texts possible because they invite challenge and critique and they provide a framework in which the intelligent discussion of specific themes and elements can occur. Like scientific theories, interpretations are scrutinized, challenged, and revised by the community of those who care about the text. Interpretations facilitate the formation of these communities, encourage communication among members, and facilitate their self-understanding. This theory of interpretation encourages more thorough scrutiny and more rational discussion of interpretations; through this process more powerful readings will usually emerge. Just as classic texts challenge later artists, classic interpretations challenge later interpreters.

Another version of this objection is that my position assumes that a work of art can be wholly known and thereby exhausted. Because the objector believes major texts to be *inexhaustible,* he rejects my effort to produce thorough interpretations of them. I agree that great works are inexhaustible. One cannot be sure one has produced the best reading even along the main lines one is proceeding, and it will always be possible that other equally powerful readings may be produced along entirely different lines. Moreover, the development of theory in all fields cannot be predicted, and such developments may open new areas to which a classic text may suddenly speak (e.g., psychoanalysis). Since the area of inquiry had not yet been conceived, these implications of the work would probably be missed and lie dormant. But this is no argument against the thoroughness demanded by my approach. Quite the contrary. This interpretive theory forces the interpreter to elucidate everything he or she may know or understand about a work and to do so in a clear and integrated fashion. But this does not presume that the work itself is exhausted, only that the interpreter's knowledge of it is exhaustively expressed. A genuine interpretation will act as a challenge or spur to other interpreters to see more and/or see better. It virtually requires them to explicate the differences between the work as they understand it and the interpretation as presently developed. This works to the advantage of all parties. The original interpretation's weaknesses get revealed (and improvement becomes possible), and the threads that might be woven into a new reading are uncovered. If a new viable interpretation emerges, then additional facets of the work stand revealed. Interpretation is an ongoing communal process, building on past achievements—sometimes transcending them, sometimes superseding them, sometimes complementing them. The whole enterprise succeeds only because each contributing interpreter strives to articulate everything she or he may see—both about the work and about existing interpretations. Finally, the thoroughness demanded by this interpretive approach may uncover insights that will contribute to the emergence of the new fields of knowledge. These fields may only be hinted at in the work itself. The interpreter can take the necessary seminal steps to initiate the discipline. If the best art really does extend the frontiers of knowledge and sensibility, then disciplined interpretation will render these extensions in a form that those (theorists and other artists) who wish to pursue these fields independently can use and develop.

All of my replies have appealed to the possibility of powerful interpretations as I define them. This is proper because one must consider the ideal case when evaluating the enterprise of interpretation itself. I have shown that such interpretations are internally related to texts and enrich and honor them just as lovers enrich, animate, and honor one another. Yet I cannot deny the current dearth of such interpretations. This theory seeks to guide us toward overcoming it.

II. Pedagogical Implications

Since I seek to create a new seriousness about interpretation, teaching this theory effectively is essential. I have developed some useful strategies to help students master this approach, but before I describe them, I shall indicate some of its pedagogical advantages.

Undergraduates, especially those in the humanities, oscillate between two attitudes toward intellectual or theoretical work, and these attitudes are related to the two extreme views from which I distinguish my position. The first attitude accepts the expertise of teachers and assumes that whatever they assert must be true and thus should be memorized. This attitude is rarely discouraged by teachers themselves, however fully they are aware of the tenuousness of their interpretations. Indeed this assumption underlies the "lecture" approach to university teaching. This attitude is related to the authorial intention theory in that both views assume that *someone* (the author, the teacher) has privileged access to the truth and that to discover the truth one must find and listen to this privileged person. The learner, on this model, is a passive receiver, and students who adopt this attitude strive primarily to master the views of the best authorities they can find. Rarely do they try to think for themselves. The second attitude is diametrically opposed to the first; it rejects all expertise and all rational efforts to validate claims. It holds that one position is as good as another and thus that any student's beliefs are as adequate as anyone else's. This attitude is closely related to radical pluralism. It can even be modulated into playful pluralism if one posits that surveying a panorama of interpretations allows one to better choose the one most compatible with one's sensibility. This position also creates passivity in learning and a withdrawal from the dialogue with other people. Since nothing can "convince" such students that a reading is inadequate, they tend to adopt whatever reading occurs to them first. Moreover, since there are no criteria for truth or validation, there is nothing to discuss with other people. If others disagree with one's reading, then they must be constituted differently (genetically or culturally). This attitude underlies the free-form discussion approach to teaching, which encourages all students to express their positions but does not seek any logical resolution of disparate or contradictory views.

My position supports an alternative pedagogy and fosters an attitude toward the life of the mind different from either of these. By outlining a method and some criteria for evaluation, this approach opens the way toward serious collective interpretive work. No one is *presumed* to have the truth, although the possibility of discovering viable (even the *most* viable—given existing alternatives) interpretations is presupposed. Students learn that interpretation takes considerable effort, and even after careful reflection and immense labor, their results may not be on target. The teacher's reading is not necessarily correct; it must satisfy the same criteria of evaluation that students' readings must satisfy. Students and teachers should thus begin to take an active interest in the genuine reactions of one another to their readings. Students' intellectual discipline matures as they master the method. They learn that only arguments, evidence, and convincing insights support interpretations and that no one has a privileged pipeline to the truth. Published readings can be shallow or inept, and students have a responsibility to locate weaknesses and problems in them so that they can improve upon them. This responsibility extends to other students as well. By hearing and actively evaluating each other's interpretations, they learn both to hold positions with less ego-involvement and to raise questions about fellow-students' readings without threatening their budding intellectual identities. In effect, the serious application of rationality opens the possibility of communal work resembling the best research situations in the sciences.

Just as importantly, students can apply this same attitude of continuous refinement and reevaluation to the development of the theory of interpretation itself. Much more could be said about the way organizing principles relate to regional theses and regional theses to elements, and students can contribute to further elaborating these matters. Beyond this, they may discover problems in the theory, e.g., they may demonstrate that one of the criteria of evaluation should be excluded and/or others included. They might further examine the foundations of the theory as they reflect on its differences from other interpretive practices to which they have been exposed. Teaching the theory thus becomes an open inquiry in which students actively participate—testing its dicta against their own interpretive experience and examining its logic and support according to their best lights. The spirit in which the class is conducted is thus more inviting and more conducive to serious critical reflection than most approaches.

An additional benefit of this approach is that the kind of intellectual discipline it fosters can be used in other humanities and social science courses. Because this approach to interpretation unites both an analytic moment and a synthetic moment and extensively develops both skills, it should help students determine their own responses to theories in many other areas. Because they learn to accept the authority of teachers only insofar as they can provide convincing arguments, students will seek independent rational evaluation of theories offered in other courses. They will thus become more active participants in the constitution of knowledge, will better comprehend what they have come to accept because they have studied it from the inside, and will better understand the strengths and weaknesses of current work in a wide variety of areas.

Finally, my approach helps students understand how difficult it is to formulate a plausible, defensible, theoretical position or interpretation. They learn to struggle to articulate their own positions and defend them. They come to realize that developing an interpretation involves considerable work. They may even come to better appreciate their teachers' readings once their defense and the thoroughness with which alternatives have been examined have been made explicit. Students should thus accept new responsibility for the positions they hold and for the quality of argument supporting the positions of their friends. Only if students accept this kind of responsibility do their own minds begin to take shape. Only if they realize the importance of criticism for their own development will they see the importance of expressing their criticisms to others with a view to similar development. My position, in facilitating a new kind of attitude to interpretation, also forges a more critical, active, and articulate interpreter. This is an ideal to which much lip service is paid in liberal education but which is rarely realized in our graduating seniors.

Another virtue of this approach is the demand for clarity and explicitness it issues. It forces interpreters to state what they regard as their deepest insights in terms lucid enough to be comprehended and evaluated by any serious reader of the text. Some people believe that art itself can only address the most important matters of human life indirectly. Perhaps so. But the obligation of the interpreter is to recover these intuitions and subtleties in prose that may stretch current conceptual schemes but that is nonetheless clear enough to be comprehended. Interpretation makes known what initially is only implicitly grasped. The direction of interpretation is always toward greater explicitness and clarity; only when something is stated clearly can one be sure one truly understands what one has previously only intuited. Casting one's insight into language does not degrade it; it makes it testable and active. It helps one refine it, sharpen it, and relate it to the rest of one's beliefs. Making the basis of one's passion for a work explicit does not deflate that passion; it reinforces it, concretizes it, and allows others to share it. To write clearly is not to write in clichés or to limit oneself to the well-trodden. Often it requires one to invent new, apt metaphors and symbols. It allows others to see the unfamiliar on the basis of the familiar, but this forces one to render the familiar in new ways. Obfuscation simply prevents serious reaction to one's ideas and threatens the quality of one's own self-understanding. Leaving something implicit simply doubles the effort readers must make; not only must they interpret the text under discussion for themselves, they must also interpret the reading one has given. Too easily they become exhausted in the latter process and are then unable to offer serious critical commentary on one's work. Explicitness and clarity are the best antidotes to self-inflation and pretension, and they are the best means of generating an ongoing critical dialogue.

Some might object that this approach assumes that students are far more advanced than in fact they are. They might argue that to bring the abstract theoretical issues discussed in professional journals into the classroom is simply to expect too much from students, to demand a level of involvement that even teachers can sustain only on their best days. At best one can introduce only the basics of interpretation; to try for more will only discourage and demoralize everyone. I would offer several responses to this objection.

Not only does one cheat and patronize one's students, one reduces one's own engagement in the class if one tries to separate the theory one practices in one's research from the one which one teaches in the classroom. One cheats one's students because one bores them with oversimplified versions of theories and prevents them from becoming intellectually involved in the development of the theories. One also protects one's ideas from serious challenge (and thus loses the opportunity for refinement and correction) if one refuses to teach students the best version of the approach one uses in actual practice. Real dialogue about method is rare enough in the humanities without having to eliminate opportunities for it. Most of our students are mentally asleep because they are not treated as independent thinkers.

Most students approach the kind of interpretation I teach with some trepidation, but invariably most find their final product more rewarding and worthwhile than their papers for other classes. Most find my explicitness about criteria of evaluation refreshing, and most appreciate the opportunity to criticize my readings in the same way that I criticize theirs. By participating in the kinds of evaluative exercises I require, most students begin to learn the meaning of genuine self-evaluation. Most also appreciate the chance to work through a methodology critically together; they look for ways to improve and challenge both the general theory and the readings it helps produce. Finally, by seriously examining one approach, they gain the tools for evaluating the many other approaches to which they will be exposed. They are less likely to accept what future teachers require of them in an unexamined way.

Students are also willing to work harder for a teacher they believe is working hard for them. If one offers one's best reading of a text, if one tries to present one's own effort as a rationally defended work of art, then they will aim for a similar standard in their own work. Only when students work to their fullest potential can the criticisms a teacher offers have genuine impact. Under these conditions, when they see the point of the teacher's recommendations, their capacities are expanded. They realize they have more to master. Similarly, if teachers put everything into their lectures and can still acknowledge flaws and shortcomings in the result, they teach students how to receive and respond to criticism in a productive fashion. This process also forces teachers to think through their methodological assumptions and make explicit their own contributions to the school or style of interpretation they adopt. One's teaching and research begin to support rather than conflict with one another. Thus for both students' and teachers' sake, the theory one uses in one's research should not be segregated from the methodology one teaches in the classroom.

Someone might still object that to teach one's best readings and the most refined version of one's interpretive approach risks trivialization by one's students. Teachers may hesitate to put themselves so vulnerably on the line when students are unlikely to share their interest, enthusiasm, and appreciation of nuance. My reply here is that someone must break the cycle of silence and self-withholding if humanities education is ever to recover its passion. Trivialization by one's audience is a risk one always takes, even when reading papers to professionals. It is a risk balanced by the possibility of genuine dialogue, serious reaction and criticism, and the consequent possibility of self-improvement. Moreover, the teacher plans the course of study. Complexities and nuances can be given adequate preparation. Necessary building blocks can be provided. The teacher should be able to prevent unnecessary misunderstandings and oversimplifications. Even students who are required to take a course can be motivated toward genuine interest if the right texts are chosen and the right level of presentation is adopted at the outset. One may have to work up to complex views, but this does not mean one should not try to get there. Who really appreciates one's work anyway? Do colleagues or scholars shower us with letters of recognition or congratulation? By offering our best efforts to students, we may inspire those who have talent to devote themselves seriously to the course and possibly to their studies generally. To those who remain indifferent to one's work, one can adopt the same attitude one already assumes to the rest of the world. Even if none of the students responds, this will be no worse than what already occurs; and the chance that something powerful might happen in the classroom is sufficient to make the risk worth taking.

How can the interpretive approach described above be most effectively taught? When one teaches this theory for the first time, two principles are useful. First, because students are either oblivious to or fearful of the demands of interpretation, one needs to approach the finished product in small steps. Often short, trial assignments can help students become familiar with each phase of the enterprise. Allowing the class to work through the entire process collectively can also be helpful. Second, if one does proceed slowly and in small steps, nearly everyone can produce a genuine interpretation. Though their work will vary in quality, most students will produce a paper well beyond what they might have expected of themselves at the outset of the course. I shall describe a typical sequence of class sessions and assignments which facilitate mastery of this skill.

Initially I present the theory clearly and slowly and encourage students to raise doubts and questions. Several sessions are needed to familiarize people with the terminology and to exemplify the procedures. Typically I will then apply the procedures of analysis, of formulating regional theses, and developing organizing principles for the same text. I indicate the limits of my evidence for each aspect of the interpretation, and I also suggest places where alternative readings might be pursued. In this way I try to produce a reflective, open, self-critical approach to the enterprise. Once a first attempt at interpretation is complete, I evaluate it using the seven criteria discussed above and thus suggest how it might be improved.

Next, the class takes a short text through these phases of interpretation collectively. Often we begin with a subsection of the text and examine it closely. The whole class explores all eight elements for that chapter, act, or sequence. This restriction of scope allows disputes to be more readily resolved and insures that everyone assimilates the concepts involved in analysis. The scope is then widened to the entire text, and different people are asked to explicate different elements of the text. Questions about the meaning and application of the categories usually emerge from this exercise. Once the entire class has reviewed these efforts, most have a clear working conception of what analysis involves, and most are sensitive to the kinds of disputes it engenders.

The class then turns to the formulation of regional theses. Again, students are divided into subgroups, and each group concentrates on a particular regional theme. Initially groups meet separately to formulate the most plausible, alternative regional theses. The entire class then discusses the efforts of each subgroup, and I examine the differences in the kinds of disagreements that arise here and the kinds of evidence used to resolve them. Though agreement is much harder to achieve in this phase, I at least try to indicate the considerations that might produce it. Most important in this section of the course is assessing the reasons for accepting or rejecting alternative formulations.

Once some reasonable regional theses are discovered, I ask everyone to consider how they might be synthesized into an interpretation. Typically the whole class first canvasses alternatives. Then the most promising paths are pursued and discussed by the entire class. Each is evaluated according to the seven criteria. Once the class has produced and discussed some genuine interpretations, I ask them to read published critical readings on the text. The flaws and insights of these essays are noted, and this helps students to assimilate the ultimate aim of the course: to improve the overall quality of interpretations.

If the class is having difficulty with a particular phase of the process, I will take a new text up to that phase and have students continue to work collectively until most have a reasonable mastery of it. Before asking for a complete interpretation in writing, I encourage students to turn in short ungraded papers that attempt an analysis and a formulation of regional theses. I also duplicate one or two exemplary interpretations from previous terms and have the class critically examine them. Then I assign an interpretation paper on a new text. Through it the previously learned skills are absorbed and integrated. I encourage class discussion of the general problems of interpreting this text so that everyone is aware of the main options on the difficult questions.

I ask for two copies of students' papers and require them to exchange the second copy with a partner. Partners evaluate each other's work in writing using the seven criteria. This helps students to grasp them more vividly. I also duplicate the best two papers and allow the class to discuss the merits and problems of each. All this evaluation prepares people for my thorough evaluations of their work.

When I return the papers, I suggest some possible ways to resolve the major issues and may even offer an interpretation of my own, which I then encourage them to criticize. No interpretation is declared definitively correct. The relative merits and difficulties of the main contenders are reviewed, and the issues that demand additional attention are isolated. I do not pretend to have all the answers about either the particular text or the general theory. Once everyone has seriously attempted to create an interpretation, the questions about the process and its value are often more penetrating. I invite criticisms of my theory as well as supplements to it.

Because this is a course in intensive textual work, I restrict the number of texts to be covered. At least three, but no more than five, is a good rule. The theory takes about nine weeks to teach. In a semester course, I typically proceed to discuss a particular philosophical problem common to the texts for that term because my courses seek to introduce students to philosophy as well as explore the philosophical aspects of literary theory. I can thus present interpretation as a necessary prerequisite to intelligent philosophical discussion of the issues raised by the texts. If I were teaching a literature course, I would probably consider some alternative critical approaches and complete the course by examining some of these in detail. When the course is finished, students possess an important skill, and they have a basis for evaluating many of the critical essays they will read in other literature or film courses.

III. A Conclusion

Since Susan Sontag published her famous broadside against interpretation, interpreters have been on the defensive.[33] The skepticism implicit in most forms of pluralism and the antiintellectualism of some recent cultural movements have contributed to this posture. It is hoped that this ambiance has begun to change. Instead of celebrating the diversity of critical projects for their own sake, the time has come to sift through the options and more intensively pursue those showing genuine promise. I hope I have demonstrated that interpretation bears such promise. It is not merely compatible with important recent developments in criticism, it seeks to integrate them.[34]

Defensiveness in contemporary interpreters has allowed the resources of contemporary narratives to lie fallow. Literature, drama, and film offer distinctive attempts to identify and address some of the deep dilemmas of the contemporary era.[35] By striving to comprehend the most penetrating contemporary texts, we may achieve more perspicuous understanding of these issues. Often they are so pervasive that we barely register them. Interpretation, like art, can help us face the problems we all too humanly seek to avoid.

NOTES

1. Two recent theorists who adopt this approach are E. D. Hirsch in *Validity in Interpretation* (New Haven, Conn.: Yale University Press, 1967) and P. D. Juhl in *Interpretation: An Essay in the Philosophy of Literary Criticism* (Princeton, N.J.: Princeton University Press, 1980).

2. Two recent theorists of this school are Hans Georg Gadamer in *Truth and Method* (New York: The Seabury Press, 1975) and Paul Ricoeur in *Interpretation Theory* (Fort Worth, Tex.: Texas Christian University Press, 1976).

3. Though these two schools are in conflict on many issues, one should note that their underlying projects are compatible. One can simultaneously seek criteria for evaluating or validating interpretations and also uncover explanations for the emergence and persistence of diverse readings.

4. My theory provides procedures for ranking the quality of different interpretations and for rejecting some of them without appealing to the author's intention. The main argument in favor of the authorial intention theory is that it establishes objectivity and rigor for interpretation that can be provided *in no other way*. I show that the italicized phrase is incorrect.

5. The intent of this distinction is to restrict the scope of my claims in this paper. I am *not* trying to develop a theory of interpreting any possible object in any sense of "interpret" (this would be the most global theory). Moreover, some claims I make here might not hold if one were considering rules for interpreting other kinds of objects. For example, if I were considering the interpretation of historical events, the role of the actor's intentions might be larger than the one I argue for here. If I were interpreting the psyche of a person, the acknowledgment by the person of the hypotheses I had formulated might well play a more central role than the one I allow here. I take no stand on whether a theory like this one can be developed for music or painting. What about poetry? I suspect that most of my claims could be extended to poetry without great modification, but I prefer to remain silent about poetry because my experience in interpreting it is minimal. The reader should also realize that the theory developed here is not as local as it could be. I do not, for example, address the important differences in interpreting novels, narrative films, and

drama. There are differences, but I am ignoring them for present purposes.

6. This definition is quite similar to, and elaborates upon, the one offered by John Ellis in his *Theory of Literary Criticism: A Logical Analysis* (Berkeley: University of California Press, 1974), especially pp. 202–8. Though I do not agree with Ellis's views in the early and later chapters of this book, I concur with the positions in chapters 5 and 6. I have benefitted from his clarity and his arguments.

7. Moreover, the discipline of the confirmation process (both in interpretation and in science) often indicates areas in which such paradigms need correction or reformulation. The conduct of inquiry introduces self-correction into both activities.

8. Cf. Ellis, *Theory of Literary Criticism*, pp. 192–99.

9. Recall that the theory in this paper concerns interpretations of *particular texts*. A literary theorist might also identify and elucidate conditions of a genre. Such a theory will apply to many different texts. This activity has closer affinities with scientific theorizing. To interpret a text within a genre is to understand its distinctive contribution to it.

10. This may be a function of the previous point. Interpreters face a complete text; they gain a definite "feel" for its themes and its direction while reading it. But scientists observe only a small fragment of the data they ultimately seek to explain. This is one reason why the data are less suggestive. Another is that the system must be altered—experiments performed—before nature's organization begins to reveal itself. The interpreter may imaginatively vary some of the elements of the text to appreciate its structure, but the organic coherence of a text is usually more readily apparent. Of course, I admit that scientists develop hunches based on adjacent theories or minimal observations and that interpreters create new hypotheses and refashion their experience of the work as they interpret. Thus the difference here is one of degree, not kind.

11. In a recent essay, Ronald Dworkin has challenged this position ("Law as Interpretation," *Critical Inquiry* 9 [September 1982]: 179–200). He claims that evaluation is central to interpretation because interpreters attempt to read texts in ways that make them the best works of art they can be. Thus, better interpretations reveal texts as better works of art; quality in interpretation logically depends on quality in art. Disputes about the nature and appropriate style of interpretation are really disputes about excellence in art. Dworkin emphasizes that interpreters must clarify the text at hand, not create a wholly new text. Consequently, their activity is constrained by coherence conditions that insure the identity of the text being interpreted. He claims that even these conditions are logically dependent on aesthetic values. As he develops his theory of interpretation in law, he acknowledges two distinct kinds of constraints

on interpretation: formal matters like coherence and substantive matters like political (for law) and aesthetic (for literature) value. These work hierarchically. Formal considerations first limit the number of acceptable interpretations; then value considerations determine which among them is the most promising or viable one.

This position is the most challenging and intriguing view of interpretation I have encountered in some time. Since I cannot address all the issues it raises here, I will restrict myself to six observations. First, Dworkin admits that even on his view there is a difference between evaluation and interpretation (my main point in the text). Saying how good a text *can be* is different from saying how good *that is*. One can do the former without doing the latter—that is, one can interpret a text without evaluating it (but not vice versa, presumably).

Second, I would then add that one can evaluate a text without (explicitly and thoroughly) interpreting it, at least if one is willing to ignore cognitive value. The excellences and faults of a work are often readily apparent without thorough interpretation. Journalist-critics could not do their jobs if this were not true. Such judgments may be revised in the light of subsequent interpretation, but they need not always be. On my view, one first grasps the qualities of a text exhaustively and then provides an integrated account of them in one's interpretation. One does not first imagine the qualities a work might have and then construct a reading that generates those qualities. The latter procedure too easily leads to creating an entirely new text.

Third, my central disagreement with Dworkin is over the relative importance of coherence (formal) considerations and aesthetic value (substantive) considerations. Consider three cases: (a) Interpretation 1 is strong formally but generates only a fair work of art while interpretation 2 is weak formally but generates an excellent work of art. Serious interpreters will prefer interpretation 1 on the grounds that the second reads too much into the text. Dworkin sometimes seems to suggest otherwise. (b) Interpretation 3 and interpretation 4 are equally strong formally, and both make the text an impressive work of art, but along different value dimensions (say, psychological and political; also, assume the two readings cannot be synthesized). On my view, one has two different, equally good interpretations. There is no necessity to rank them evaluatively and choose the best. In literary interpretation, unlike legal interpretation, one is not forced to select the *best* reading. I think it would be quite a feat to produce two readings that are equally good formally, but if it could be done, this is how I would view the result in most cases. (c) Exactly the same conditions as (b), except interpretation 5 produces an excellent work of art while interpretation 6 produces a mediocre one. In this situation, I *agree* with Dworkin. Serious interpreters would opt for interpretation 5. Our disagreement concerns the weight I put on formal considerations before allowing aesthetic merit to enter consideration.

Fourth, my theory competes with Dworkin's as the best comprehension of the enterprise of *interpretation*. My approach takes the notion of a text's meaning(s) (as distinct from its value[s]) seriously and tries to clarify a non-author-based means of explicating it. The various formal criteria I outline below clarify the nature of this (these) meaning(s). Even if my position were subsumed by Dworkin's, however, I think it would fare quite well against the available competitors. Dworkin would claim that my approach presupposes the value of organic unity. But I think my interpretive approach would stand even if one did not accept that value, and I can (and do) certainly acknowledge a greater diversity of aesthetic values than organic unity without making radical changes in my theory of interpretation. Dworkin's theory seems to require a multitude of interpretive strategies, one for each kind of text with distinctively different aesthetic value. Such a view would only generate mass confusion in interpretive theory.

Fifth, Dworkin may be trying to account for the whole wide diversity of reading practices in the history of criticism; he may be operating with the widest possible notion of 'interpretation.' I am not. Instead, I am elaborating and rendering coherent one specific type of practice that has considerable value. It may be that our theories have a different scope. I note with interest that my project in this paper functions exactly as Dworkin thinks all 'interpretations' do. It seeks to reconstruct an existing practice and render it in the most meritorious fashion. However, I am not *interpreting* the enterprise of interpretation in any straightforward sense. Whatever I am doing seems qualitatively different from the sort of interpretation I am trying to clarify.

Finally, if one, for some reason, had to interpret a bad work of art (or even a work that was only marginally art), one's first task would not be to make it *better,* but to clarify what it means or comes to. My theory better captures what this involves; in such cases one can "bracket" value considerations and proceed with the interpretation. This is what Dworkin seems to deny. A different way to see the distinction between meaning and value is to consider the difference between a work that is intellectually profound but aesthetically mediocre and one that is intellectually flat-footed but aesthetically brilliant. The first demands interpretation, but the second may not be worth the effort despite its great merit and impact.

12. It should, however, offer criteria for evaluating *interpretations*. I shall discuss this topic below. I should add that in practice a *thorough* evaluation of a text requires an explicit and astute interpretation of it.

13. Juhl, *Interpretation*, p. 12.

14. Some examples: Roland Barthes, *S/Z* (New York: Hill and

Wang, 1974), and Cary Nelson, "Reading Criticism," *PMLA* 91 (October 1976): 801–15.

15. See Juhl, *Interpretation*. Also see Steven Knapp and Walter Benn Michaels, "Against Theory," *Critical Inquiry* 8 (Summer 1982): 723–42. I elaborate these objections and others in my "Reflections on the Philosophy of Literary Interpretation," *Alaska Quarterly Review* 1: 3–4 (Spring 1983): 109–20.

16. See Juhl, *Interpretation*, chapter 3. Hirsch's distinction between meaning and "significance" excludes the kind of significance I am referring to here. For him significance is the pragmatic import the text has for particular readers; for me significance exists for all readers who seek a genuine interpretation. His type of "significance" also exists, but "meaning" and "significance" in his sense do not exhaust the objects of interpretation.

17. Ellis, *Theory of Literary Criticism*, pp. 116–18.

18. This point can be strengthened. I would argue that one cannot comprehend (interpret) an author (and thus his or her intentions) without already having interpreted the author's major works. Thus, the precondition for comprehending authors is adequate interpretations of their various texts. Similarly, in studying historical eras, one learns about the tensions and deep dynamics of a period via thorough interpretation of its texts. One should not read antecedent assumptions about a period into every text that emerges from it. See Ellis, *Theory of Literary Criticism*, pp. 133–43.

19. This view has been proposed by Alexander Nehamas in "The Postulated Author: Critical Monism as a Regulative Ideal," *Critical Inquiry* 8 (Autumn 1981): 133–50.

20. Juhl makes this kind of attempt on pp. 67–80 and 114–27.

21. This is one central point of disagreement between by position and that of Sigurd Burkhardt, as expressed in "Notes on the Theory of Intrinsic Interpretation," the Appendix to *Shakespeare's Meanings* (Princeton, N.J.: Princeton University Press, 1968), pp. 285–313. Burkhardt believes that the intrinsic approach depends on the assumption of infallibility—i.e., that a constituting author has created the text as an ordered whole which can thus be known completely. I have been defending my position without this assumption. My claim is that organic coherence is a regulative principle of the activity of interpretation despite one's assumptions about authorship or infallibility.

Other major differences between our positions concern the output of interpretation, the value of simplicity, and explicit criteria of evaluation. In my view, the output of interpretation is an integrated system of organizing principles and regional theses. In Burkhardt's view, it is a single all-encompassing law. Perhaps for a short poem (his example) a single statement could constitute an adequate interpretation, but for a play or a novel, a much more elaborate set of hypotheses will be needed to capture the entire meaning of the text. In general, I resist the idea that interpretation produces capsule formulas. I also object to Burkhardt's emphasis on simplicity, which has been discredited even in philosophy of science (see Mario Bunge, *The Myth of Simplicity* [Englewood Cliffs, N.J.: Prentice-Hall, 1963]), even though I agree that arbitrary, ad hoc assumptions should be minimized when an interpretation is being reformulated in response to criticism. "Simplicity" is virtually impossible to define in any useful manner, and in many cases, attempting to abide by it will produce misleading results in both science and literary interpretation. Finally, although I agree that a method is ultimately proved by its results, I also suggest some specific criteria for evaluating interpretive hypotheses. Burkhardt neglects this. I at least make an effort to elucidate what would count as interpretive success.

Nevertheless, there are many similarities in our positions, and I regard Burkhardt as a kindred spirit. He too believes that the age of serious interpretation has hardly begun, that interpretive hypotheses must account for every detail of the text, that only inquiries that seek the text's inner law (what I call its organizing principles) are genuine interpretations, that the activities of science and literary interpretation have more similarities than differences, that interpretive claims about the author are posterior to the interpetation of the author's works, and that analysis differs from interpretation. My efforts in this essay are not intended to offer a *new* theory, but to provide a more perspicuous statement, elaboration, and defense of a theory that many in this century have accepted and used.

22. The favored example in the literature is a grammatically intelligible poem typed accidentally by a group of monkeys; see Juhl, *Interpretation*, pp. 71–76 and 82–86. Juhl believes that interpreting such a document would be absurd. I think it would be perfectly plausible. We interpret many phenomena in which authorship is questionable—e.g., dreams, anonymous texts, large-scale historical phenomena. For all we know, many ancient texts might have been written collectively and over long periods of time. In such cases the notion of "*the* author's *intended* meaning" has no application; if this were the primary aim of interpretation, then interpreting such texts (e.g., the Bible) would be unintelligible.

23. All the considerations discussed above are essential to my position. If one is confused about the aim of interpretation (say, if one seeks the author's intention), then one's orientation to the text and one's search for evidence will be misguided. Similarly, one's energies will be exhausted in preliminaries if one confuses analysis with interpretation. I mean to

exclude considerations about authorial intent *at every point*. Mixed theories that adjudicate readings via both formal criteria and the author's apparent intention are, on my view, mistaken. True statements of the author's intention, however these are discovered, will be adequate interpretations only if they fulfill the seven criteria explicated above (and just *because* they fulfill those criteria).

24. The idea that the primary product of interpretation is the text's *theses* will no doubt meet some resistance. Does this view not make texts too pedagogical and interpretation too moralistic? Are there not many texts that—eschewing "instruction"—seek only to delight? Are there not many texts that consciously defy interpretation as I envision it? By 'thesis' I mean something general and inclusive like "what the text is ultimately saying" or "its central implications." Sometimes texts may address (underline, reconstitute, challenge) interpretive or reading processes explicitly; their response to these processes will then be among their theses. Sometimes the delight of a text has a distinctive impact or resolution; this might, in some cases, be construed as a 'thesis'. Texts which defy organicity often are asserting something important about it. The broad character of my concept of 'thesis' is best revealed in the many distinct types of elements theses must explain. Texts may produce an alternative sensibility, a new vision of the world, or a heightened sense of paradox; all of these can be incorporated by the concept of 'thesis' I am adopting. I do assert, however, that interpretation requires more than merely identifying themes.

25. There are probably more than eight types of elements, and if one were to concentrate on one of the three kinds of art I am limiting myself to here, then much more elaboration of these elements could be offered. For example, in film, "world" might include everything from mise en scene, to lighting, to depth of field, to color schemes, to spatio-temporal editing relations, and much else. Since further elaboration of the elements is the task of *analysis,* which is not my focus here, I am deliberately offering only the most general and rudimentary observations about each element.

26. Drama often lacks a narrator, but both the staging and the rhetoric of the play can serve similar functions.

27. The philosopher-writer who most closely studies this aspect of narrative fiction is William H. Gass; see "The World Within the Word" in *The World Within the Word* (New York: Knopf, 1978), pp. 308–37.

28. Pierre Macherey, *A Theory of Literary Production* (London: Routledge and Kegan Paul, 1978), pp. 13 and 19. See also Susan Sontag, "Against Interpretation" in *Against Interpretation* (New York: Farrar, Straus and Giroux, 1966), section 5.

29. Sontag, "Against Interpretation," sections 8, 9, and 10.

30. Macherey, *Literary Production,* pp. 15–19, and Sontag, "Against Interpretation," sections 3 and 6.

31. This objection was offered by professors Cary Nelson and Lawrence Grossberg, University of Illinois, in personal communication.

32. Someone might object that few critics have taken these arguments seriously. My reply would be that they may have been dismissed without being given a full or convincing response. They do articulate some reasons for the ambivalence toward and resistance to interpretation. Responding to these arguments is of paramount importance for my purposes because as long as they motivate people to avoid rigorous interpretation, they prevent the kind of disciplined rationality and devoted communal inquiry my approach seeks to foster. See section II above.

33. See Sontag, "Against Interpretation." I do not claim that she *convinced* the critical establishment with her arguments. Rather her essay marked a moment when a paradigm shift in literary theory was about to occur. A plenitude of diverse activities became legitimate, the common aim of which was to find alternatives to a more impoverished conception of interpretation than the one I am explicating here. Sontag intuited and perhaps anticipated this shift in the temper of the time.

34. Several areas of current research can be construed as efforts to more fully elaborate some of my "elements" of analysis. For example, narratology can be seen as an in-depth effort to explore "narrative point of view." See Wayne Booth, *The Rhetoric of Fiction* (Chicago: University of Chicago Press, 1961) and Gerard Genette, *Narrative Discourse* (Ithaca, N.Y.: Cornell University Press, 1980). In addition, various forms of reader response criticism can be seen as elaborations of "notable effects." See Susan Suleiman and Inge Crosman, *The Reader in the Text* (Princeton, N.J.: Princeton University Press, 1980). Finally, the philosophically oriented aesthetic investigations of William Gass and Nelson Goodman can be construed as efforts to clarify how "the world" of a text is created and ordered. See William H. Gass, "Philosophy and the Forms of Fiction" and "In Terms of a Toenail: Fiction and the Figures of Life" in *Fiction and the Figures of Life* (New York: Random House, 1972), as well as the essay cited in note 27, and Nelson Goodman, *Languages of Art* (Indianapolis, Ind.: Bobbs-Merrill, 1968), especially chapters 1, 2, and 5, and *Ways of Worldmaking* (Indianapolis, Ind.: Hackett, 1978) especially chapters 1, 2, and 6.

35. I attempt to demonstrate this in a manuscript in progress on philosophy and film.

VINCENT B. LEITCH

Deconstruction and Pedagogy

Within the domain of present-day deconstructionist studies, reflections on pedagogy typically focus on the historical and contemporary roles of power, authority, and language. Teaching happens in the school and in the university—in a cultural institution situated amidst a network of financial, political, and intellectual interests and concerns. That the university *serves* culture and society becomes, in deconstructive thinking, the grounds for a critique and positive transformation of educational institutions and pedagogical practices.

Taking Positions on Institutional Structures

Let us first consider Jacques Derrida's writings on the scene of pedagogy, particularly in relation to his work with GREPH. GREPH, the Group for Research on Philosophic Teaching, is an organization, established in Paris in 1974 and spearheaded by Derrida, that has sought, among other things, to resist the preemptive intrusions over the past decade of the State into the teaching of philosophy. Briefly, GREPH saw that a proposed government "reform," introduced in the early 1970s, would have shrunk the teaching of philosophy in the French secondary schools, cut drastically the number of future teaching positions, and reduced the ranks of philosophy majors in the universities. In short, GREPH foresaw the diminution and eventual death of academic philosophy. Almost immediately large numbers of people, 600 professors and students and twenty work groups, began to inquire into the economic and political links amidst various social and pedagogical institutions—into the nature and history of modern education. Derrida himself wrote a half-dozen critical essays during the 1970s on the scene of pedagogy—all stemming from his work with GREPH.

In an essay of 1975 Derrida states that "deconstruction . . . has, then, always borne in principle on the apparatus and the function of teaching in general."[1] In Derrida's view, deconstruction is, and has been, "inherently" related to and concerned with pedagogical theory and practice—despite what some narrow-minded American "readers" of Derrida may believe. Derrida goes on in the essay to suggest three general strategies for concerned academics: (1) don't abandon the "old" university, (2) create a critique of it, and (3) develop a positive and extensive transformation of it (pp. 66–67). Speaking generally, Derrida is less interested in protecting the university from the play of powers than in taking positions in regard to such power plays. In matters pedagogical, neutrality is unacceptable and activism is essential (p. 74). Basically, Derrida recommends that every constituted hierarchy and criterion, of any sort, be investigated as a prelude to any transformation.[2]

The approach of GREPH is characteristic of deconstructive inquiry: it starts with a local issue and quickly expands its critical investigation into the system of hierarchical relations underlying the institutions involved in the issue. Thus in the GREPH statutes of 1975 we read: "We don't think that reflection on the teaching of philosophy is separable from the analysis of the historical and political conditions and functions of the system of teaching in general."[3] And in the document that takes a position against the government "reform," GREPH seeks "a veritable recasting of the teaching of philosophy—and of school in general—."[4]

What distinguishes Derrida's work with GREPH is not only a broadened set of concerns but a special tone. Where we would expect, finally, apocalyptic and angry accusations and prognostications, we discover here and there an intractable gaiety—reminiscent of a certain radical strand in Nietzsche. This tone follows from several deconstructive fundamentals: (1) every field is a site of contending, differential forces; (2) every such site is historically constituted as a set of hierarchical values and apparatuses—an institutionalized axiomatics; (3) there is no outside such a systematics—only a transformation from within; and (4) apocalypse and revolution, sometimes tempting and irresistible, tend to reconstitute more firmly preexisting forms and practices. To catch a glimpse of Derrida's distinctive tone, we can turn to his opening remarks to the Estates General of Philosophy, a convention of 1200 people who met at the Sorbonne in June 1979 in order to combat the deteriorating situation of philosophy teaching in France. Noting a certain tranquillizing complicity between academia and officialdom, Derrida urges: "It is this complementarity, this configuration—everywhere that it appears—which we must, it seems to me, combat. Combat simultaneously, and joyously, without accusation, without trial, without nostalgia, with an intractable gaiety. Without nostalgia for more discreet forms, sometimes (sometimes only) more distinguished, less noisy, which *in large part* will have prepared yesterday what we inherit today."[5] The necessity of struggle, of vigilance, of noisy assertion—opposed to discretion and nostalgia—override accusations and recriminations in favor of intractable gaiety in joyous combat. It's almost as though Derrida appreciated threat, which fosters inquiry and transformation, not simply on the local but on the systemic level.

By the time Derrida in 1980 delivered "The Conflict of Faculties," an address at Columbia University in honor of the founding of the Graduate School, he could describe the project of deconstruction as avowedly activist: "What is somewhat hastily called deconstruction is not, if it is of any consequence, a specialized set of discursive procedures, still less the rules of a new hermeneutic method, working on texts or utterances in the shelter of a given and stable institution. It is also, at the very least, a way of taking a position, in the work of analysis, concerning the political and institutional structures that make possible and govern our practice, our competencies, our performances."[6] Between the founding of GREPH in 1974 and the planning for a new International College of Philosophy—which Derrida coordinated[7]—following the publication of *Glas* (1974), Derrida has increasingly turned deconstruction toward sociopolitical and pedagogical inquiry and critique while maintaining and furthering its work of "narrowly" textual analysis. Or rather, he has situated institutions as well as texts more fully within their political and historical networks—grids that create and control our activities.

Given Derrida's progressive elaboration or broadening of the deconstructive project, we should not be surprised to hear his call to arms and tone of gaiety in the 1980 address delivered at Columbia, where he ties the work of deconstruction firmly to the critique of academic institutional structures: "But I *do* say that today, for anyone who belongs to an institution of teaching and research, the minimal responsibility, and also the newest, most powerful, and most interesting, is to make as clear and thematically explicit as possible such political implications, their system and its aporias" (pp. 54–55).

The Depropriation of Pedagogical Discourse

The focus on pedagogy in Derrida's work has the broadening effect of bringing into the foreground the potential of deconstruction to become activist *cultural* criticism. In the work of Roland Barthes, on the other hand, reflections on pedagogy often lead to a narrowing and intensifying of normally broad cultural concerns into a concentrated attention to and focus on the powers of classroom language. Where Derrida gazes more and more at the array of cultural institutions, Barthes focusses more and more on a limited range of effective teaching strategies available to the professor in the classroom. Let us consider Barthes's reflections on pedagogy as expressed during his decade of deconstructive work.

When asked at the close of an interview published in 1971 about what would constitute a valid teaching of literature, Barthes responded:

> I don't quite know what to answer. I don't know if literature *should* be taught. If one thinks that it should, then one should accept, shall we say, a reformist perspective, and in that case one becomes a "joiner": one joins the university to change things, one joins the schools to change the way literature is taught. In the main, I would be more or less inclined, by personal temperament, to this provisional, localized reformism. In this case, teaching would be directed toward exploding the literary text as much as possible. The pedagogical problem would be to shake up the notion of the literary text and to make adolescents understand that there is text everywhere, but that not everything is text; I mean that there is text everywhere, but repetition, stereotype, and *doxa* are also everywhere. That's the goal: the distinction between this textuality, which is not to be found only in literature, and society's neurotic, repetitive activity. People should be made to realize that we have a right of access to texts that are not printed as texts, as I did with Japan, fo. example, by learning to read the text and fabric of life, of the street.

> We should perhaps even redo biographies as writings of life, no longer based on real or historical referents. There would be a whole spectrum of projects, tasks that would be directed roughly toward a *disappropriation* of the text.[8]

Here in the early stages of his involvement with deconstruction, Barthes transforms the task of critical work into a pedagogical goal. We should free the ubiquitous text from stereotype, repetition, and opinion—formations of a neurotic society. And we should through such *depropriation* unleash or explode the text: textuality (linguistic determinism) should spread across everything. In the process, "literature" undergoes decomposition, replaced by the "text." The general movement here is from text as frozen form, stereotype, "literature," to text as licentious play of signifiers. The general activity involves exploding, throwing into disorder, and depropriating. These, of course, are fundamental practices of deconstruction.

The pedagogical scene that Barthes characteristically describes includes two elements: neurotic society in the background and the subversive professor in the foreground of the classroom. With Derrida we typically glimpse, not the individual professor in the classroom, but the teaching corps and the university in their relations to the State and to society. Because the classroom is always a problematic arena, Barthes early grappled with the difficulties of teaching deconstructively. Almost all such difficulties for Barthes have to do with language—its powers, its writing, its speaking.

In the well-known essay "Writers, Intellectuals, Teachers," published in *Tel Quel* in the fall of 1971, Barthes observes, "Language is always a matter of force, to speak is to exercise a will for power; in the realm of speech there is no innocence, no safety."[9] In effect, *"All speech is on the side of the Law"* (p. 191) and "The Law appears *not in what is said but in the very fact of speech"* (p. 192). That speech, the teacher's medium, is inherently violent and authoritarian means that the depropriation demanded by deconstructive teaching is difficult, if not impossible, to attain in the classroom. Barthes considers four options for the classroom teacher. First, he can capitulate and accept the role of authority and *speak* "well." Second, he can remain mute and fall prey to the stereotype either of the "great silent mind" or of the "recalcitrant militant" who dismisses discourse as useless. Third, he can alter delivery, pace, and rhythm or add copious corrections and capricious revisions as a way to nudge speech toward writing (textuality), but then he courts the stereotype of the "fumbling, weak and ineffective speaker." Fourth, he can practice "peaceable speech," which for Barthes is the closest he can come to deconstructive teaching. Trying to *suspend* the violence and authority of speech, the "peaceable speaker" is never "the actor of a judgement, a subjection, an intimidation, the advocate of a Cause" (p. 214). As in a drugged state or in an ascetic posture, the speaker generalizes himself, "tracing out a pure form, that of a *floating* (the very form of the signifier); a floating which would not destroy anything but would be content simply to disorientate the Law" (p. 215).

Whether or not "floating discourse" can be effected, Barthes, we see, is working toward a classroom practice of deconstruction. In doing so, he shifts from throwing the (literary) text into disorder to exploding professorial speech itself. The critic turned professor is pressed to depropriate pedagogical discourse. Society fades into the background and returns embodied in a violent and authoritarian language, which must undergo decomposition and pacification.

When he assumed the first Chair of Literary Semiology at the Collège de France in January of 1977, Barthes delivered the traditional *leçon*, ending with a peroration on pedagogy. Here we encounter a further elaboration of deconstructive teaching:

> What I hope to be able to renew, each of the years it is given me to teach here, is the manner of presentation of the course or seminar, in short, of "presenting" a discourse without imposing it. . . . For what can be oppressive in our teaching is not, finally, the knowledge or the culture it conveys, but the discursive forms through which we propose them. Since . . . this teaching has as its object discourse taken in the inevitability of its power, method can really bear only on the means of loosening, baffling, or at the very least, of lightening this power. And I am increasingly convinced, both in writing and in teaching, that the fundamental operation of this loosening method is, if one writes, fragmentation, and, if one teaches, digression, or . . . *excursion.*[10]

Again, Barthes affirms that the main job of deconstructive pedagogy is to suspend the oppressive forces of discursive language—to loosen, baffle, or lighten its power. And, once more, he devises a strategy to accomplish the job—a strategy that attempts to textualize discourse, to transform speech into writing. In place of "floating" discourse is now "fragmentation," "digression," "excursion." Pedagogical discourse, ideally, should become chronic linguistic sidetracking—randomized movement. The discourse of the professor, partial rather than totalized, should be, at its best, discontinuous.

Near the end of his *leçon*, Barthes observes that the practice of deconstructive digression or excursion describes "the comings and goings of desire . . ." (p. 15). And he notes that the professor of desire, this body, occupies, not the place of the Father, but that of the son. Barthes here links the project for a deconstructive pedagogy with his well-known contemporaneous psychoanalytic project for a libidinal textuality.[11] He seeks, in effect, a pedagogical practice of *jouissance* (libidinal bliss) beyond simple *plaisir* (pleasure). In Barthes's view, "Pleasure is linked to a consistence of the self, of the subject, which is assured in values of comfort, relaxation, ease—and for me, that's the entire realm of reading the classics, for example. On the contrary, bliss is the system of reading, or utterance, through which the subject, instead of establishing itself, is lost, experiencing that expenditure which is, properly speaking, bliss."[12] Here we find an extension of the earlier ideas of the "generalization of the subject," of the drug state, of the ascetic posture ("WIT," pp. 214–15). *Jouissance,* in the scene of pedagogy, names a system of enunciation in which the teaching body abandons itself: this excursion of the blissful son's discourse is staged in opposition to the coherent and steadfast speech of the authoritarian, violent Father.[13]

Barthes's whole pedagogical project goes in the direction of deracination and desedimentation, on one hand, and pleasure and play, on the other: uproot the frozen text; break down stereotypes and opinions; suspend or baffle the violence and authority of language; pacify or lighten oppressive paternal powers; disorient the Law; let classroom discourse float, fragment, digress; seek ascetic or libidinal abandonment of the teaching body/self. Between its early expression in *Tel Quel* and its later formulation in the Collège de France *leçon,* this project, like Barthes's texts, becomes increasingly libidinal and "lyrical" while remaining antiauthoritarian and "anarchist."

Playful and mischievous, Barthes's project for a deconstructive pedagogy, for the depropriation of discourse, contrasts with Derrida's contemporaneous project for a critique of institutional structures leading to the taking of positions. Derrida's activist and engaged commitment, unlike Barthes's solitary radicalism in its mobility and libidinal floating, aims to take or to stick so as to alter existing hierarchies and pedagogical institutions. To transform only personal classroom practice is to limit the effort; Derrida maintains solidarity with the workers of GREPH—a group seeking to criticize and transform *the* system. Yet both deconstructors attempt to break down the prevailing cycles of educational (re)production and both manifest a certain stubborn joy or gaiety in their struggles. Finally, both men, playing at moralist, call all teachers to their consciences—to the obligation to extend critical inquiry beyond a textual hermeneutics toward a critique of institutional values, arrangements, and practices.

Toward a Practice of Deconstructive Teaching

In the early 1980s a growing American interest not only in deconstruction but in its potential pedagogy manifested itself in several ways. *Yale French Studies* devoted an issue to pedagogy, which consisted of fifteen essays, many of which were deconstructive critiques of educational theories and practices. In the same year the Society for Critical Exchange offered a session on "deconstruction and pedagogy" at its annual meeting held in conjunction with the Modern Language Association. In 1983 the International Association for Philosophy and Literature convened a conference on "Deconstruction and Its Alternatives," which featured a panel and discussion on "Deconstruction and the Institutions of Learning in Philosophy and Literature." The journal *Social Text* began a special series in 1982 on "Critical Theory of Education," aiming to clarify "the political stakes of the struggle over education. . . ."[14]

What would a pedagogical practice, derived from the "principles" of deconstruction, entail? Can one teach deconstructively? How?

A preliminary step would require something akin to "attitude adjustment" or, more grandly, "epistemological transformation." We can start by affirming an obvious, though sometimes forgotten or overlooked, point: in the realm of knowledge, everything is constituted during a certain time by one or more people. Some "things" are included, some are excluded, some are marginalized. Boundaries are set up. The "made up" quality of knowledge, its fictitious character, evidences itself as inscription. Knowledge is recorded or registered in some way, even if only in an individual's memory cells. In deconstructive terms, everything we know is written or, more dramatically, *writing* produces all our knowledge. The adjustment, the transformation, here is twofold: first, traditional epistemological matters are transferred to the ground of philosophy of language or to linguistics; second, *writing* is understood in the widest possible sense to include all forms of inscription, ranging from carving a path through a forest to recalling a dream to penning a legal code. The incommensurability of our "written texts" and the "things and ideas" written about reveals, once again, the "fictitious" quality of our knowledge: its differential character. The effect of this whole operation, which traces a key paradigm shift of our time from world as orderly array of substances and things to world as differential text, is to defamiliarize or denaturalize our knowledge. Knowledge is constituted as *historical* writing. Our knowledge, in its present and past formations and branches, could have been, and may yet be, constituted in other ways. Our relation to "facts," disciplines, departments, and hierarchies of knowledge is less "natural" or "normal" than concocted and thus alterable.

Out of such deconstructive thinking comes a certain strategic stance and practice for pedagogy. Nothing is ordained, natural, unalterable, monumental. Everything is susceptible to critique and transformation. "Arrangements," whether traditional or contemporary, can be "rearranged." To criticize is to cause crisis. In order to be successful this teaching—suspicious, critical, discriminating, optimistic—must pass to students. What distinguishes such a pedagogy is its grounding in *writing*. It is precisely the power of writing, in the broad sense, to ordain, create, naturalize, monumentalize, which produces the grounds for critique and transformation.

As classroom discourse, deconstructive teaching ought in turn to submit its own language to depropriation. There might follow tactical assaults on and transformations of pedagogical grammar and syntax through excursive rhetorics and impure styles. Socratic dialogue, dialectical conversation, would probably be disrupted. Intelligibility would be put in constant jeopardy. If not "depropriated," pedagogical discourse risks ordaining and naturalizing its own critiques. In this case, criticism would remain discreet cultural conversation.

Another tactic for classroom discourse is possible. Here relentless, lucid inquiries into the constituting powers of *language* would reveal its "creative" and "monumentalizing" functions, teaching active suspicion of all language formations. All writing, one's own especially, becomes subject to depropriation—deconstruction. Lucidity pushed far enough engenders vigilance about language—its productions, slippages, congealings.

The *politics* of such "deconstructive teaching" moves beyond traditional liberal tolerance; it is usable with certain socialist, libertarian, and anarchist ideals. That this pedagogy could serve "right" or "left" political ideologies is, one would suppose, incriminating. Such heterogeneity or undecidability, however, is the hallmark of deconstructive productions. To purify such duplicity, to turn this new pedagogy toward *a* political doctrine or dogma, would be precisely to turn away from deconstruction, to end its teaching, which, nevertheless, is not apolitical, as Derrida makes clear.

The focus of deconstruction on language, on its potential to "make up" and "maintain," to create and monumentalize, is inherently historicist. Language is historical. Not surprisingly, the archeological examinations performed by deconstructors are frequently corrosive insofar as the formations of history are subject to irreverent critiques of founding categories and operations. (The deconstructive trajectory is from text to textual system as historically constituted.) What we get is often a sort of counter-historiography. This revisionist impulse, respectful of history in an unconventional way, must lead to a certain pedagogical embrace of cultural history. Thus deconstructive teaching would be characterized precisely by an "historical" as well as a "linguistic" orientation.

NOTES

1. Jacques Derrida, "Où commence et comment finit un corps enseignant," *Politiques de la philosophie,* ed. Dominique Grisoni (Paris: Bernard Grasset, 1976), p. 65. All translations of previously untrans-

lated texts are my own. For a brief overview of the mission of GREPH, see James Kearns and Ken Newton, "An Interview with Jacques Derrida," *Literary Review* 14 (18 April–1 May 1980): 22.

2. Jacques Derrida, "L'âge de Hegel," *Qui a peur de la philosophie?* (Paris: Flammarion, 1977), p. 91. This text lists no editor, containing instead the names of seventeen contributors on its title page and the designation "GREPH." A "Liminaire" (pp. 5–11) offers a short history of GREPH, and a fourth section (pp. 427–71) collects ten GREPH documents, ranging from statutes to interviews to manifestos.

3. GREPH, "Modes de fonctionnement du GREPH (Statuts)," *Qui a peur . . .*, p. 441.

4. GREPH, "Prise de position contre la Réforme Giscard-Haby," *Qui a peur . . .*, p. 459.

5. Jacques Derrida, "Philosophie des États Généraux," *États Généraux de la philosophie (16 et 17 juin 1979)* (Paris: Flammarion, 1979), p. 43. No editor listed. A Committee of Preparation—twenty-one members listed on pp. 16–17—compiled this book from tapes of conference sessions. Among the committee members are Derrida, Gilles Deleuze, Philippe Lacoue-Labarthe, Jean-Luc Nancy, and Paul Ricoeur.

6. Jacques Derrida, "The Conflict of Faculties: A Mochlos," trans. Cynthia Chase, Jonathan Culler, Irving Wohlfarth, p. 56. I thank the author for the loan of this English-language typescript. This text is forthcoming in a collection edited by Michael Riffaterre entitled *Languages of Knowledge and of Inquiry* (New York: Columbia University Press, forthcoming).

7. See Jacques Derrida, Letter to Colleagues, 18 May 1982, published in *SubStance* 35 (1982): 80–81. This letter by Derrida, on stationery from the State Minister of Research and Technology, is an international call for suggestions, advice, and participation. On the program of the College, see François Châtelet, Jacques Derrida, Jean-Pierre Faye, and Dominique Lecoury, *Rapport pour le Collège International de Philosophie* (Paris: Ministre de la Recherche et de l'Industrie, 1982) and my "Research and Education at the Crossroads," *SubStance* (forthcoming).

8. Roland Barthes, *The Grain of the Voice: Interviews 1962–1980,* trans. Linda Coverdale (New York: Hill and Wang, 1985), p. 149.

9. Roland Barthes, "Writers, Intellectuals, Teachers," *Image-Music-Text,* ed. and trans. Stephen Heath (New York: Hill and Wang, 1977), pp. 192 (hereafter "WIT"). On this topic see also Jean-François Lyotard and Jean-Loup Thébaud, *Au juste: Conversations* (Paris: Christian Bourgois, 1979), pp. 16–19. See also Lyotard's reflections on contemporary university education in his *The Postmodern Condition: A Report on Knowledge,* trans. Geoff Bennington and Brian Massumi (Minneapolis: University of Minnesota Press, 1984), pp. 47–53.

10. Roland Barthes, "Lecture" (in Inauguration of the Chair of Literary Semiology, Collège de France, January 7, 1977), trans. Richard Howard in *October* 8 (Spring 1979): 15. Consider also Michel Foucault, "The Discourse on Language" (*Leçon* presented at the Collège de France, December 2, 1970), trans. Rupert Swyer in Foucault's *The Archaeology of Knowledge,* trans. A. M. Sheridan Smith (New York: Harper & Row, 1972), p. 227: "Every educational system is a political means of maintaining or of modifying the appropriation of discourse, with the knowledge and the powers it carries with it."

11. See my "From a Poetics to an Erotics of the Text," *Deconstructive Criticism: An Advanced Introduction* (New York: Columbia University Press, 1983), pp. 102–15.

12. Roland Barthes, *The Grain of the Voice,* p. 206.

13. Barthes contrasts older paternal theories of literature as *mathesis* and *mimesis* with the new theory of literature as *semiosis,* which produces "the bliss of the symbolic" in his "Literature/Teaching," in *The Grain of the Voice,* pp. 237–38.

14. To sample American reflections on "deconstruction and pedagogy," see, for instance, J. Hillis Miller, "The Function of Rhetorical Study at the Present Time," *ADE Bulletin* 62 (September-November 1979): 10–18; Jonathan Culler, "Literary Theory in the Graduate Program," *The Pursuit of Signs: Semiotics, Literature, Deconstruction* (Ithaca, N.Y.: Cornell University Press, 1981), pp. 210–26; *The Pedagogical Imperative: Teaching as a Literary Genre,* special issue of *Yale French Studies* 63 (1982), ed. Barbara Johnson; Michael Ryan, "Reason and Counterrevolution," in *Marxism and Deconstruction: A Critical Articulation* (Baltimore and London: The Johns Hopkins University Press, 1982), pp. 132–58, esp. pp. 152–58; William V. Spanos, "The End of Education: 'The Harvard Core Curriculum Report' and the Pedagogy of Reformation," *Boundary 2* 10 (Winter 1982): 1–33; Paul de Man, "The Return to Philology," *TLS,* 10 December 1982, pp. 1355–56, which is one of nine contributions to a symposium entitled "Professing Literature"; and, most recently, Gregory L. Ulmer, *Applied Grammatology: Post(e)-Pedagogy from Jacques Derrida to Joseph Beuys* (Baltimore: Johns Hopkins University Press, 1985), which appeared after this essay was completed.

To sample British thinking about contemporary critical theories and pedagogical practices, see *Re-Reading English,* ed. Peter Widdowson (London: Methuen, 1982), which contains sixteen essays by diverse hands. One essay in this collection is particularly concerned with deconstruction—Peter Brooker, "Post-Structuralism, Reading and the Crisis in English," pp. 61–76.

P A U L A A . T R E I C H L E R

Teaching Feminist Theory

Feminist theory seeks to illuminate, and to change, the social organization of sex and gender, the structure and reproduction of male dominance, and women's experiences as subjects in the world.
  —Feminist Theory Course Syllabus, Barrie Thorne, 1983[1]

The grand theorists hardly bothered to look at us, or, when they did, they looked at us through the most vicious and hostile lenses. Well, *we're* here now, and *we're* looking.
  —Naomi Weisstein, Virginia Blaisdell, Jesse Lemisch, 1975, p. 87

Black women could not exist consciously until we began to name ourselves.
  —Gloria T. Hull and Barbara Smith, 1982, p. xviii

We understand what we are and where we are in the light of what we are not yet.
  —Sandra Lee Bartky, 1977, p. 26

Feminist theory is not recent. The history of feminism is in part a history of theory. Even the word *feminism,* with its ideological marker *-ism,* presupposes a theoretical analysis that enables us to say something about women as a group or class. But in the last decade, feminist theory has become newly visible in the form of a wide-ranging body of ambitious and controversial writing. As this body of work grows, U.S. women's studies programs—and some traditional departments as well—have increasingly welcomed the teaching of feminist theory at both the graduate and undergraduate level. New courses, scholarship, and standing-room-only conference sessions all signal the charged atmosphere surrounding feminist theory and make clear that the resources for teaching are rich indeed. Yet simultaneously there is resistance to feminist theory within the feminist community as well as outright hostility to its claims. Also resisted is the privileging of academic theoretical writing over the feminist political theorizing which has taken place largely outside the academy. These tensions have special significance for the feminist classroom, where traditional notions of "theory" may appear to threaten hard-won feminist pedagogical practices and to undermine women's studies' longstanding independence from the male academic establishment.

This essay concerns the current teaching of feminist theory. More precisely, it explores how the term "feminist theory" functions, what its tensions are, and how its intellectual and pedagogical claims are variously inscribed, perceived, and credited. First, I describe the intellectual projects encompassed by current feminist theoretical writing. Second, I explore relations between feminist theory and feminist pedagogy, examining how feminist theory actually functions in the academic curriculum and in the classroom. Here I draw on my own experiences and on conversations with other feminist theory teachers. Finally, I explore how many feminist theory projects seem to be theoretically positioned. What does "theory" mean? What does it mean to "do" feminist theory? Can feminist theory reproduce the theoretical pluralism characteristic of U.S. feminism and women's studies and still be "theory"? Is pluralism an illusion constructed to disguise the real controversies in feminist theory and their potential divisiveness? I examine how current theoretical writing bears on these questions and on teaching. I conclude that feminist theory is a broad project, with diverse theoretical roots and connections, whose ultimate configuration makes unique contributions to our understanding of what it means to be in the world, particularly as a female. Certainly feminist theory belongs at present to no one; preempting the designation for one project or another, or contesting the production of theory by feminists, is considerably less interesting at this stage than seeking to illuminate various theoretical projects and to position them with greater precision in relation to one another.

I. Current Feminist Theory: Seven Basic Plots

> The first question to pose is therefore: how can women analyze their exploitation, inscribe their claims, within an order prescribed by the masculine? Is a politics of women possible there?
> —Luce Irigaray, cited by Mary Jacobus, 1981, p. 207

Given . . . the history of women's studies; its origins in the women's movement; its dependence on faculty with marginal status in the academy; and its practical, opportunistic, and immensely successful method of growth, essential abstract questions have understandably received sustained attention only recently.
—Marilyn J. Boxer, 1982, p. 683

Until very recently, feminist criticism has not had a theoretical basis; it has been an empirical orphan in the theoretical storm.
—Elaine Showalter, 1981, p. 180

The measure of [a theory's] success is just how much sense it makes of what did not make sense before.
—Marilyn Frye, 1983, p. xii

Feminist theory is blossoming at colleges and universities for several reasons: (1) as more feminist students and teachers enter all areas of academic life and mature in their thinking, a larger constituency exists to press beyond the particularities of feminist analysis toward a more general and hence more theoretical account—one that will also help us illuminate diverse and often contradictory intellectual and political positions; (2) at the same time, the existence of feminist theory demonstrates that women's studies can now legitimately claim academic and professional legitimacy and intellectual distinctiveness; (3) though theory generally does not dominate the academic curriculum in the United States, it is active within the social sciences and humanities; this gives feminist theory (especially interpretive theory) special intellectual affinities with other current teaching and research projects; (4) as feminists, we desire to explore theory in our teaching and research in part because it is theory that has been repeatedly denied us; (5) we continue to believe that we can build bridges between academia and activism and that theory will help us do so.

What is feminist theory? Rooted in the reality of women's circumstances, feminist theory, whatever else it may do, attempts to take a macroscopic view of women in culture. It examines the interlocking oppressions based on sex, gender, race, class, sexual preference, national origin, and ethnicity, and speculates about possible futures.[2] Though for some readers, "feminist theory" may have come to designate a particular enterprise (Marxist-feminism, feminist psychoanalytic writing, or feminist literary criticism, for example), the fact is that theory is being produced in so many areas that any single equation is inaccurate. In such a fluid field it follows that it is impossible to specify constitutive content. Sample syllabi and current theoretical writing yield a dizzying array of themes, projects, and positions from across the disciplines. As Barrie Thorne and her colleagues have written, however, "A good course, like a novel, has a plot, or an underlying framework which gives coherence to more specific detail" (1983). Deliberately foregoing a more conventional organization (such as the one based on political commitments proposed by Alison M. Jaggar and Paula S. Rothenberg, for example[3]), I offer the following "seven basic plots" (with subplots) as one way of representing current theoretical activity—an underlying framework that groups theoretical writings around specific intellectual concerns and questions.

1. Feminist theory takes sex and gender as its basic organizing categories and sets forth what the world looks like from this new perspective. Why do men drink wine, asked Virginia Woolf in 1929, and women water? (p. 25) On what grounds is sexual difference repeatedly inscribed in the world's social order? Who benefits by a social and political construction that holds women in subjugation? What relations exist and have existed between men and women, and between women and other disempowered members of society? How do the oppressions built into a given social structure relate to economic, political, and sexual practices? It is given in feminist theory's analysis that the subjugation of women has been a powerful force in the world's history, that it is wrong, and that it must change. What kind of analysis, then, is needed to bring an end to the subjugation of women? What kind of political power? Work which attempts a general account of women's situation includes the writings of our "foremothers" (Mary Wollstonecraft and Elizabeth Cady Stanton, for example) and that of current feminists (Shulamith Firestone, Catharine A. MacKinnon, Juliet Mitchell). Mitchell, for example, in her germinal 1966 essay "The Longest Revolution," analyzes the potential for feminist revolution in terms of four structural elements of the social system: production (work patterns and the ideologies which support them), reproduction (including both contraception and the demographics of populations), socialization (including the psychosocial function of the family), and sexuality (especially the current liberation of sexual experience from such traditional bonds as procreation and

family structure). Powerful contributions by lesbians and women of color during the early 1970s prevented U.S. theoretical writing from concentrating exclusively on male versus female as the only crucial dichotomy, insisting that analysis examine other differences as well.[4]

2. Upon what foundation is the notion of "sex" or "gender" grounded? How does sex become gender? How are male and female behaviors shaped and by whom? What are the mechanisms of the socialization process? But there is a prior question. From the ambiguity and complexity of biological sex (a complexity far from universally recognized), how does it happen that two dichotomous genders are constructed? What processes of recognition and identity construct female and male persons? As a conceptual tool for the study of these processes, psychoanalysis has been perceived to be "a revolutionary one. If we are afraid to use it—and using it is frightening—we have only ourselves to blame" (Dorothy Dinnerstein, p. xi). Its use is frightening because psychoanalysis itself has been faulted for the hierarchical fortification of sexual difference. Some feminist writers thus appropriate psychoanalytic theory, seeking to explain the genesis of female identity by way of a revised and more open-ended account of psychological and social processes (Dinnerstein, Gayle Rubin, Nancy Chodorow). Others have returned to Freud's own writings, and those of the French psychoanalyst Jacques Lacan, renewing their interrogations of these texts at the point at which "masculinity" and "femininity" are created within existing social and symbolic structures (e.g., Juliet Mitchell and Jacqueline Rose, eds.). But, finally, are there two sexes? Anomalies continually threaten dichotomous division in favor of the possibility of genetic, physiological, and psychological continuums, thus dissolving into a series of particulars a conception of dichotomous biological sex that is increasingly tenable only within particular contexts (see Tobach and Rosoff, eds.). These projects, which challenge traditional notions of sex and gender, in turn call for a rethinking of motherhood and mothering, of our relations to others in the world, and of the family.[5]

3. The feminist struggle takes place within a complex of existing power relations and against a larger panorama of class struggle. Or does the class struggle reenact an older, and more universal, system of patriarchal oppression? Does the traditional notion of

class struggle enshrine a mode of analysis no longer useful or even plausible as a foundation for feminist revolution? The oppression of women under capitalism, argues Michèle Barrett, "must be seen in the light of the enduring oppression of women throughout the world as we know it. . . . It must be stressed that male domination, and the struggles of women against it, precede and go beyond that context. As Gayle Rubin so refreshingly puts it, 'No analysis of the reproduction of labour power under capitalism can explain foot-binding, chastity belts, or any of the incredible array of Byzantine, fetishized indignities, let alone the more ordinary ones, which have been inflicted upon women in various times and places . . .' " (p. 39). Feminist writers, especially in England, have emphasized the relations between economic, social, and ideological structures: Is the notion of ideology reconstituted if we analyze it from a feminist viewpoint? What are the gaps within the dominant ideology that allow for feminist struggle? How are particular representations of women articulated into relations of power? How do representations of gender relations reinforce a patriarchal hegemony?[6]

4. After more than a decade of struggle to create a collective, unified feminist movement, it now seems important to begin more carefully to honor differences, particularities, and divisions. This struggle for "common differences" has often marked relations in U.S. feminism between white women and women of color: "It is, apparently, inconvenient, if not downright mind straining," writes Alice Walker, "for white women scholars to think of Black women as *women*, perhaps because 'woman' (like 'man' among white males) is a name they are claiming for themselves, and themselves alone" (p. 44). Now, increasingly and inescapably, "sisterhood is global." Anthropological writings were the first source through which women in the west gained knowledge about women in third-world countries; as third-world women increasingly speak for themselves, questions intensify about the reproduction by U.S. feminists of colonialist and imperalist impulses and ways of seeing. There is insistence that the category "woman" not be totalized to obscure difference, nor that the dynamic of difference itself be reproduced to establish third-world women as "the other." "It is necessary to emphasize that theoretical reflections concerning the status of women must be linked to the study of the *specificity of*

the condition of women" (Alya Baffoun, p. 227). What are these specificities? How can specific practices (like veiling in some Arab countries) be understood within the history of that culture? How are they linked to religious practices? What are the relations between women's rights, religion, and patriarchy? Is an international feminism possible? To that end, what international channels can maintain communication and solidarity among women in the face of widespread government control of publishing, mass media, freedom of speech, and freedom of movement?[7]

5. *Whose Body?* (the title of Dorothy L. Sayers's first detective novel) signals a point where biology, science, and sexuality intersect—the embattled female body. As biology deconstructs our notion of "woman," women deconstruct our notion of biology (Hubbard, Henifin, and Fried). What is "natural"? "Normal"? (See Ruth Herschberger, Donna Haraway.) How can we describe and interpret female sexuality, on its own terms and in relation to male sexuality (Snitow, Stansell, and Thompson, eds.)? How have theoretical and "scientific" accounts of female sexuality functioned to construct as well as explain sexual phenomena (Sander Gilman)? What happens when we ask why people become heterosexual, not why they become homosexual (Adrienne Rich, 1980)? What do we discover when we reopen discussion of so-called "perversions" within a feminist context *(Diary of a Conference)?* How do theories of the nature of female sexuality reflect and construct social, economic, religious, and medical policies and practices (Jacqueline Rose, Nawal el Saadawi)? Is the "right-to-life" movement a plot whose ostensible obsession with individual fetal annihilation distracts us from global progression toward nuclear genocide (Zoë Sofia)?[8]

6. A growing body of writing—in sociolinguistics, literary criticism, film theory, cultural studies, and psychoanalysis—looks at language as the site where female subjectivity is inscribed. Through what processes do women learn to use language? Do they have equal access to linguistic resources? How are women represented within the symbolic order? How do words, images, and patterns of discourse intersect to construct our notions of "femininity"? How are these systems of representation linked to cultural "facts" and internalized as cultural knowledge? What does it mean to say that language is patriarchal? Woman in patriarchal culture

63

stands, writes Laura Mulvey "as signifier for the male other, bound by a symbolic order in which man can live out his phantasies and obsessions through linguistic command by imposing them on the silent image of woman still tied to her place as bearer of meaning, not maker of meaning" (p. 7). But do women make meaning? By whose authority are particular meanings "authorized"? As feminists "seize the language," they move away from inquiry which privileges "sex differences" and ask instead about the meaning of language, speech, and silence for women under patriarchy. Nélida Piñon writes: "You must know who is the object and who is the subject of a sentence in order to know if you are the object or the subject of history. If you can't control a sentence you don't know how to put yourself into history, to trace your own origin in the country, to vocalize, to use voices" (p. 74). How do particular words and sentences relate to "conditions for speaking"? Is there something that can be called "women's writing" or "women's film" that disrupts the assumptions and codes of patriarchy? What is the function of gossip? Politeness? Assertiveness? How do particular words acquire meaning, and whose meaning do they acquire? Is the power of language in part the power of naming? How can women's texts be written and read as the locus of political, cultural, and biological experience? Through self-conscious attention to language, feminist theory seeks to build its own house with its own tools and to create new writing, reading, and interpretive practices.[9]

7. In a sense all feminist inquiry could be called "rethinking history," a process that underlies feminist inquiries in other areas. Yet a number of questions about theory and method are specific to the field of women's history and explore what happens when we place women at the center of our inquiries. "A new conceptual framework for dealing with the subject of women in American history is needed," wrote Gerda Lerner in 1969; "the feminist frame of reference has become archaic and fairly useless" (p. ix). Though agreeing with Lerner, Berenice A. Carroll noted that for some historians, the call for "theory" in women's history reflected a reluctance to accept work in women's history for its own sake; in contrast, she argued, "theory cannot wholly precede the detailed monographic, descriptive, and narrative work which, in the field of women's history, has been so badly neglected" (1976, p. xi). What do empirical findings about women's history, then, suggest

for theory? Are the language and categories of traditional historical writing—categories such as "civilization," "period," and "class" which are built on the historical experience of men—largely inapplicable to the historical experience of women? To what extent do all women share a historical existence? "If women's oppression cannot be denied, neither can it be denied that its character varied greatly by time, place, and class; nor that women have also played powerful roles in history" (Carroll, p. xii). Important historical research is at present examining women in different historical periods as well as the history of particular groups of women: lesbians, Afro-American women, Hispanics, Native American and Asian-American women, Jewish women, professional women, working-class women, and others. Initially motivated by a desire for greater empirical knowledge (and, perhaps, for a greater sense of identity), these studies collectively make important contributions to a theoretical understanding of historical processes. Thus historical studies of black women in the U.S., which trace the imprint of an African cultural tradition reshaped by the institution of slavery, suggest revisions in a traditional view of black history. Angela Y. Davis writes, for example: "Required by the masters' demands to be as 'masculine' in the performance of their work as their men, Black women must have been profoundly affected by their experiences during slavery." Despite their oppression, "they must have been aware nonetheless of their enormous power—the ability to produce and create. . . . Their awareness of their endless capacity for hard work may have imparted to them a confidence in their ability to struggle for themselves, their families and their people" (p. 11). Historical studies have also attempted to place women's history within a broad framework of human evolution.[10]

8. I need now to add an eighth "plot" that emerges from and in turn seeks to ground the others. These inquiries necessarily raise issues of ontology and epistemology: How is nature constructed? How do we gain knowledge? Do women have particular means available for knowing? Does this give access to a different kind of knowledge about the world? Feminists in both science and philosophy are asking these questions (among them Donna J. Haraway, Evelyn Fox Keller, Sandra Lee Bartky, Janet Radcliffe Richards, and Naomi Scheman). Feminist theory in relation to research methodology is increasingly a pressing issue (e.g., Gloria Bowles and Renate Duelli Klein, eds., Angela McRobbie, Liz Stanley). And

here, too, go questions and concerns that do not fall easily into the classification above.[11]

Even this incomplete list communicates the scope of this field and makes clear that the term "feminist theory" encompasses work of great diversity. This is reflected in the many ways feminists approach teaching feminist theory: (1) teaching feminist theor*ists;* (2) teaching a body of feminist work centered around existing bodies of theory (e.g., psychoanalytic theory); (3) teaching feminist challenges to existing theories and methodologies in a variety of academic disciplines (e.g., feminist literary criticism); (4) teaching core themes or central issues that engage feminist theoretical writers across disciplines (e.g., labor, sexuality, race, power and powerlessness); and (5) teaching feminist theoretical work in an attempt to construct *a* feminist theory—that is, a unified theory of women's experience and sexual difference.[12]

For many of us, the question of approach intimately connects *what* we teach to *how* we teach. This in turn leads us to the relationship between feminist theory and women's studies, where a well-developed pedagogy is anchored to a feminist philosophy.

II. Feminist Theory and Women's Studies

[Feminist teachers] were not set up as knowers among a group of nonknowers. They were more like part time assistants. They helped as much as they could by giving information about their experiences. . . . The 'teacher' did not remain the same person. In sharing our knowledge, our thoughts and experiences, the 'teacher' rotated among us. Each functioned as teacher at times because each had something to offer. There was no knower/nonknower, judge/judged hierarchy.
—Janet Robyns, 1977, p. 53

I really do wonder whether buying into theoretical discourse doesn't mean buying into just the kind of abstract language that so much of feminism has been opposed to.
—Susan Gubar, 1981, p. 10

I'm convinced that one can learn to lecture in a 'feminist' style—that one can speak publicly in a way that includes and involves the audience, and is not necessarily a form of 'male discourse.'
—Feminist theory teacher

The closer one gets to the truth the better the cause of women will be served. At the core of the feminist critique of the various

disciplines is the attempt to fashion intellectual tools that are freer
from the distortions of present male scholarship and that allow us
to seek the truth while we recognize our commitment.
—Margaret Benston, 1982, pp. 49–50

In the women's studies classroom, theory meets practice. Though
the principles and pedagogical goals of individual women's studies
courses may differ greatly, there is a kind of meta-formulation of
the project which connects feminist theory, feminist scholarship,
women's studies, and women's experience.[13] The words of wom-
en's studies practitioners help to communicate the flavor of these
discussions:

> As we try to understand more deeply women's experience under
> patriarchy, it becomes apparent that our venture is more profoundly
> radical than most of us had imagined (or even secretly wished).
> Eventually, it becomes clear that the venture is more than filling in
> the blanks with missing nuggets of information about women. No
> longer can we be satisfied just with critiques of the biases and blind-
> ness of our disciplinary theories, our religions and our ideologies.
> Finally, the frightening and exhilarating fact can no longer be de-
> nied—we are together embarked on a journey which has as its goal
> the complete reconstruction of human knowledge and human ex-
> istence. (Jill McCalla Vickers, p. 28)

Not every feminist teacher or scholar would endorse this ambitious statement nor even interpret it in the same way. For some,
"the complete reconstruction of human knowledge and human
existence" may mean an epistemological revolution and an end to
universities as we know them. For others, it may signal a much
more modest effort—mainstreaming the women's studies curriculum, for example. For still others, it may have nothing to do with
universities. Nevertheless, the statement includes a number of features that connect women's studies with feminist theory and help
define our collective vision of the general enterprise. First, these
projects—doing women's studies, doing feminist theory—*are* collective; there is a "we" in this statement that implies a community
with shared goals. (This "we," however, has always been problematic and becomes more so for feminist theory.) Second, as a
result of our practice of women's studies and feminist scholarship,
we have changed our original goals; we see that simply adding
women to existing institutions (curricula, disciplines, committees,

research protocols, etc.) will not bring about sufficient change. Instead, writes Adrienne Rich, women and women's studies programs need to become "woman-centered"; they then find themselves embarked on a quite different path. Spatial metaphors often express this vision of women engaged in a journey, entering new territory, crossing borders, dancing through a minefield, entering a wilderness, transforming a landscape. The journey entails the reconstruction of human knowledge and human existence.

This is a visionary project with, nevertheless, firm pedagogical consequences and commitments. The interdisciplinary nature of women's studies is one of its essential elements. By demanding "that the study of women become a central focus of the university curriculum," women's studies crosses boundaries and undoes "narrow disciplinary specialization" (Bowles, p. 7, 9). Gerda Lerner (1972b) argued that women's studies and feminist scholarship, by transcending individual disciplines, could illuminate the entire range of women's experiences; in turn, wrote Linda Gordon (1975), by transforming both scholarship and methodology, women's studies could more fully describe the human experience. But women's studies and feminist scholarship must go beyond description. The aims of women's studies, in Catharine Stimpson's view, are (1) to deconstruct false axioms, logic, and conclusions; (2) to reconstruct reality; and, finally, (3) to construct new theories and ideas.

Thus a second element in the women's studies agenda involves a view of feminism as a "philosophy of knowledge" (Marilyn Salzman-Webb and see Dorothy E. Smith). On the one hand this occurs as the disciplinary structure of existing knowledge is transformed (Florence Howe). But in addition, as we develop a "gynocentric vision" (Cheri Register), we find our consciousness changed and the processes of teaching and doing scholarship constituted in new ways. From this vantage point, no position is privileged, even our own. A rigorous and at times seemingly relentless program of self-scrutiny, with its wellspring the larger women's movement, is a part of many women's studies projects. For some feminists, the ideological nature of feminist activity demands such ongoing self-criticism as a safeguard (Rita Kipp).

In women's studies (particularly in the United States), perhaps the single most critical source of knowledge has been women's personal experience; feminist "consciousness raising" is in fact a kind of epistemological revision which seeks to restore personal observation and interpretation as trustworthy sources of information about the world. Thus quite early on, feminist pedagogy explored ways of incorporating personal experience into women's studies classes. This challenged traditional classroom hierarchies and values, as well as traditional approaches to what and how to study: personal experience was not opposed to intellectual experience but rather inextricably linked to the processes of discovery and of testing truth (Spender, 1981a). Catharine A. MacKinnon (1982) places consciousness-raising at the core of a feminist epistemology.

To the personal is linked the political, and this, too, was part of the classroom. As Marilyn J. Boxer sums it up,

> The double purpose of women's studies—to expose and redress the oppression of women—was reflected in widespread attempts to restructure the classroom experience of students and faculty. Circular arrangements of chairs, periodic small-group sessions, use of first names for instructors as well as students, assignments that required journal keeping, "reflection papers," cooperative projects, and collective modes of teaching with student participation all sought to transfer to women's studies the contemporary feminist criticism of authority and the validation of every women's experience. These techniques borrowed from the women's movement also were designed to combat the institutional hierarchy and professional exclusiveness that had been used to shut out women. (P. 667)

The power of these changes should not be underestimated. The notion that "sisterhood is powerful" gave strength to many women in their individual and collective development. For many women teachers, traditionally trained, it meant unlearning what they were used to; for some, it legitimated their own sense of what education should be and made possible an ease in the classroom that traditional formats discouraged. Many women students felt comfortable in university classrooms and able to participate actively for the first time. A voluminous literature documents these successes of women's studies classrooms. What is important for our purposes is that they introduced personal experience into the academic setting as simultaneously a mode and an object of inquiry.

Feminist theory and research methodology, likewise, are for many women anchored in the lives and experiences of individual women or women as a class. Muriel Dimen contrasts "masculine theory" with "feminist theory," which arises out of women's experience: "From women's way of being in the world grows a theory which tells of its origins—the simultaneity of similarity and differences, connections and separations, process and product, linearity and contradiction, that is, the multiply-faceted character and determination of all social existence." "Feminism reconceptualizes the connection between being and thinking," writes Catharine MacKinnon (1982, p. 535). This view of women's relationship to the world suggests for feminist research a different kind of relationship between the scholar and the object of study. Feminist researchers, writes Gloria Bowles, "hope for a dialogue between researcher and researched in order to learn more about the inner and outer lives of all of us" (p. 10).

Finally, because the personal is political, women's studies is also—must necessarily be—"a pledge of resistance" (Adrienne Rich, 1976), inseparable from feminist culture and feminist politics. Though teachers differ in the degree to which they would call women's studies "frankly political" (Ann Fitzgerald and see Dale Spender, 1981b), few would deny that feminist teaching and scholarship are linked inextricably to the larger women's movement. For it has opened the channels for information about women to flow in, and with it come certain inescapable realities. Marilyn Frye writes, for example, that feminist theory requires us to try to make many women's lives and experiences intelligible. To do this requires acknowledging the patriarchal structures in which these experiences take place: "Trying to make sense of one's own feelings, motivations, desires, ambitions, actions and reactions without taking into account the forces which maintain the subordination of women to men is like trying to explain why a marble stops rolling without taking friction into account . . ." (pp. xi–xii). The women's movement requires, as well, that we take a stand with respect to our discoveries and not merely document but also explicitly seek to change the subordination of women. By demanding that "apolitical objective knowledge" no longer be privileged, feminist teachers and scholars make a commitment to both "the search for Truth" and "social change" (Bowles; Duelli Klein; Howe and Ahlum; Deborah Rosenfelt).

There has always been a fair amount of skepticism about

whether these visionary goals have a place in the academic world. In some sense, writes Gloria Bowles, women's studies within the university is already an internal contradiction. Feminist scholarship has also been seen as incompatible with academia (Jo Freeman). The university, it is charged, is inhospitable to the woman scholar and has consistently betrayed her interests: "The Alma Mater is a woman of ill repute" (Joanne Spencer Kantrowitz, p. 15). Just as women's studies has consistently challenged the nature of the academic institution, feminist activists have consistently challenged the nature of women's studies. Frye, who has been resolutely self-reflective on this point, notes that feminist academics are a privileged group and that shedding privilege is not a voluntary action: even the choice not to exercise privilege is a privilege. "The master's tools," charged Audre Lorde at an academic conference in 1979, "can never dismantle the master's house" (1981a). Not only do many academic feminists learn to use the master's tools; they sometimes do so at the expense of the larger women's community. An early indictment was made by three academic feminists: "Academic women command politically useful resources unavailable to nonacademic women. This gives them disproportionate power in defining the movement. They are not, however, accountable to the movement. There is a name for such a group: an elite" (Leffler, Dair, and Gillespie, p. 17). The view of academic feminists as coopted elitists is not limited to the U.S. Christiane Makward describes the attitude of certain radical French feminists: for them, "the wickedness of academic feminism is so obvious as to need no proof" (p. 99).[14]

A problem related to that of privilege is power. Indeed, suggests Constance Penley (in this volume), the aim of the feminist classroom to disperse or even eliminate authority may merely disguise the hierarchical distribution of power embodied by the university's institutional structure. "The risk," she writes, "in aiming toward or claiming the eradication of power relations, is that the force and pervasiveness of those relations may be overlooked, 'out of sight, out of mind.'" As a result, the feminist classroom is the site of a number of contradictory demands around authority. Gayatri Chakravorty Spivak argued at a conference that while attempts toward "nonauthoritarian" structure do not displace the power relations of institutional hierarchies, neither does an "authoritarian" structure like the lecture format wholly inscribe the power of the teacher over the students; a well-prepared lecture is also a service for which students have paid tuition, conference fees, or whatever, as are other aspects of the teacher's role.[15]

The perceived irrelevance or sterility of much academic research has also been seen to be at odds with feminist goals. What looks revolutionary to the feminist academic working to transform her discipline may look stunningly trivial to the nonacademic or even the scholar in a different field. Women of color have charged repeatedly that many aspects of the academy are antithetical to their experience. The intellectual predisposition of mainstream scholarship, writes Michele Russell, "is to regard anything dead as good, and the living as suspect and intrusive. Like any suburb, it is clean—pruned, well-manicured, sanitary—but psychotic." The academy is especially barren for women of color, she goes on, and asks white feminists whether their work will be different: "how will you refuse to let the academy separate the dead from the living, and then, yourselves, declare allegiance to life? . . . This is not a call for mindless activism, but rather, for engaged scholarship." "What chou mean *we,* white girl?" asked Lorraine Bethel in a poem critiquing the relations between Black and white women in the academy, especially white feminists' privileging of their own concerns and assumptions. Audre Lorde (1980), in another context, wrote, "I am myself, a black woman warrior poet doing my work, come to ask you, are you doing yours?"

Women's studies has thus, for more than a decade, been explosive with controversy—controversy by no means in the past.[16] Attacked by activists as sterile, attacked by conservatives as irresponsibly political, women's studies has survived and thrived through a variety of strategies and practices: healthy enrollments, alliance with other programs such as those for reentry students and continuing education, research productivity, and the project of "mainstreaming" the women's studies curriculum as a way of revitalizing the liberal arts curriculum. Boxer suggests that the very name "women's studies" is a form of protection: in contrast to the overtly political "feminist studies," it purports to reflect traditional academic "objectivity." On quite different grounds, Gloria Bowles and Renate Duelli Klein (1980) argue that women's studies should become a separate academic discipline; accordingly they routinely write "Women's Studies," using initial caps. Spender ironically titles a collection on women's studies *Men's Studies Modified*. Susan Groag Bell and Mollie Schwartz Rosenhan don't like the name at all; arguing that "women's studies" is ambiguous because it means both studies *by* women and studies *of* women, they advocate a more restrictive "women studies"—studies whose object is women. (This name would be just as ambiguous in speech, where it is virtually indistinguishable from "women's studies.") Jane Gallop (1982a) takes issue with their argument, claiming that the ambiguity of that "apostrophe *s*" embodies the power of women to be both subject and object—knower and known—and thus reflects a crucial source of strength.[17]

This discussion of the name "women's studies" displays a final characteristic of the field—its close attention to language. Whether women's studies is viewed as a liberating force in higher education or as a movement which is inappropriately political and confessional, it clearly has made the classroom a place where new voices can be heard. Many feminist writings, significantly, have titles like *Another Voice, Voices from Women's Liberation, In a Different Voice*. At the same time that they struggle to find their own voices, feminists seek to take apart the language around them—the language of the academy, of the disciplines, of traditionally male theory—to reveal the mechanisms of substance and structure that function to keep women in their place. For many feminists, deconstruction is nothing new; it has been a mode of survival for years. The tensions which mark the existence of women's studies programs within academic structures mark our language as well: what we say, what we do not say, what we cannot say, and what does not yet exist to be said. These tensions are particularly intense in feminist theory classrooms.

The name "women's studies" is thus powerfully connotative as well as denotative: "feminist theory" picks up some of the same symbolic load, bringing with it additional complexities that further problematize its definition and practice. Like women's studies, its name both announces and protects it. What this name encompasses, what counts as "feminism," what counts as "theory," and how links are made to the elements of women's studies I have been describing, can vary considerably. The next section describes some of these variations.

III. Implications for Teaching

At the beginning of the course, I tell the students that the whole field of feminist criticism is *totally* speculative, that there are no answers, that they can disagree with one another, that there is lots of room for work in this area. This tends to short-circuit clashes with conventional literary analysis.

—Teacher, graduate seminar in feminist literary criticism

I use bits and pieces of everything in my course, including the work of Black women activists. But there are basic conceptual differences between feminist theory and the Black agenda. It can't all be just subsumed under a kind of monolithic Woman.

—Teacher, Black Studies course

When I teach theory, I'm very up front about the difficulties I have with the material myself. I don't put myself up as an expert. I share with the students the fact that many of these texts are very, very hard.

—Teacher, women and literature course

I think we ought to read the text not with anticipation for quote Truth with a capital 'T' or Understanding with a capital 'U' but rather attempt to make some sense of it, given our individual histories.

—Student, feminist theory course

Feminist theory classes are fashioned from a complex fabric, with many threads. Talking with feminist theory teachers made clear that "feminist theory" has complex connotations. Responding to the word *feminist,* one feminist theory teacher calls her course "Sexual Inequality" to avoid "the classificatory issues ('is x feminist or not?') and start with substantive questions ('what is the nature of sexual inequality?')" "Theory," however, has associations quite different from "women's studies" and may mitigate some of the connotations of "feminist." Theory suggests abstraction, conceptualization; it invokes something "academic," not in the "real world." Some feminists are suspicious of theory because they perceive it as incompatible with activism; for others, theory has traditionally been used by males to obfuscate, mystify, and appropriate. Yet others—women and men, students and faculty— may be comfortable with feminist theory in a way that they are not comfortable with "women's studies." Once a course is elevated to the status of theory, particularly if it's a graduate course, they may not have the same apprehensions that the classroom will

feature "feminist process" (a student asked me whether participants in a feminist theory seminar would "have to sit in a circle")
or stress personal experience. The teacher's responsibility in feminist theory courses may also be differently perceived. A faculty
member at a research university contrasted the kind of intellectual
and political exploration that would take place in her theory class,
commitments more closely linked with her own research, with the
emphasis on personal experience important in her undergraduate
women's studies course. It also seems likely that the very word
theory—which designates what has traditionally been a male domain in most fields—gives males a sense of access to feminism,
quite in contrast to their relationship to "women's studies." For
some people, theory seems to be linked semantically to the masculine academic intellectual enterprise. Theory is not uncommonly
distinguished from activism, personal experience, and accessibility.
The commitment of some male academics to theory enables them
to incorporate or appropriate feminist theoretical writings as part
of their larger project. In contrast, other academics may perceive
the trend toward theory in their fields as excluding or devaluing
traditional scholarship.

While it is easy to argue that these are false equations, they
recur in conversations about feminist theory. In the classroom, as
in theoretical feminist scholarship, there may be a dichotomy between those whose background is primarily in "feminism" and
those whose background is in "theory." One feminist theory
teacher comments that some theory is "overly mystified": "This
is especially a problem when we study Marxist-feminism; the language of Marxism is unfamiliar to many, and highly abstract. Since
radical feminist writings dovetail with experience, that's less of a
problem."

Polarization between feminist theory and feminist experience
may be exacerbated by the linguistic equation of theory with specialized jargon and personal experience with confessional speaking
and simple language. Indeed, conversation on the subject sometimes comes to a standstill. At a 1983 conference on third-world
women and feminist perspectives, the use of "I" came to signal
personal experience ("lived experience") and to be seen as incompatible with strategically responsible analyses of particular conditions and actions in the third world; it came further to be equated
with the exploration of sexuality. In contrast, other speakers of-

fered "position papers," framing their remarks in Marxist-socialist language highly dependent on factual recitations, narratives of conditions, proper nouns, and abstract nominal compounds. One woman commented, "When a woman speaks in the first person, people call her language 'confessional' and thus trivialize it in the way women's experience has always been trivialized. A man who was poor and Black could tell his story in the first person and not be called 'confessional.' " Another woman described conference speakers who used this mode as "holy rollers." "I," of course, carries with it the baggage of a bourgeois romantic and humanistic tradition which privileges the individual and grounds discussion in an ideology which makes certain kinds of analysis impossible.[18]

Even as we strive to speak, we find language there ahead of us, already waiting, already contaminated. The notion of "theory in the flesh" (Moraga and Anzaldúa, p. 23) attempts to root theoretical analysis in concrete "flesh and blood experiences." But what is theory supposed to look like? A feminist who teaches literature and women's studies talks about the pervasiveness of the dichotomy between "theory" and "feminism": "It took me a long time to acknowledge that what I was teaching was theory. Because my language was simple and accessible, I thought it must not be theoretical. But as I continued to think about what made my teaching of women in literature a 'women's studies' course, I realized that not only was it political, it was theoretical as well. I now teach many things under the heading of 'theory'—a poem like Marge Piercy's 'Unlearning to Notspeak' is as theoretical as something more conventionally labelled 'theory.' " Another teacher includes Judy Grahn's *The Queen of Wands* and other creative writing in her theory course.

But another teacher who has offered courses on feminism and psychoanalysis includes as 'theory' work that contributes to the detailed examination of how sexual difference is constructed through language and the unconscious. Thus she includes the work of some men as more relevant to her enterprise than that of certain women—for example, Jacques Lacan or Stephen Heath rather than Karen Horney or Nancy Chodorow, since the latter tend to reduce the psychical to the social. Her goal is to help students learn to find their way through complex and often difficult texts. In fact, she says that for her there is a specific pleasure in doing theory and she does not consider this pleasure to be antithetical either to feminism or feminist research.

A feminist who teaches courses in Chicana literature talks about this question somewhat differently:

> I have sympathy with structuralism and the Baroque writing traditions characteristic of Borges and other Latin American writers. I think the French feminist writers are exciting and fascinating, and I love the things they do with language. Theory therefore informs my work and the way I read. But I don't write in that way myself. I write to be accessible, and I publish in journals where poststructuralist language would not be appropriate. For example, I might read many texts, read a lot of theory, and then write a piece on grandmothers—something clear and concrete. No doubt it would be nice to have my colleagues think I am doing important theoretical work. But I have made my choices: it's more important to me that the secretary who typed my paper on grandmothers wants a copy to read to her family than that my work be acclaimed for its theoretical complexity.

"I believe in reading theory," says a graduate student with a background in both theory and in feminist activism, "but at the same time, like Virginia Woolf, I read looking for myself."

A woman who teaches and studies Black women writers criticizes much current feminist theory for failing to specify the terms of its own claims. "I read an analysis of nineteenth century French women's autobiographical writings that purported to offer a theory of women's literature—all women, all forms of literature. In my own work on nineteenth and twentieth century Black women writers, I would never make such a claim. Much feminist theory reproduces the same false notions of universality that we criticize in male theories." The essentialist arguments of some French feminist writers create a similar queasiness over universal claims. Some feminist scholars resist theory in general because its claims seem so broad. Who has authority to speak for all women? What kind of background equips one to make or evaluate such claims? The breadth of writings cited in my opening section is formidable. Can one speak of "women" without some knowledge of all these fields?

Women I talked with handled these questions in various ways. Several teachers adopted the familiar mode of women's studies classrooms and became learners along with their students. One teacher emphasized the speculative nature of feminist theory and urged students to argue, question, disagree; she provided occasional short lectures to clarify discussion but otherwise was a participant rather than an expert. A teacher who looked forward to teaching a graduate theory seminar in her research area felt she would not be comfortable teaching interdisciplinary feminist theory. She indicated that team teaching—which might resolve her discomfort—was relatively rare at her university, as it is at most. Many of the teachers I spoke with ask other feminist academics to contribute to their courses, sometimes to talk about their own research and sometimes to cover certain topics—most typically the French feminist writers, whom some American teachers do not find readily teachable. One teacher said, "Sometimes I do the French feminists myself, but when someone else is available who can more sympathetically address work that takes place within a male theoretical tradition, I prefer to let them do it." "I personally have a lot of problems with the French feminists," said another, "and basically find the project of 'writing the body' bizarre. So I invited in a guest lecturer who gave background on the history of psychoanalysis in France, talked about Derrida and Lacan and what they're trying to do, and placed the French feminist theorists within that context; the students ended up thinking the French feminists were marvelous and the most revolutionary of all the feminist writers we studied."

Just as the relationship to male theorists varies widely from course to course, so does the relationship to feminist activism. Not everyone would include radical feminist theoretical writing in a course on theory. Yet some courses emphasize this work. One course in feminist theory and research methodology became a kind of practicum in university politics: as one of the teachers said, "We had to ask ourselves hard questions about the Women's Studies Program and its function within the university: how do you survive if your students are learning to critique every other academic department?" The students also critiqued the research of feminist faculty members which, said the teacher, they found "very much in the mainstream and nothing very revolutionary: but then how could a feminist academic be very different and survive?"

Finally, some courses encourage students to attend to personal experience and respond to the readings with their feelings as well as their intellects. One teacher drew on her experience in women's studies: "There is always the problem/resource of strong passion in feminist teaching, and I've found that by including readings about anger, these issues can be part of our collective self-reflection." "It is easy to intellectualize this material," said another; "I include readings which are accessible and controversial to try to subvert that process." "My only ground rule was that they had to come prepared each day with three questions about the readings; apart from that, I said, anything goes, but I wanted them to argue and get emotionally involved with this material."

These positions raise interesting questions for feminist theory classes. Can we preserve feminist activism within the demands of graduate-level academic work? How do we reconcile material which uses highly theoretical abstract language with the accessibility that many feminists expect of feminist texts? In what context do we present certain theoretical work (Julia Kristeva, Hélène Cixous) that seems to directly challenge the activist orientation of many American feminists and trigger their discomfort with a feminism not clearly allied to feminist social concerns and not clearly committed to a nonelitist, nonexclusive community of women? How do we address the issues and concerns raised by women of color, who may themselves be even more excluded from theoretical feminist discourse than from the women's studies curriculum? How is the breadth and diversity of "lived experience" to be credited when the experience of white middle-class women is continually privileged? Can we critically evaluate theoretical readings without embracing a traditionally combative mode of argumentation? Can we explore our "common differences" without overemphasizing the divisions that currently seem to characterize the feminisms of the United States and of the world? How do we link feminist theory with other theoretical analyses and at the same time explore and celebrate the characteristics that make *feminist* theory unique? What kind of courses enable us to explore these questions most fruitfully?

Many of the teachers and students I have spoken with encounter these issues as genuine problems and see them as closely linked to both theoretical and practical feminist questions. Each person, like each classroom, addresses them differently. In the following section, I describe our experience of teaching an interdisciplinary feminist theory course at the University of Illinois at Urbana-Champaign.

IV. Notes on Teaching a Feminist Theory Course

Three of us on the faculty collaborated to teach a feminist theory course in 1982. The course, titled Feminist Theory and Research Methodology, met two hours per week for lecture-discussion, student presentations, or guest presentations by faculty colleagues. Students met outside the class in study groups to prepare in-class presentations.[19] Special events, like an open discussion session with Sandra Gilbert and Susan Gubar, were occasionally scheduled, and several evening classes were held near the end of the term. We provided a substantial bibliography of required and recommended readings as preparation for our own introductory lectures and as further reading for the study groups. After the first six weeks, most classes involved study group presentations followed by class discussion. Written assignments included a long research paper. On the last day, students wrote anonymous evaluations of the instructors and the course. Besides myself, the teachers were Berenice A. Carroll in political science and Cheris Kramarae in speech communication. Our syllabus and readings were structured around a series of themes, which coincided only in part with academic disciplines:

> Beyond the Godfathers: Feminism, the Social Sciences, and Marxism
>
> The Master's Tools Will Never Dismantle the Master's House: Language, Critical Theory, and Women's Experience
>
> A Thief in the House: Language, Gender, and Communication Theory
>
> The Main Enemy: Patriarchy and Its Friends
>
> This Bridge Called My Back: Race, Sex, and Feminist Theory
>
> The Phallic Age: The Feminist Struggle with Psychoanalysis
>
> Between Money and Love: The Politics of Housework and Dependency
>
> The Glorious Age: Female Bonding and Matriarchy
>
> Writing the Body: Toward a Feminist Phenomenology
>
> Sinister Wisdom: On Lies, Secrets, and Silences
>
> Whose Body? Toward a Theoretical Understanding of Definition and Control
>
> What Would We Choose If We Had A Choice? Sexuality and Freedom
>
> Power and Powerlessness

Rethinking the Family

The Public Sphere and the Private Sphere

Methodicide and Journeyings: Research Applications

We did not, of course, do justice to this imposing lineup, partly because our own interests and those of the class members focussed more readily on some issues than others and partly because the study group presentations did not conform to this structure very neatly. Ongoing developments in feminist theory also of course alter the ways in which it can most fruitfully be taught.[20]

Several measures indicated that the course was successful, including written evaluations, quality of student work, continued attendance, and student comments both in and out of class. Most features of the class were praised, including the collaborative teaching process, the readings, the structure which combined introductory faculty presentations with subsequent student presentations, and the guest lectures and special events. Yet the most intense responses were to those aspects of class structure that maximized student-student interactions: in-class discussion and out-of-class small study group meetings. Responses to in-class discussion were widely variable, ranging from "*much* better than anything I've experienced in other classes" and "great!" to "overly intellectualized," "bad atmosphere in terms of tensions," and "when? I didn't notice very much." In contrast, students unanimously applauded the value of their small study groups, even when their particular group experienced problems. "Fantastic!" wrote one student. "Best part of the class. Not only in terms of in-depth study of material but warm atmosphere conducive to exploring different viewpoints. I learned a *lot* and made new friends." "An excellent experience," another wrote. "I've made good friends as well as acquired intellectual comrades." A number of these points may be briefly expanded.

Collaborative Structure

Collaborative teaching was a particular pleasure and enabled us to teach a broader body of material than any one of us could comfortably have included in a syllabus. Our various backgrounds and departmental affiliations probably drew a more diverse student population than any of us would have alone. We did not find the logistics of teaching together a burden, nor were we often in disagreement. Each of us gave a presentation introducing ourselves and the major issues in our fields; we then took turns being primarily responsible for individual classes. All of us read and commented on each student paper; we met together to work out final grades. Though we did have differences of opinion and perspective in evaluating the papers, we were not in substantial disagreement about quantity and quality of student work.

This tolerance for pluralism might not be to everyone's taste. Though it might be expected of three teachers with experience in teaching women's studies, it is not entirely compatible with the more competitive and combative interaction that sometimes accompanies critical thinking in graduate courses. At the graduate level, furthermore, both team teaching and true collaboration are relatively rare. It was important to us, then, to let graduate students see three academics teaching collaboratively by sharing teaching responsibilities and interacting intellectually in a productive way. As I note below, there was some tension among the students as they sought appropriate modes for their own classroom interaction with us and with each other.

It is also worth noting that we had three very different styles of interaction and of presenting material, and thus demonstrated (successfully I think, though perhaps not all the students would agree) that different forms of interaction and communication can fruitfully coexist in one classroom. As academics struggling with our disciplines and the academic setting, we were engaged intellectually with the students. Yet in functioning as "working academics," so to speak, we were less personally engaged with the class than a teacher of an introductory women's studies course might be.

Study Groups

The study groups grew out of students' own intellectual commitments. In the second week, we distributed a list of topics with bibliographies and asked students to choose by the third week an area for concentration. Five or six small working groups were thus created. Our initial thought in designing the study group structure was to transmit *content* in a "feminist" way: unconsciously guided by the illusion that a graduate course in feminist theory was not altogether a "women's studies" class, we sought to balance "required" content with freedom and responsibility for students to define and pursue their own interests. We liked the idea of asking students to collaborate—as we were collaborating—but saw collaboration as a way for students to address content in a more ambitious way. As it turned out, the study group structure enabled women students to engage in a *process* to which most of them felt clearly suited. Despite our attempts to focus primarily on content, process—as one of the instructors put it in a final class session— "kept sort of hitting us over the head." As we have suggested elsewhere (Treichler and Kramarae), this course structure successfully integrated a number of features of women's interaction patterns into a traditional academic format, not as a gesture toward a friendlier atmosphere but as a real contribution to the way teaching and learning occurred. The study group structure made it possible for a large class with a relatively traditional lecture-discussion format to coexist with another structure which facilitated an entirely different pattern of interaction. As the study groups developed, the two types of structures worked together: ideas could be explored and refined in the "warm atmosphere" of the study groups, then presented more formally to the larger class. At the same time, ideas and events from the large group could be mulled over in greater depth and with more ease in the study groups. This was crucial to the process of encountering and digesting large quantities of diverse theoretical material and of beginning to work out one's own theoretical positioning.

Classroom Interaction

As students noted in their evaluations, classroom interaction was frequent, lively, and sometimes tense. The fact that we taped each class session made it possible for students to listen to the tapes afterwards, and some of them did this to arrive at a better sense of what had happened in a given discussion. Classroom interaction was sometimes but not always what might be expected in a women's studies course. At the first class meeting, for example, each person present gave her or his name and field; though standard practice in a seminar, it seemed not altogether appropriate for people in a women's studies course to present themselves solely in their academic personae—as though "graduate student in philosophy" or "political science major" encompassed their identities. Nevertheless, everyone followed this format, including the instructors. When his turn came, one of the men students departed from the formula in order to describe his motives for enrolling in the course in the light of his own intellectual goals; his description, offered in a poststructuralist vocabulary, was briskly interrupted by one of the women students, who asked him, "Why don't you just say your field like everybody else?" Though in a regular graduate seminar his remarks would have been quite appropriate, he seemed to be perceived in this course as displaying inappropriate self-importance and an insensitivity to the egalitarian interaction characteristic of women's studies. The fact that he was male probably heightened this perception; a woman student who departed from the name-and-field formula with similarly abstract remarks a bit later was not interrupted.

Intersections among contrasting linguistic modes were often evident. Tension between academic versus nonacademic styles of talk created perceptions of commitment to an intellectual versus an activist orientation toward feminism. Yet it was actually more complicated than that, as student discussion of Julia Kristeva's "Women's Time" suggested, since a number of constituencies asserted their presence in the class discussion. During the initial discussion, only four or five students ventured to contribute; since the piece was difficult, I was pleased that at least a few students spoke up. During a break, several students who had remained silent expressed their frustrations privately to me. After the break I said that some students had found Kristeva "impossible." One student, who had spoken initially, challenged their experience of frustration, expressing her view that some of these students were not reading the text with enough care or with enough appreciation of its complexities: "If you reject the text simply because 'it's complicated,' you're doing yourself a disservice for any further reading you might do within a feminist literary tradition." But another student took issue with this, citing her own irritation with Kristeva's "jargon" and her sense that the requirement for understanding it was to plough through the tradition of male scholarship from which it derived. She felt this undermined the status of "Women's Time" as a "bona fide women's studies" piece: "I really resent that." Her first-person language seemed deliberately to avoid the impersonal, academic tone of the first student. Further, in reporting her own experience of frustration, she validated the experience reported by the women who had remained silent. In turn, a third student challenged her: "So what is the distinction between a woman's text and a man's text? One between simplicity and difficulty? . . . That I would object to." A fourth student addressed the first student who had spoken: "I'd like to speak on what *you* said. I do think there's validity in attempting to get something out of these things that we're assigned to read or that are available to us. . . . So, you know, I tried to read it and I found it very difficult. There were some things in there I could take with me—and some stuff I was unwilling to work hard enough to really get into. But I think that *that's* not necessarily a bad thing *either*—you know, we have a *right* to reject some of this stuff." This student addressed the earlier speaker directly and seemed deliberately to use nonacademic, even deflating, language, calling Kristeva's writing or perhaps French feminist writing in general "this stuff." She avoided poststructuralist vocabulary, used colloquial language, and freely admitted that she found the text "very difficult." Notable in this exchange was the fact that students addressed each other directly in a way more typical of women's studies than of regular university classes. Toward the end of the session, I expressed sympathy with each student's right to make individual evaluations of the material, checking it against her own experience and learning to take what was useful for her own purposes and reject what was not. Outside class, two students who had been active in this discussion suggested to me that this was not an appropriately intellectual attitude toward difficult theoretical material and that it encouraged nonserious reading among the students; despite a view encouraging behavior characteristic of a graduate seminar, their coming to me directly was, again, characteristic of women's studies interaction. At the same time, I learned, two other students dropped the class because it was "too academic." At a couple of final class sessions, where people were freely sharing their views of the course, several students who had remained silent during the Kristeva discussion expressed their view that much of what we had read and said was "intellectual bullshit" and "mental masturbation" that would not—could not—speak to the oppression of women. Others countered with the view that language *is* action and as much a site for activist activity as other arenas of behavior. Further, it was argued, there must be interplay between theory and practice; even when the theory exists in a relatively inaccessible form, time should be taken to understand it and explore its applicability as a guide to change. No, ran the counter-counter-argument: theory must not be inaccessible. It is only inaccessible to conform to a tradition of male mystification which dictates what theory has to look like.

These perspectives and the impasse they lead to will be no surprise to teachers of women's studies and feminist theory. But to find a balance among them in actual classroom practice—quite literally to transcend the contra-dictions of talk itself—is not easy. Empirical evidence suggests that for women there are still no truly acceptable forms of talk. Studies find that women students are penalized for using language that is not assertive, yet equally penalized when they do assert themselves. Studies of teachers find that, at every educational level, women tend to generate more class discussion, more interaction, more give-and-take between students and teacher and among students. In direct relation to the degree to which this is true, (1) students evaluate these classes as friendlier, livelier, less authoritarian, and more conducive to learning, *AND* (2) students judge the teacher to be less competent in her subject matter. Thus behaviors judged as traditionally male—a lecture format, little student give-and-take, the transmission of a given body of content, little attention to process—seem also to signal professional competence. Conversely, students in women's studies classes may evaluate the teacher and the classroom experience according to whether it conforms to the egalitarian ideal and avoids "male" teaching behaviors. Other students may be subjected to similar evaluative criteria, and those who exhibit "male" classroom interaction patterns may be distrusted and judged by non-feminists as aggressive and domineering and by feminists as non-feminist. For students and teachers who draw intellectual and professional support from the feminist community, the quest for an appropriate mode of academic self-expression may be excruciating. The problem may be exacerbated in theory courses where unfamiliar and technically difficult material often exerts its own strong linguistic life. But perhaps the feminist theory classroom is precisely the theater in which these issues can be enacted and fruitfully explored.

V. Enacting the Theoretical

Is theory not always theatrical, a rhetorical performance as well as a quest for truth?
—Jane Gallop, 1985, p. 220

It is crucial that feminism move beyond the opposition between essentialism and anti-essentialism. This move will entail the necessary risk taken by theories which attempt to define or construct a feminine specificity (not essence), theories which work to provide the woman with an autonomous symbolic representation.
    —Mary Ann Doane, 1981, p. 33

Theory is, by nature, legalistic; infractions—the wrong theory, theoretical errors, or insouciant disregard for theoretical implications—are crimes; theory is a form of policing.
    —Nina Baym, 1984, p. 45

Theory, in all its manifestations, feeds back into everyday life and exerts a conceptual imperialism over it, so that we believe the theory and disbelieve ourselves.
    —Liz Stanley, 1984, p. 53

Mainstream white feminists must realize that feminist theory, feminist organizing, women's conferences, and women's studies courses generally lack an ideological philosophy capable of systematically encompassing the histories, experiences, and material needs of Black and working-class women.
    —Gloria I. Joseph, 1983, p. 136

There is no such animal as a uniquely feminist research methodology.
    —Feminist teacher and scholar, social sciences

A theory in the flesh means one where the physical realities of our lives—our skin color, the land or concrete we grew up on, our sexual longings—all fuse to create a politic born out of necessity.
    —Cherríe Moraga and Gloria Anzaldúa, 1981, p. 23

Women's way of being in the world, made public, thus becomes revolutionary. . . . We have found that process is our most important product.
    —Muriel Dimen, 1979, p. 62

Feminist theorizing about science is of a piece with feminist theoretical production. Unlike the alienated abstract knowledge of science, feminist methodology seeks to bring together subjective and objective ways of knowing the world. It begins with and constantly returns to the shared experience of oppression.
    —Hilary Rose, 1983, pp. 87–88

No rigorous definition of anything is ultimately possible, so that if one wants to, one could go on deconstructing the opposition between man and woman, and finally show that it is a binary opposition that displaces itself.
    —Gayatri Chakravorty Spivak, 1985, p. 119

> It seems to me that whatever else feminism might be, and whatever ends it might think of itself as serving, by the time it enters literary studies as critical discourse it is just one more way of talking about books.
> —K. K. Ruthven, 1984, p. 8

> I have had to bury my father to set my tongue free.
> —Francine Du Plessix Gray, 1982, p. 46

The term *feminist theory* suggests a unity that does not exist. Indeed, the term has become a dense point of linguistic intersection among competing discourses where meanings are produced and almost immediately contested. These contestations are irrevocably built into the deceptively generic rubric "feminist theory." In writing about the teaching of feminist theory, I am really writing about the nature and scope of these contestations, including the tensions between "feminism" and "theory" that can be heard in feminist voices throughout this essay.

The word *theory* originally, and most broadly, meant "a looking at, a viewing, a contemplation."[21] *Theory,* a noun, is derived from the notion of seeing, a connection preserved in the first two meanings, now more or less obsolete: (1) "a speculation—also a sight, a spectacle" (Christ's crucifixion was described in 1631 as "a theory") and (2) "a mental view, a contemplation" (Sir Thomas Browne writes in *Religio Medici,* "I thinke I have the true Theory of death when I contemplate a skull"). Modern definitions move away from the immediacy of seeing toward more abstract conceptualizations: theory is (3) "a conception or mental scheme of something to be done, or of the method of doing it; a systematic statement of rules or principles to be followed." The shift from the process of looking-at to conceptualizations of that process in turn prescribes the rules or principles for future looking-ats. This third definition also links the conception of goals with the method for achieving them. The link to a scientifically based positivism is spelled out more clearly in the language of the fourth definition: "A scheme or system of ideas or statements held as an explanation or account of a group of facts or phenomena; a hypothesis that has been confirmed or established by observation or experiment, and is propounded or accepted as accounting for the known facts; a statement of what are held to be the general laws, principles, or causes of something known or observed." Here the chain of nouns takes us away from the immediately observable world and obscures the number of verbs required, in practice, to make one's way from "facts" to "theory" (law, principle, system of ideas): one discovers, identifies, isolates, observes, teases out, synthesizes, assembles, collects, organizes, formulates, arrives at, forges, constructs, explains, accounts for, builds, makes, creates, achieves, systematizes, and encompasses. Faced with this weighted chain of theory-building, some feminists might feel an affinity for the fifth definition, which notes that "in theory" is sometimes contrasted to "in practice": lives concentrated on practice have often precluded theory; at the same time, what looks appealing in theory may founder in practice. Finally, a sixth definition documents our democratic extension of *theory* in common parlance to mean speculations, hypotheses, conjectures, ideas, and individual views or notions.

Even before venturing beyond the dictionary into connotation or practice, we can see that "theory" is open to multiple interpretations. Disagreement about the status of feminist theory is thus partly semantic: the word *theory* is in fact used in all these ways, often without specification. Some feminists use it disparagingly (in the sense of the fifth definition) to mean speculation without a clear agenda for practice. Sometimes it is used about writing that is primarily metaphorical or that sets forth the grounds for a feminist political agenda. Sometimes it serves as shorthand for feminist writing grounded in Marxism, deconstruction, or psychoanalysis. Sometimes it refers to the principles underlying specific intellectual paradigms (rationalism, positivism, poststructuralism). Indeed for many U.S. academics only positivist theoretical paradigms—produced more or less in accordance with the third and fourth definitions above—can really claim to be called Theory, with a capital *T;* anything else is discredited a priori. When the social scientist quoted above says "there is no such animal as a unique feminist methodology," what she really means is that in her view feminist studies do not constitute a paradigm capable of being evaluated by established positivist social science tradition; at best, feminist scholarship merely adds the variable of gender to a well-established tradition of inquiry. In contrast, at least some of what we teach as feminist theory falls into the broader category of conjectures and ideas described in the sixth definition and cannot be "validated" or "discredited" in the positivistic sense. For other feminists, the women's movement has nothing to do with theoretical production; a social and political movement, it has forced certain academic fields to view women in strikingly new ways and to incorporate women as practitioners; though this may change what the profession looks like, it does not constitute a new theory or research methodology.

But these diverse usages are not merely the function of a complex term with multiple meanings available. There are nonsemantic reasons why feminist theory is the scene of ongoing contestation, why there is tension between feminism and theory, and why feminist theory is not immediately identified as Theory with a capital *T*. These reasons are closely bound up with what feminist theory is itself about: the question of how sexual differences are constituted, how they function in specific contexts, what social and historical institutions preserve them, whose interests they serve. Theory—that spectacle, that contemplation, that constructed mental scheme—is deeply implicated in these questions of sex and gender. When we teach feminist theory, we are inescapably implicated as well.

Most theoretical traditions as we now know them in the west feature a Founding Father, with a capital *F*. Though there is a *tradition* of feminist thought, there is no "Femina" that "Feminist Theory" will ever derive from as Christian thought derives from Christ, Marxism from Marx, psychoanalysis from Freud, the theory of evolution from Darwin, the theory of relativity from Einstein.[22] Of course, despite the fact that a number of influential theories have the work of a single founding figure at their core, most people working within these theories insist on a diversity of positions within the theory and often on their own radical divergence from the work of their compatriots; a body of theory like Marxism or psychoanalysis actually exists as a group of widely different theories. Yet a central father figure serves as a continuing point of regeneration and departure: the Name of the Father is the patronym that unifies the enterprise.

The nonexistence of Femina—and consequent absence of core texts (Femina's early, middle, and late writings, together with commentaries by her students)—obscures the existence of feminist theorizing as a coherent and continuing activity. But in fact we do not really understand the nature of women's theoretical production. Because most women enact their lives within social relations that mark sexual difference in a variety of (often oppressive) ways, their ability to participate in a structured chain of theory building has typically been materially constrained. As studies of many fields document, such production not only requires access to training, space, and resources, it also requires time and some freedom from the responsibilities of daily living, including domestic labor and child care. When a woman does produce theory, she is often dependent on a male theoretician in some way, and her work may be subsumed under his name. Thus the conditions for theory-production may be different for women than for men.

In some cases, women (primarily white, middle-class, educated women) have had independent access to resources and have produced theoretical writing. Yet the fate of a given theoretical production is immensely unpredictable and by no means determined by its intrinsic characteristics (Kuhn, 1970). For example, by virtue of an evaluation process Berenice A. Carroll calls "the class system of the intellect," women's theoretical productions are not equally valued in the market of ideas but rather neglected, depreciated, or distorted (Carroll, 1984; and see Spender, 1982, 1983). The fourth definition above makes clear that what is acceptable as theory is also dependent upon the Name of the Father—that is, what we already accept about the world. As history tells us, this has often made things difficult for male theory-builders; for feminists, whose writings propose an often unfamiliar and almost always unwelcome world-view, the problem of producing theoretical writing and getting it heard is magnified. A couple of rules seem to guide the assessment of theoretical writing by females. One reads: if it is theory, it must look like a male produced it—that is, it must in some respects take the shape of the dominant discourse. The other reads: if a women produces it, it cannot be theory.

I repeat these familiar observations about women and theory to emphasize the paradox we encounter again and again: if women follow the rules of the dominant theoretical traditions and produce something that looks like theory, their work will not be feminist; if they depart from the rules of these traditions, which are generally policed by men, their work will probably not be judged theoretical. Because they are women, whatever they do will be subjected to different rules of interpretation and evaluation. The generic name "feminist theory" falls into the middle of this paradox and becomes for some a coopted elitism, for others an impossibility, for still others a transcendent challenge.

Given all this, it is not surprising that feminists take diverse positions on what feminist theory is, whether it is useful, how it is to be evaluated, and even whether it exists at all. In the spirit of the humanistic pluralism that has characterized women's studies, you can apparently teach a feminist theory course without precisely addressing or resolving these questions: you can practice the teaching of feminist theory, that is, without fully theorizing its practice. A very general statement can serve as a theoretical starting point: feminist theory seeks to understand women's historical and present condition and to envision and bring about change; feminist theory requires us to place the question of gender at the center of our inquiry; feminist theory is rooted in the history of women's oppression, seeks to link that oppression to other divisions based on race and class, and aims to reverse the conditions of that oppression; and so on. Such central feminist aims carry the course along, offering ample space for many theoretical approaches and positions. If there is a final position at the conclusion of the course, it is likely to involve implications for practice: a body of writing called feminist theory better empowers us to carry out our work (enabling the feminist literary critic, for example, to use the insights of feminist theory in her analysis and the feminist activist to more fully formulate and execute her mission). Within the universe of teachers of feminist theory in the U.S., most would probably be relatively comfortable with this pluralistic approach to classroom activity; most would not, I think, feel it was their right or responsibility to privilege one theoretical position or to present the diverse positions within feminist theory as a unified, universal account of women's experience.

But there are other possibilities here. As Muriel Dimen and others have written, feminist theory is *theory* as well as feminism and thus does seek to provide a general account of the nature of things. A pluralistic approach, resisting the temptations toward such an account, generates a certain amount of impatience: "We can't even agree on what a 'Feminist' is, never mind what she would believe in and how she defines the principles that constitute honor among us. In key with the American capitalist obsession for individualism and anything goes so long as it gets you what you want, feminism in America has come to mean anything you like, honey. There are as many definitions of Feminism as there are feminists, some of my sisters say, with a chuckle. I don't think it's funny" (Carmen Vasquez, cited in Bell Hooks, 1984, p. 17). Of course pluralism itself makes choices that simultaneously privilege and omit: it, too, can distort as well as inform more immediate reality, impose false universality on experience, and suppress or discourage the articulation of positions that do not celebrate plurality.

If "women's studies" embodies the fundamental ambiguity of women's experience as subjects in the world, "feminist theory" embodies the paradox of women's experience as theory-producers. This paradox requires, I think, that the teaching of feminist theory be more than the presentation of a pedagogical product. Just as the women's studies classroom represents theorized practice, the feminist theory classroom needs to be a space for self-conscious attention to the nature, scope, traditions, and consequences of theorizing itself. What follows is an attempt to sketch out this argument.

1. The production of theory takes place within a culture and involves in several respects the production of meanings. Jane Gallop (1985) links the word *theory* and the word *theater* to emphasize the significance of theory as rhetorical performance. Teaching theory also produces meanings. The feminist theory classroom becomes a place where we can explore not only the "objective content" of theoretical writing but how it is "performed" and how we, culturally situated, "read" it. Part of this task involves the interpretation of practices that claim to be nontheoretical. They, too, may be read as a rhetorical performance: ultimately, one cannot *not* do theory. But what is the stage? Who are the players and who the audience? What rhetorical strategies are employed and for what purposes? How does discourse tell a story, shore up an argument, deflect our scrutiny, ensure its survival? What designs does a given theoretical production have upon us? What are our designs upon it? How will it come out in the end?

2. Many feminists enter theoretical debates equipped with skepticism and a knowledge of history. For them "feminist theory" is not simply a body of knowledge that replaces Theory X. Feminist literary theory, for example, is not, as Ruthven claims, "just another way of reading books" but rather entails a feminist politics

as well. In describing and explicating the construction of sexual difference, feminist theory goes on to call for an end to the oppression of women. Though empirical investigation and theoretical analysis increasingly problematize any simple or universal definition of "oppression," the political agenda and programmatic activism of feminism cannot simply be stripped away and left outside the classroom door. Feminist theory would not exist without the feminist movement. This may not be clear to the reader of feminist theory who begins with Luce Irigaray but has never read Valerie Solanas. To address this question pedagogically is not (necessarily) to politicize the classroom nor to insist that students evolve a feminist politics but rather to illuminate the political commitments and consequences of feminist theoretical writing. Feminist politics is also part of feminist theory's appeal to other theoretical positions. Poststructuralists, for example, may be attracted to feminism not only because destabilizing sexual binarism is one of the most radical projects in the current critical scene, one with apparent real-world effects; they are also attracted because feminism provides a moral and political grounding not offered by a theory that calls into question the very possibility of meaning. Now whether a feminist politics is to be taken as a given or as an outcome of theoretical analysis may itself be a question of politics (or temperament or rhetorical preference); but in either case it can be used to maintain the tradition, sketched in section 2, of feminist pedagogy as a subversive activity.

3. As a theory that places gender at the center of inquiry and successfully charts the social construction of sexual difference, feminist theory's explanatory power and methodological contributions are as great as those of any other body of theory in the humanities and social sciences. Feminist theory has no less coherence and no fewer common ordering concerns and terminologies. Taken together, feminist theoretical writings constitute a coherent body of contemplation: to return to the original definition of theory, it is a vigorous "looking-at," in which many women and men over many centuries have participated. But for *feminist* theory, this "looking-at" is not sufficient. Instead, the classroom has the potential to be the site where the construction of sexual difference can be enacted and theorized. Obviously, one goal is (as the quotation above from Mary Ann Doane argues) to move beyond bald dichotomies to some greater understanding of female specificities.

We might, for example, review our own engagement with theory in terms of the gendered traditions and discourses it invokes together with our own (often contradictory) desires to mark or disguise sexual difference. We can also use feminist theory to examine the teacher-student relationship: see the discussions of transference by Constance Penley (this volume) and Michèle Le Doeuff (1977), of maternal and paternal roles (see Robert J. Bezucha and Margo Culley, in Culley and Portuges, eds., pp. 89, 212), and the description of a feminist film theory class in which "the spectacle of gender" unfolded with unexpected results (Catherine Portuges, 1985).

4. My presentation of feminist theory in this essay—as centered around a series of intellectual concerns—artificially constructs a sense of a coherent project that is in some ways quite false. It places people together who may never read each other's work: although they are working on "the same" content area, they are in essentially different theoretical universes. A classification based on political positions (liberal feminist, etc.) similarly misrepresents the ways in which practitioners of feminist theory are actually doing work. One might rather group people according to their faith in the power of language: Is language a "tool" we use to "transmit content"? Is language a gendered system we inevitably inherit and inhabit as female subjects within a patriarchal society? Is language incapable of "representing" female experience? Is language a site within which an unstable subject is constituted and reconstituted within given discursive practices? Does language shape all that we know of and can say about the world? Do we use language or does language use us? To ask these questions— and the feminist theory classroom is the place where they can be asked—presupposes that a theory is constituted within discourse. Such discourse is not generated in a vacuum; accordingly, theoretical writing cannot be read and interpreted on formal grounds alone. Its social, historical, cultural, and institutional contexts are crucial determinants of its production, of our reading, and of whether it could have come to be as a formal object in the first place.[23] No language is "uncontaminated" or "entirely new," though there may be good reasons for making the claim. (Feminists in a variety of fields, for example, are drawing on psychoanalytic accounts of the development of female sexuality: to dismiss such projects because they play on a tradition of male discourse is

nonsense. All language is contaminated by its existence in the world, by its interaction with other language, by its past, by its future. Projects that seem more closely linked to feminist activist concerns may be equally contaminated. A feminist health network based in Washington, for example, investigates and protests the irresponsible use of U.S. drugs on women in third-world countries. To lobby effectively, network members must steep themselves in alien, technical, and offensive terminology. Linguistic pollution is inevitable: the process of protest is always embedded in its opposing structure.) Yet as linguistic relations and positions are clarified, writing produced in diverse contexts (e.g. in different disciplines) becomes accessible for theoretical interpretation and use. At the same time, my discussion of classroom interaction in section 4 was intended to highlight the politics of classroom speaking and its relation to theory. What is the reward, what the punishment, for speaking theoretically? Must language play out the politics of the One and the Other? What is the significance of the quest for metaphor characteristic of feminist theoretical language? Again, the classroom is a space where we can enact and scrutinize tensions inherent in the name "feminist theory." We need to be attentive to language—to pronouns, for example: after critiquing for more than a century what Wendy Martyna (see Kramarae, 1982) has called he/man language, we are now problematizing our notions of and faith in *I, you, she,* and *we.* Attending to our own speech and what it inscribes is a necessary part of theorizing and one that serves to correct false universalities. We need to attend to how we name ourselves and others, what labels we give, what we appear to signify when we use words like *women, oppression,* and *feminist theory.*[24]

5. There are legitimate grounds for resisting a given theoretical model. A theory has the potential to colonize practice, shape research, dictate language, create stars, and dominate discourse to the exclusion of other voices. Therefore the judgments, cited above, by Nina Baym and Liz Stanley. But the production and consequences of a theory within the context of specific institutional structures should not be simply equated with the value and pleasure of working out a theoretical account. The explosion of feminist theoretical writing across different fields makes clear that feminists are increasingly gaining access to the means of theory production. Its practitioners do not seem to feel themselves to be dupes of the

patriarchy. In contrast to the formulaic character of much intellectual production, this is a field in the process of creating itself. Self-conscious attention to theorizing in the classroom can become part of the theoretical spectacle, an impetus for raising questions of responsibility, accountability, intentions, interests, and rewards. Thus there can also be self-conscious attention to existing institutional structures and their alternatives (see Hilary Rose, Cheris Kramarae, and Mary Helen Washington). Feminist theory practitioners often call for the interplay between subjective and objective types of knowledge. What does this mean? In part, it involves synthesizing subjective accounts of experience with other kinds of information. It involves analysis that examines and challenges the separation of public and private labor. Examination in feminist theory courses of "the class system of the intellect," the different evaluations of male and female classroom performance, and the relationship between personal and professional experience may deepen this analysis. In contrast to those theories formulated around a central figure, feminists are generally comfortable with a collective, multiply-historical founding figure—the voices of women now and throughout history. Footnotes, references, bibliographies—new formats and collective resources increasingly mark a different paradigm for scholarship. The collective foundation of feminism requires us to build more than a diversity of voices into our construction and practice of feminist theory. As Mary Helen Washington has noted, "The class imitates the syllabus" (1985, p. 228), thus the structure of the class can begin to spell out specific mechanisms: collaboration within the classroom, for example, encourages recognition and negotiation of competing vocabularies as well as continued collaborative work. Like all theory, feminist theoretical productions can have "real world" applications and consequences that need to be anticipated and articulated. Rosalind Coward (1982) attempts to work out such an account for psychoanalysis; Pauline Bart (1985) addresses the question of foreseeing the ways one's published work will be used.

6. Finally, feminist theory is a pledge of resistance. With increased access and control comes the right to name. Theoretical feminist writing of many kinds can be given the name of feminist theory. In the classroom, this naming process should not be taken for granted, but debated. The name *feminist theory* resists the historical decree that women cannot do theory as well as more

general social decrees about who can do what. The continual questioning of "whether men can do feminist theory" or whether they are, at the least, appropriating feminist theoretical writing as their own is involved here. If a male produces it, reads one inversion of the rules commonly applied to women, it cannot be feminist theory. Only superficially does this function as simple retribution for past exclusion. Nor should it really be taken as an essentialist position about a biological male's ability to understand and produce genuinely "feminist" thought. Rather it articulates a recognition that our constructions of sexual difference influence how theoretical productions are produced and interpreted. By continually calling into question the sex of the producer or interpreter, it disrupts the smooth operation of traditional processes. It is not intended—nor can it function—literally to preclude participation. At the same time, many women are already actively participating in constructing theory: women of color, women of different ethnic groups, disabled women, women of different ages, third-world women, white middle-class women, working-class women. This is not just a feminist ideal but a theoretical necessity. The growing body of work by women of color, for example, makes clear that much "white" feminist theory to date is limited in its appeal and applicability. This is not a political observation that theory-builders can choose to ignore but rather a testimony to the inadequacy of current practices. But to work out a comprehensive theoretical account is an ambitious project, and it is important that the voices contributing toward this collective enterprise be situated in relationship to one another—within a web, perhaps (in Gilligan's terms), if not a hierarchy. How we interpret and use each voice may vary, but there are none we can choose not to hear. For theory is both process and outcome: to assert that some voices are theoretically more pure, more useful, or more "feminist" than others is to theorize far beyond our current data. The feminist theory classroom, however, offers a site where these questions can be examined in some detail.

Conclusion

In this essay, I have explored the current teaching of feminist theory in terms of its intellectual concerns and political claims. I have argued that the teaching of feminist theory is more than the presentation of a pedagogical product. Rather, the term *feminist theory* is a falsely generic rubric incorporating diverse and sometimes contradictory discursive practices. We need not seek to resolve or disguise contradictions and competing claims: these contests are inherent in the notion of feminist theoretical production. The classroom is an ideal site for investigating how theory works, what languages it speaks, what claims it makes, what strategies it adopts. When the classroom itself is made the site for self-conscious theorizing, it becomes difficult to sustain a belief that nontheoretical practice is possible. It also becomes difficult to sentimentalize feminist theory by reading it as a series of metaphorical assertions about women. Feminist theory, emphasizing the importance of women's individual and shared experience and their political struggle in the world, necessitates the analysis of how sexual difference is constructed within given intellectual and social traditions; at the same time, it seeks to build general accounts of experience from these particularities. We are still discovering the nature and scope of these particularities and exploring what kind of theory we are able to create; at present, all productions, of information and of theory, are potentially important. Strategically, then, pluralism enables us to proceed in many different directions at the same time. But pluralism is not equivalence. If our task in teaching is not to privilege one theoretical project over another, neither is it to treat them all as identical contributions. We need to use the principles of feminism, of theory, and of feminist theory, to place them structurally and strategically in relationship to one another and to the overall enterprise. As for that enterprise itself, there now seems little doubt of its enormous scope or of its radical power to transform our understanding and experience of the world.

NOTES

1. Because this essay is both an overview of the field and a resource for teaching feminist theory, references are documented internally by author's name and, as appropriate, date and page number; the full list of references appears at the end of the essay. The list is suggestive, not comprehensive. In collections of theoretical essays, individual essays are not always cited.

This essay has been shaped by my own experiences as a teacher and scholar of feminist theory, by reading, and by dialogue with other teachers, students, and scholars. I will not offer a disclaimer about the ways in which my comments are skewed by my individual perspective; in the vast and interdisciplinary field of feminist theory, humility is obligatory. I would, however, like to thank the following people for their conscious or unconscious contributions to this effort: Bettina Aptheker, Nina Baym, Evelyn Beck, Gloria Bowles, Marilyn Carlander, Berenice Carroll, Virginia Cyrus, Judith Kegan Gardiner, Sally Green, Larry Grossberg, Grace Holt, Joan Huber, Mary Jacobus, Cheris Kramarae, Marlene Longenecker, Deborah McDowell, Cary Nelson, Constance Penley, Tey Diana Rebolledo, Deborah Rosenfelt, Ann Russo, Beth Stafford, and Barrie Thorne.

2. "Consider a birdcage," writes Marilyn Frye; "If you look closely at just one wire in the cage, you cannot see the other wires. If your conception of what is before you is determined by this myopic focus, you could look at that one wire, up and down the length of it, and be unable to see why a bird would not just fly around the wire any time it wanted to go somewhere" (p. 4). In writing this essay, I talked with a number of feminist theory teachers, examined syllabi, and read theoretical writing in many fields, but no doubt missed some important current work. I would be very glad to hear about it.

3. Jaggar and Rothenberg classify current feminist thought in terms of five theoretical positions: liberal feminism (with its roots in the social contract theories of the sixteenth and seventeenth centuries and its current emphasis on equality of opportunity); radical feminism (a more recent position that takes the domination of women as a fundamental oppression whose abolition requires revolutionary change); Marxist-feminism (which is committed to some form of historical materialist analysis); the position of women of color (who have insisted upon an analysis that links sex to race and class); and conservatism (which in Jaggar and Rothenberg's analysis includes such theoretical frameworks as psychoanalysis and sociobiology, which function to preserve traditional gender arrangements). Related discussions of feminist theoretical positions include Josephine Donovan, Jean Bethke Elshtain, Maggie McFadden, Ann Oakley (1981), Mary Anne Warren, Angela Weir and Elizabeth Wilson, Elizabeth Whitelegg et al., and Ellen Willis.

4. The study of the theoretical foundations of current feminisms might include the writings of Crystal Eastman, Beatrice Forbes-Robertson Hale, Emma Goldman, Olive Schreiner, Mary Wollstonecraft, and Virginia Woolf. Foundations of the current feminist movement might include these writings: Ti-Grace Atkinson, Sidney Abbott and Barbara Love, Simone de Beauvoir, Tony Cade, ed., Mary Daly, Christine Delphy, Andrea Dworkin (1974), Shulamith Firestone, Betty Friedan, Marilyn Frye, Carol Hanisch, Anne Koedt, Ellen Levine, and Anita Rapone, eds., Audre

Lorde (1981), Del Martin and Phyllis Lyon, Kate Millet, Juliet Mitchell (1971, 1984), Juliet Mitchell and Ann Oakley, eds., Robin Morgan, ed., Redstockings, ed., Adrienne Rich (1979), Barbara Smith, Valerie Solanas, Susan Sontag, Celestine Ware, and Naomi Weisstein.

5. Writings on sex and gender—more precisely on the social and cultural construction of sexual difference—include Joseph S. Alper, Sandra L. Bem, Jessie Bernard, Nancy Chodorow, Hélène Cixous, Dorothy Dinnerstein, Mary Evans and Clare Ungerson, eds., Shulamith Firestone, Jane Gallop (1982b), Carol Gilligan, Susan Gubar (1981b), Colette Guillaumin, Berard Haile, Carolyn G. Heilbrun, Luce Irigaray, Noreene Z. Janus, Mary Kelly, Julia Kristeva (1980), Michèle Montrelay (1978, 1980), Jean Baker Miller, Juliet Mitchell (1974, 1984), Juliet Mitchell and Jacqueline Rose, eds., Linda Putnam, Adrienne Rich (1976), Laurel Richardson and Verta Taylor, eds., Jacqueline Rose, Gayle Rubin (1975), Lillian Rubin, Carol Stack, and Barrie Thorne with Marilyn Yalom, eds.

6. Catharine A. MacKinnon (1982), summarizing the claims Marxists and feminists make against each other, notes that "Marxists and feminists thus accuse each other of seeking (what in each one's terms is) reform—charges that appease and assuage without addressing the grounds of discontent—where (again in each one's terms) a fundamental overthrow is required. The mutual perception, at its most extreme, is not only that the other's analysis is incorrect, but that its success would be a defeat" (p. 518). Feminists who have tried to illuminate the complicated intersections of gender and class, and/or to marry feminism with socialism or Marxism, include Bettina Aptheker, Michèle Barrett, the Combahee River Collective, Angela Davis, Christine Delphy, Zillah Eisenstein, Nancy Hartsock (1979, 1981), Annette Kuhn and AnnMarie Wolpe, LACW Collective, Michèle Le Doeuff (1984), Catharine A. MacKinnon (1982), Ellen Malos, ed., Mary O'Brien (1981b), Lillian S. Robinson (1978), Sheila Rowbotham, Lillian Rubin, Lydia Sargent, ed., Barbara Smith (1982), Natalie Sokoloff, Gayatri Chakravorty Spivak (1985), Batya Weinbaum, Sylvia Wynter, and the journals *Questions feministes* [available in English translation as *Feminist Issues*], *m/f, Feminist Review,* and *Feminist Studies.* The analysis of sexual inequality in its various forms is a project at the core of feminist theory: see, for example, Roslyn L. Feldberg, Charlotte Perkins Gilman, Joan Huber, ed., Catharine A. MacKinnon (1979), Marcia Millman and Rosabeth Kanter, eds., Pauli Murray, Laurel Richardson and Verta Taylor, eds. Tracing the history of women in relation to technological change is a related project: see, for example, Margery W. Davies, Joan Rothschild, ed., Jan Zimmerman, ed.

7. Writings include Paula Gunn Allen, ed.; Bettina Aptheker; Asoka Bandarage (1983); Evelyn Torton Beck (1983); Lorraine Bethel and Bar-

bara Smith, eds.; Beth Brant, ed.; Toni Cade, ed.; the Combahee River Collective; Angela Davis; Andrea Dworkin (1974); Norma Grieve and Patricia Grimshaw, eds.; Bell Hooks (1981); Gloria T. Hull, Patricia Bell Scott, and Barbara Smith, eds.; Julia Kristeva (1977); Winona LaDuke; Jill Lewis and Gloria Joseph; Gerda Lerner (1972a); Audre Lorde (1981b); Magdalena Mora and Adelaide R. Del Castillo, eds.; Cherríe Moraga and Gloria Anzaldúa, eds.; Robin Morgan, ed. (1984); Nawal el Saadawi; Carol Lee Sanchez; Robert Stam and Louise Spence; Gayatri Chakravorty Spivak (1985); Haunani-Kay Trask; and Michelle Wallace. The exploration of differences is linked to the study of cultures, and anthropological writings are relevant—for example, Shirley Ardener, ed. (1977, 1978, 1981), Ruth Borker, Ernestine Friedl, Leith Mullings, Sherry B. Ortner, Rayna R. Reiter, ed., and Michelle Rosaldo and Louise Lamphere, eds. See also the journals *Connexions, Off Our Backs, Manushi, Women's Studies International Forum,* and the *Canadian Newsletter of Research on Women.*

8. Theoretical writings about female health and reproduction include Hilary Allen; Rita Arditti, Renate Duelli Klein, and Shelley Minden, eds.; Beverly Brown and Parveen Adams; Mary Daly; Janice Delaney, Mary Jane Lupton, and Emily Toth; Claudia Dreifus, ed.; Barbara Ehrenreich and Deirdre English (1974, 1978); Sue Fisher and Alexandra Dundas Todd, eds.; Linda Gordon (1974); Ruth Hubbard; Judith Walzer Leavitt, ed.; Adrienne Rich (1976); Helen Roberts, ed. (1981b); Janet Sayers; Nawal el Saadawi; Caroll Smith-Rosenberg and Charles Rosenberg; Judith Jarvis Thompson. Writings about female sexuality—as well as writings about the problematics of an analysis of pornography—include Charles Bernheimer and Claire Kahane, eds.; Beverly Brown; Susan Brownmiller (1984); Sue Cartledge and Joanna Ryan, eds.; Rosalind Coward (1982, 1984); *Diary of a Conference on Sexuality;* Andrea Dworkin (1976); Alice Echols; Jane Gallop (1985); Garner et al., eds., Germaine Greer (1984); *Heresies: The Sex Issue;* Ruth Herschberger; Luce Irigaray; Cora Kaplan; Chuck Kleinhaus and Julia Lesage; Laura Lederer, ed.; Robin Ruth Linden et al., eds.; Catharine A. MacKinnon (1982); Gayle Rubin (1984); Samois, ed.; Snitow et al., eds.; Carole S. Vance, ed.; Ellen Willis. Theoretical explorations of lesbian sexuality and female relationships include Evelyn Torton Beck, ed.; Elly Bulkin; Blanche Wiesen Cook (1979a, 1979b); Margaret Cruikshank, ed.; Rosemary Curb and Nancy Manahan, eds.; Mary Daly (1978); Adrienne Rich (1980); Caroll Smith-Rosenberg; and Monique Wittig. On male violence against women, see Susan Brownmiller (1975), Andrea Dworkin, Susan Griffin, and Catharine A. MacKinnon (1982, 1983).

9. Writings on language include work on the place of the female subject within discourse (Hélène Cixous, Catherine Clément and Hélène

Cixous, Verena Andermatt Conley, Hester Eisenstein and Alice Jardine, eds., Wendy Hollway, Luce Irigaray [1983, 1985a, 1985b], Alice A. Jardine, Ann Rosalind Jones [1981, 1984], Julia Kristeva, Elaine Marks and Isabel De Courtivron, eds., Cary Nelson, Claire Pajaczkowska, Paul Smith, Helene Vivienne Wenzel, Allon White, Monique Wittig); feminist criticism (Elizabeth Abel, ed., Nina Baym, Cheryl Clarke et al., Jonathan Culler, Dartmouth College Collective, ed., Mary Ellmann, Mari Evans, ed., Judith Fetterly, Shirley Nelson Garner, Sandra M. Gilbert and Susan Gubar [1979, 1984, 1985], Carol Gilligan, Myra Jehlen, Mary Jacobus, ed., Annette Kolodny [1980a, 1980b], Claire Kahane and Madelon Sprengnether, eds., Estella Lauter and Carol Schreier Rupprecht, eds., Jane Marcus [1984], Biddy Martin, Toril Moi, Marjorie Pryse and Hortense Spillers, eds., Tey Diana Rebolledo, K. K. Ruthven, Elaine Showalter [1981, 1984, 1985], Barbara Smith [1982], Hortense Spillers, Gayatry Chakravorty Spivak [1983, 1985], Erlene Stetson, Catharine Stimpson, Paula A. Treichler [1984]); analysis of language (Maria Black and Rosalind Coward, Ann Bodine, Penelope Brown, Edward Bruner and Jane Paige Kelso, Deborah Cameron, Rosalind Coward and John Ellis, Elizabeth Cowie [1976], Mary Daly [1978, 1984], Carole Edelsky, Suzette Haden Elgin [1982, 1984], Pamela Fishman, Marilyn Frye, Judy Grahn [1982, 1984], Nancy Henley, Mary Kelly [1977 and 1981], Cheris Kramarae, Cheris Kramarae and Paula A. Treichler, Robin Lakoff, Audre Lorde [1981a], Wendy Martyna, Sally McConnell-Ginet [1980, 1983, 1984a, 1984b], Sally McConnell-Ginet, Ruth Borker, and Nelly Furman, eds., Kate McKluskie, Angela McRobbie [1982b], Gillian Mitchell, Cherríe Moraga and Gloria Anzaldúa, eds., Noëlle Bisseret Moreau, Meaghan Morris, Janice Moulton, Patricia Nichols, Nélida Piñon, Adrienne Rich [1979], Rosemary Ruether, Joanna Russ, Muriel Schulz, Dale Spender [1980], Julia Penelope Stanley and Susan J. Wolfe, Una Stannard, Barrie Thorne and Nancy Henley, eds., Barrie Thorne, Cheris Kramarae, and Nancy Henley, eds., Mary Vetterling-Braggin, ed., Marta Weigle, Candace West, Terry R. Winant, Monique Wittig and Sande Zeig, and Virginia Woolf); cultural studies (Birmingham Centre for Cultural Studies, Rosalind Coward, Kirsten Drotner, Marjorie Ferguson, Betty Friedan, Katie King, Angela McRobbie, Tania Modleski, Janice Radway, Ellen Wartella and Paula A. Treichler, eds.); feminist film theory (Camera Obscura Collective, Elizabeth Cowie [1977], Mary Ann Doane, Stephen Heath [1978, 1982], Claire Johnston [1978, 1980], Annette Kuhn, Teresa De Lauretis, Julia Lesage, Laura Mulvey, and Stephen Heath [1978, 1982]); and writings about women and communications (Matilda Butler and William Paisley, Margaret Gallagher, Noreene Z. Janus, Thelma McCormack, Angela McRobbie [1982a], Lana F. Rakow [1985a, 1985b], MaryAnn Yodelis Smith, Gaye Tuchman).

10. Feminist writings on history include Mary Ritter Beard, Berenice A. Carroll, ed., Blanche Wiesen Cook (1979a), Nancy Cott, Rosalind Coward, Angela Davis, Eleanor Flexner, Estelle Freedman (1981, 1982), Catherine Hall, Mary Hartman and Lois W. Banner, eds., Marie Louise Janssen-Jurreit, Joan Kelly, Linda Kerber, Ethel Klein, Gerda Lerner, Sheila Rowbotham, Hilda Smith, Louise A. Tilly and Joan W. Scott, Carroll Smith-Rosenberg, Barbara Taylor, Mary Roth Walsh, and Elizabeth Whitelegg et al. Here also would go those speculations and theoretical commentary about the constructions of a different kind of history: Angelika Bammer, Elizabeth Gould Davis, Sarah Hrdy, Evelyn Reed, Mary Jane Sherfey, Charlene Spretnak, ed., and Barbara G. Walker. Writings on feminist theory, research methodology, and the construction of feminist (and nonfeminist) discourse include Francis Barker et al, eds.; Michèle Barrett (1982); Pauline Bart (1985); Gloria Bowles and Renate Duelli Klein, eds.; Charlotte Bunch and Sandra Pollack, eds.; Margo Cullen and Catherine Portuges, eds.; Ellen Carol DuBois et al; Jean Bethke Elshtain; Jo Freeman (1975, 1979); GLCA Women's Studies Conference Proceedings 1978–82; Bell Hooks (1984); Alison Jaggar and Paula Rothenberg, eds.; Renate Duelli Klein (1980, 1985); Cheris Kramarae and Paula A. Treichler (1985); Maria C. Lugones and Elizabeth V. Spelman; Maggie McFadden; Angela McRobbie; Mary O'Brien (1981a); Ann Oakley; Sherry Ortner and Harriet Whitehead, eds.; Constance Penley; *Quest* Staff and the *Quest* Book Committee, eds.; Janice A. Radway (1985); Shulamit Reinharz; Janice Radcliffe Richards; Helen Roberts, ed. (1981a); Sheila Rowbotham (1983); Sara Ruddick; Sheila Ruth; Julia Sherman and Evelyn T. Beck, eds.; Elaine Showalter (1983); Dale Spender, ed.; Judith Stacey and Barrie Thorne; Liz Stanley; Liz Stanley and Sue Wise; Paula A. Treichler, Cheris Kramarae, and Beth Stafford, eds.; Jill McCalla Vickers; Mary Anne Warren; and Angela Weir and Elizabeth Wilson. Writings about women in relation to science and scientific discourse include Donna Haraway, Ruth Hubbard, Hubbard et al., Evelyn Fox Keller (1982, 1984), Carolyn Merchant, Hilary Rose, and Margaret Rossiter. Feminist analyses of art history include Judy Chicago, Germaine Greer, Lucy Lippard, Linda Nochlin, and Rozsika Parker and Griselda Pollock.

11. Other fields beginning to be addressed by feminist theoretical writing are law (Sylvia A. Law, Catharine A. MacKinnon [1983]); education (Charlotte Williams Conable, Jane Roland Martin [1981, 1984], Rosalind Rosenberg, Barbara Miller Solomon, Dale Spender [1981a], Paula A. Treichler [1985]); organizational behavior (Kathy E. Ferguson, Arlie Russell Hochschild); and theology and feminist spirituality (Mary Daly, Rosemary Ruether, Charlene Spretnak, ed.).

12. Many feminists remain unconvinced that there is a distinct body

of work that can legitimately be designated "feminist theory" because they think feminist contributions have not yet challenged received male theory in their own fields, or they do not consider as "feminist" writing that builds upon the work of recognized male theorists, or they believe feminist scholarship and women's studies have contributed to our knowledge about women but not (at least not yet) to our understanding of the processes by which knowledge is acquired.

13. A number of current writings help illuminate the connections between feminist theory and women's studies, and document the challenges of the last fifteen years. These include the *Female Studies* series published by KNOW, Inc., and the Feminist Press; Dale Spender's *Male Studies Modified;* Helen Roberts's *Feminist Methodology;* many essays in journals but particularly in *Signs: Journal of Women in Culture and Society* (especially the two theory issues); the Barnard College Women's Center Scholar and the Feminist series; the Berkeley Women's Studies Program collections edited by Gloria Bowles and Renate Duelli Klein, *Theories of Women's Studies I and II;* the essays in *Black Women's Studies,* edited by Gloria T. Hull, Patricia Bell Scott, and Barbara Smith; *Gendered Subjects,* edited by Margo Culley and Catherine Portuges; *Conditions: Five, the Black Women's Issue,* edited by Lorraine Bethel and Barbara Smith; the collection from *Quest* called *Building Feminist Theory,* and assorted essays (especially a recent unpublished paper by Barrie Thorne and her colleagues about teaching the sociology of sex and gender). There are many others, but I have found these especially valuable.

14. This charge is sometimes made against nonacademic mainstream feminists as well, of course; the point is that academia is supposed to be an ivory tower, free of at least some of the oppressions of the "real world." See Treichler and Kramarae (1983) for a fuller discussion.

15. An exchange between Gayatri Chakravorty Spivak and Catharine A. MacKinnon at the 1983 conference on Marxism and the Interpretation of Culture at the University of Illinois included discussion of the structure of speaking at conferences and in the classroom. See Cary Nelson and Larry Grossberg, eds., *Marxism and the Interpretation of Culture* (Urbana: University of Illinois Press, in press). See also Audre Lorde (1981a), Catherine Clément and Hélène Cixous, (1986), and Jane Gallop (1982a).

16. I have been speaking generally of internal controversy. But it is important to remember that attacks on women's studies from outside the field continue. Walter Jackson Bate, a somewhat aging lion of literary criticism, reflected recently in the *Harvard Magazine* on the sad decline of the Modern Language Association apparent in the number of feminist programs at the annual meeting. A truly virulent attack, which must be

read to be believed and even then you won't believe it, occurs in the October 1983 issue of *Prospect* (published by "Concerned Princeton Alumni"); titled "Let's 'Mainstream' Women's Studies" and subtitled "A proposal for dealing with women of the fevered brow," the piece gets worse and worse, and it's not a joke.

17. Notions about women's subjectivity play themselves out in our language. On this question of subject and object in the term *women's studies,* a similar observation about area studies was made at the University of Illinois conference on third-world women and feminist perspectives (April 1983). Names like *Asian studies, Caribbean studies,* and the like were critiqued as seeming often to involve the first world as active subject carrying out studies on the third world as passive object of study. Though this paper does not address language in any detail, this seems to me one of the places where feminist analysis has made continuing theoretical contributions. Now, increasingly, as feminist theoretical analysis confronts male traditions of academic discourse, challenges to existing linguistic practices go hand-in-hand with innovative alternatives (Treichler, 1982).

18. I am indebted to Nina Baym for making this connection.

19. Study groups were formed around student interests, with the course syllabus and bibliographic material as a guide. The groups that actually formed included the topics of psychoanalytic theory, Marxism and other historical analyses, racism, women and politics, and biology; a few students worked individually because group projects did not work out on Kristeva, social science methodology, and other topics. Many of the groups met once a week for discussion of class sessions and readings and for planning of the group presentation; others met less frequently. One change we would make in the future is to encourage these groups to form earlier and to follow more formal guidelines for individual and group participation.

20. The lack of cross-cultural material and anthropological literature seems a real gap; so does the lack of attention to epistemology and other areas of philosophy. Teaching the same course today, I would continue to emphasize language and discourse analysis but would add feminist film theory and would try to do a better job of encouraging students to analyze the discourse of their own disciplines and of the classroom itself. Other courses cover the social sciences more thoroughly than ours did and do a better technical job of critiquing methodological issues; beyond our scope, but in my view tremendously important, are the life sciences and their interaction with feminism: the nature of biological sex, the practice of science and its relationship to women, and the possibilities for feminist science.

21. This discussion is based on the definitions of theory in the *Ox-*

ford English Dictionary. Dictionary makers both reflect and foster the false equations of a community of speakers. Though the particular language reflects the orientation of the *OED*'s editors, most other accounts are not strikingly different in substance, though some insist upon an analysis that links the theory to its theorizer. Women's words about theory have been included throughout this essay.

22. I am indebted to Berenice A. Carroll for this notion.

23. Cf. Elizabeth Bruss, Cary Nelson.

24. Although "theory" also refers to bodies of thought like Marxism, the traditional vocabulary of theory is nevertheless strongly linked to empirically based science. One of feminist theory's contributions promises to be its quest for original and illuminating language. Both Marilyn Frye (1983) and Carol Gilligan (1982), for example, seek language different from most writing in their fields. Feminist theory shares this with other current theoretical writing. Yet even within theoretical traditions more highly metaphorical than that of U.S. empiricism, feminist writers carefully explore different forms of discourse (see, for example, Christiane Makward, 1980). Nina Baym notes that she now finds the word *must* in feminist writing (e.g., "our collective project must be to . . .") "a danger signal"; "My latest operating goal is, no 'must' in feminist discourse, even go easy on the 'should' " (personal communication), and see Nina Baym (1984).

BIBLIOGRAPHY

Abel, Elizabeth, ed. 1981. *Writing and Sexual Difference*. Special Issue of *Critical Inquiry* 8, no. 2 (Winter).

Abbott, Sidney, and Barbara Love. 1972. *Sappho Was a Right-On Woman: A Liberated View of Lesbianism*. New York: Stein and Day.

Adams, Parveen. 1979. "A Note on the Distinction between Sexual Division and Sexual Difference." *m/f* 3: 51–57.

Al-Hibri, Azizah, ed. 1982. *Women and Islam*. Special issue of *Women's Studies International Forum* 5, no. 2.

Allen, Hilary. 1984. "At the Mercy of Her Hormones: Premenstrual Tension and the Law." *m/f* 9: 19–44.

Allen, Paula Gunn, ed. 1983. *Studies in American Indian Literature: Critical Essays and Course Designs*. New York: Modern Language Association.

Alper, Joseph S. 1985. "Sex Differences in Brain Asymmetry: A Critical Analysis." *Feminist Studies* 11, no. 1 (Spring): 7–37.

Aptheker, Bettina. 1982. *Women's Legacy: Essays on Race, Sex, and Class in American History*. Amherst: University of Massachusetts Press.

Ardener, Shirley, ed. 1978. *Defining Females: The Nature of Women in Society*. New York: John Wiley and Sons.

Ardener, Shirley, ed. 1977. *Perceiving Women*. London: Malaby Press.

Ardener, Shirley, ed. 1981. *Women and Space: Ground Rules and Social Maps*. New York: St. Martin's.

Arditti, Rita, Renate Duelli Klein, and Shelley Minden, eds. 1984. *Test-Tube Women: What Future for Motherhood?* London: Pandora Press.

Atkinson, Ti-Grace. 1974. *Amazon Odyssey*. New York: Links.

Baffoun, Alya. 1982. "Women and Social Change in the Muslim Arab World." In *Women and Islam*. Special issue of *Women's Studies International Forum* 5, no. 2: 227–42.

Bammer, Angelika. 1981. "Utopian Futures and Cultural Myopia." *Alternative Futures* 4, no. 2/3 (Spring/Summer): 1–16.

Bandarage, Asoka. 1983. "Toward International Feminism." *Brandeis Review* 3, no. 3 (Summer): 6–11.

Barker, Francis, et al., eds. 1983. *The Politics of Theory*. Colchester: University of Essex.

Barrett, Michèle. 1981. *Women's Oppression Today: Problems in Marxist Feminist Analysis*. New York: Schocken.

Barrett, Michèle. 1982. "Feminism and the Definition of Cultural Politics." In *Feminism, Culture and Politics,* ed. Rosalind Brunt and Caroline Rowan. London: Lawrence and Wishart, pp. 37–58.

Bart, Pauline. 1985. "Being a Feminist Academic: What a Nice Feminist Like Me Is Doing in a Place Like This." In *For Alma Mater: Theory and Practice in Feminist Scholarship,* ed. Paula A. Treichler, Cheris Kramarae, and Beth Stafford. Urbana: University of Illinois Press, pp. 402–18.

Bartky, Sandra Lee. 1977. "Toward a Phenomenology of Feminist Consciousness." In *Feminism and Philosophy,* ed. Mary Vetterling-Braggin, Frederick A. Elliston, and Jane English. Totowa, N.J.: Rowman and Littlefield, pp. 22–34.

Baym, Nina. 1984. "The Madwoman and Her Languages: Why I Don't Do Feminist Literary Theory," *Feminist Issues in Literary Scholarship*. Special issue of *Tulsa Studies in Women's Literature* 3, nos. 1/2 (Spring/Fall): 45–59.

Beard, Mary Ritter. 1946. *Woman as Force in History*. Rpt. New York: Collier Books, 1972.

Beauvoir, Simone de. 1953. *The Second Sex*. Trans. H. M. Parshley. Rpt. New York: Bantam, 1961.

Beck, Evelyn Torton, ed. 1982. *Nice Jewish Girls: A Lesbian Anthology*. Boston: Persephone.

Beck, Evelyn Torton. 1983. " 'No More Masks': Anti-Semitism as Jew-Hating." *Women's Studies Quarterly* 11, no. 3 (Fall): 11–14.

Bell, Susan Groag, and Mollie Schwartz Rosenhan. 1981. "A Problem in Naming: Women Studies—Women's Studies?" *Signs: Journal of Women and Culture* 6, no. 3 (Spring): 540–42.

Bem, Sandra L. 1974. "The Measurement of Psychological Androgyny." *Journal of Consulting and Clinical Psychology* 42, no. 2: 155–62.

Benston, Margaret. 1982. "Feminism and the Critique of Scientific Method." In

Feminism in Canada: From Pressure to Politics, ed. Geraldine Finn and Angela Miles. Montreal: Black Rose Books, pp. 47–66.

Bernard, Jessie. 1964. *Academic Women.* New York: New American Library.

Bernheimer, Charles, and Claire Kahane, eds. 1985. *In Dora's Case: Freud—Hysteria—Feminism.* New York: Columbia University Press.

Bethel, Lorraine. 1979. "What chou mean *we,* white girl?" *Conditions: Five,* ed. Lorraine Bethel and Barbara Smith: 86–92.

Bethel, Lorraine, and Barbara Smith, eds. 1979. *Conditions: Five.* The Black Women's Issue.

Birmingham Centre for Cultural Studies. Numerous working papers and publications (see Stuart Hall).

Black, Maria, and Rosalind Coward. 1981. "Linguistic, Social and Sexual Relations." *Screen Education* 39 (Summer): 69–85.

Bodine, Ann. 1975. "Sex Differentiation in Language." In *Language and Sex: Difference and Dominance,* ed. Barrie Thorne and Nancy Henley. Rowley, Mass.: Newbury House, pp. 130–51.

Borker, Ruth. 1980. "Anthropology: Social and Cultural Perspectives." In *Women and Language in Literature and Society,* ed. Sally McConnell-Ginet, Ruth Borker, and Nelly Furman. New York: Praeger, pp. 26–44.

Bowles, Gloria. 1980. "Is Women's Studies an Academic Discipline?" In *Theories of Women's Studies,* ed. Gloria Bowles and Renate Duelli Klein. Berkeley: University of California Women's Studies, pp. 1–11.

Bowles, Gloria, and Renate Duelli Klein, eds. 1980. *Theories of Women's Studies.* Berkeley: University of California Women's Studies.

Bowles, Gloria, and Renate Duelli Klein, eds. 1981. *Theories of Women's Studies II.* Berkeley: University of California Women's Studies.

Boxer, Marilyn J. 1982. "For and About Women: The Theory and Practice of Women's Studies in the United States." *Signs* 7, no. 3 (Spring): 661–95.

Brant, Beth, ed. 1983. *A Gathering of Spirit.* Special issue on North American Indian Women. *Sinister Wisdom* 22/23.

Brown, Beverly. 1981. "A Feminist Interest in Pornography—Some Modest Proposals." *m/f* 5/6: 5–18.

Brown, Beverly, and Parveen Adams. 1979. "The Feminine Body and Feminist Politics." *m/f* 3: 35–50.

Brown, Penelope. 1980. "How and Why Are Women More Polite: Some Evidence from a Mayan Community." In *Women and Language in Literature and Society,* ed. Sally McConnell-Ginet, Ruth Borker, and Nelly Furman. New York: Praeger, pp. 111–36.

Brownmiller, Susan. 1975. *Against Our Will: Men, Women and Rape.* New York: Simon and Schuster.

Brownmiller, Susan. 1984. *Femininity.* New York: Linden Press/Simon and Schuster.

Bruner, Edward M., and Jane Paige Kelso. 1980. "Gender Differences in Graffiti: A Semiotic Perspective." In *The Voices and Words of Women and Men,* ed. Cheris Kramarae. Oxford: Pergamon Press, pp. 239–52.

Brunt, Rosalind, and Caroline Rowan. 1982. *Feminism, Culture and Politics.* London: Lawrence and Wishart.

Bruss, Elizabeth. 1982. *Beautiful Theories.* Baltimore: Johns Hopkins.

Bulkin, Elly. 1981. "Heterosexism and Women's Studies," *Radical Teacher* 17 (Winter): 25–31.

Bunch, Charlotte, and Sandra Pollack, eds. 1983. *Learning Our Way: Essays in Feminist Education.* Trumansburg, N. Y.: The Crossing Press.

Burke, Carolyn. 1981. "Irigaray through the Looking Glass." *Feminist Studies* 7, no. 2 (Summer): 188–306.

Butler, Matilda, and William Paisley. 1980. *Women and the Mass Media: Sourcebook for Research and Action.* New York: Human Science Press.

Cade, Toni, ed. 1970. *The Black Woman: An Anthology.* New York: Signet.

Camera Obscura Collective. 1976. "Feminism and Film: Critical Approaches." *Camera Obscura* 1: 3–10.

Cameron, Deborah. 1984. *Feminism and Linguistic Theory.* New York: St. Martin's Press.

Carroll, Berenice A., ed. 1976. *Liberating Women's History: Theoretical and Critical Essays.* Urbana: University of Illinois Press.

Carroll, Berenice A. 1984. "The Politics of Originality: Women and the Class System of the Intellect." Paper presented at the Unit for Criticism and Interpretive Theory Colloquium, University of Illinois at Urbana-Champaign, April.

Carter, Angela. 1978. *The Sadeian Woman and the Ideology of Pornography.* New York: Pantheon.

Cartledge, Sue, and Joanna Ryan, eds. 1983. *Sex and Love: New Thoughts on Old Contradictions.* London: The Women's Press Limited, pp. 48–66.

Chicago, Judy. 1975. *Through the Flower.* New York: Doubleday.

Chodorow, Nancy. 1978. *The Reproduction of Mothering.* Berkeley: University of California Press.

Cixous, Hélène. 1976. "The Laugh of the Medusa," *Signs: Journal of Woman and Culture* 1, no. 4 (Summer): 875–93.

Clarke, Cheryl, Jewelle Gomez, Evelynn Hammonds, Bonnie Johnson, and Linda Powell. 1983. "Black Women on Black Women Writers: Conversations and Questions." *Conditions: Nine:* 88–137.

Clément, Catherine, and Hélène Cixous. 1986. *The Newly Born Woman.* Trans. Betsy Wing. Minneapolis: University of Minnesota Press. Originally published as *La jeune née* (Paris: 10/18, 1975).

Cocks, Joan. 1985. "Suspicious Pleasures: On Teaching Feminist Theory." In *Gendered Subjects,* ed. Margo Culley and Catherine Portuges. London: Routledge and Kegan Paul, pp. 171–82.

Combahee River Collective. 1982 [April 1977]. "A Black Feminist Statement." In *But Some of Us Are Brave: Black Women's Studies,* ed. Gloria T. Hull, Patricia Bell Scott, and Barbara Smith. Old Westbury, N.Y.: The Feminist Press.

Conable, Charlotte Williams. 1981. *Women at Cornell.* Ithaca: Cornell University Press.

Conley, Verena Andermatt. 1984. *Hélène Cixous: Writing the Feminine.* Lincoln: University of Nebraska Press.

Cook, Blanche Wiesen. 1979a. "The Historical Denial of Lesbianism." *Radical History Review* 20 (Summer): 60–77.

Cook, Blanche Wiesen. 1979b. "Women Alone Stir My Imagination: Lesbianism in the Cultural Tradition." *Signs* 4, no. 4 (Summer): 718–39.

Cott, Nancy. 1977. *The Bonds of Womanhood: "Women's Sphere" in New England, 1780–1835.* New Haven: Yale University Press.

Coward, Rosalind. 1982. "Sexual Politics and Psychoanalysis: Some Notes on Their Relation." In *Feminism, Culture and Politics,* ed. Rosalind Brunt and Caroline Rowan. London: Lawrence and Wishart, pp. 171–87.

Coward, Rosalind. 1983. *Patriarchal Precedents: Sexuality and Social Relations.* London: Routledge and Kegan Paul.

Coward, Rosalind. 1984. *Female Desire: Women's Sexuality Today.* London: Paladin.

Coward, Rosalind, and John Ellis. 1977. *Language and Materialism: Developments in Semiology and the Theory of the Subject.* London: Routledge and Kegan Paul.

Cowie, Elizabeth. 1976. "Woman as Sign." *m/f* 1: 49–63.

Cowie, Elizabeth. 1977. "Women, Representation and the Image." *Screen Education* 23: 15–23.

Cruikshank, Margaret, ed. 1982. *Lesbian Studies: Present and Future.* Old Westbury, N.Y.: The Feminist Press.

Culler, Jonathan. 1982. "Reading as a Woman." In *On Deconstruction: Theory and Criticism after Structuralism.* Ithaca: Cornell University Press, pp. 43–64.

Culley, Margo, and Catherine Portuges, eds. 1985. *Gendered Subjects: The Dynamics of Feminist Teaching.* London: Routledge and Kegan Paul.

Curb, Rosemary, and Nancy Manahan. 1985. *Lesbian Nuns: Breaking Silence.* Tallahassee, Fla.: Naiad Press.

Daly, Mary. 1978. *Gyn/Ecology: The Metaethics of Radical Feminism.* Boston: Beacon.

Daly, Mary, 1984. *Pure Lust.* Boston: Beacon.

Dartmouth College Collective, ed. 1981. *Feminist Readings: French Texts/American Contexts.* Special Issue of *Yale French Studies* 62.

Davies, Margery W. 1982. *Woman's Place Is at the Typewriter: Office Work and Office Workers 1870–1930.* Philadelphia: Temple University Press.

Davis, Angela Y. 1981. *Women, Race and Class.* New York: Random House.

Davis, Elizabeth Gould. 1971. *The First Sex.* New York: G. P. Putnam's Sons.

Delaney, Janice, Mary Jane Lupton, and Emily Toth. 1977. *The Curse: A Cultural History of Menstruation.* New York: New American Library.

De Lauretis, Teresa. 1984. *Alice Doesn't: Feminism, Semiotics, Cinema.* Bloomington: Indiana University Press.

Delphy, Christine. 1984. *Close to Home: A Materialist Analysis of Women's Oppression.* Trans. and ed. Diana Leonard. Amherst: University of Massachusetts Press.

Diary of a Conference on Sexuality. 1983. New York: Faculty Press.

Dimen, Muriel. 1979. "Theory from the Inside Out." Paper presented at the Second Sex Conference, New York. N.Y.

Dinnerstein, Dorothy. 1977. *The Mermaid and the Minotaur: Sexual Arrangements and Human Malaise.* New York: Harper Colophon.

Doane, Mary Ann. 1981. "Woman's Stake: Filming the Female Body." *October* 17: 23–36.

Donovan, Josephine. 1985. *Feminist Theory: The Intellectual Traditions of American Feminism.* New York: Ungar.

Dreifus, Claudia, ed. 1977. *Seizing Our Bodies.* New York: Vintage.

Drotner, Kirsten. 1983. "Schoolgirls, Madcaps, and Air Aces: English Girls and Their Magazine Reading between the Wars." *Feminist Studies* 9, no. 1 (Spring): 33–52.

DuBois, Ellen Carol, Gail Paradise Kelly, Elizabeth Lapovsky Kennedy, Carolyn W. Korsmeyer, and Lillian S. Robinson. 1985. *Feminist Scholarship: Kindling in the Groves of Academe.* Urbana: University of Illinois Press.

Duelli Klein, Renate. 1980. "How To Do What We Want To Do: Thoughts about Feminist Methodology." In *Theories of Women's Studies,* ed. Gloria Bowles and Renate Duelli Klein. Berkeley: University of California Women's Studies, pp. 48–64.

Duelli Klein, Renate, ed. 1985. *Rethinking Sisterhood: Unity in Diversity.* Special Issue of *Women's Studies International Forum* 8, no. 1.

Dworkin, Andrea. 1976. *Our Blood: Prophecies and Discourses on Sexual Politics.* New York: Harper and Row.

Dworkin, Andrea. 1983. *Right-wing Women.* New York: Perigree Books.

Dworkin, Andrea. 1974. *Woman-Hating.* New York: E. P. Dutton.

Eastman, Crystal. 1978. *On Women and Revolution,* ed. Blanche Wiesen Cook. New York: Oxford University Press.

Echols, Alice. 1984. "The Taming of the Id: Feminist Sexual Politics, 1968–83." In *Pleasure and Danger: Exploring Female Sexuality,* ed. Carole S. Vance. Boston: Routledge and Kegan Paul, pp. 50–72.

Edelsky, Carole. 1982. "Who's Got the Floor?" *Language and Society* 10: 383–421.

Ehrenreich, Barbara, and Deirdre English. 1974. *Complaints and Disorders: The Sexual Politics of Sickness.* London: Compendium.

Ehrenreich, Barbara, and Deirdre English. 1978. *For Her Own Good: 150 Years of the Experts' Advice to Women.* Garden City, N.Y.: Doubleday/Anchor.

Eisenstein, Hester, and Alice Jardine, eds. 1980. *The Future of Difference.* Boston: G. K. Hall. Rpt. New Brunswick, N.J.: Rutgers University Press, 1985.

Eisenstein, Zillah R., ed. 1979. *Capitalist Patriarchy and the Case for Socialist Feminism.* New York: Monthly Review Press.

Elgin, Suzette Haden. 1982. "Why a Woman Is Not Like a Physicist." *Aurora: Speculative Feminism* 8, no. 1 (Issue 21, Summer): 30–34.

Elgin, Suzette Haden. 1984. *Native Tongue.* New York: DAW.

Ellmann, Mary. 1968. *Thinking About Women.* New York: Harcourt Brace Jovanovich.

Elshtain, Jean Bethke. 1981. *Public Man, Private Woman: Women in Social and Political Thought.* Princeton: Princeton University Press.

Evans, Mari, ed. 1984. *Black Women Writers (1950–1980): A Critical Evaluation.* Garden City, N.Y.: Anchor/Doubleday.

Evans, Mary, and Clare Ungerson, eds. 1983. *Sexual Divisions: Patterns and Processes.* London: Tavistock.

Feldberg, Roslyn L. 1984. "Comparable Worth: Toward Theory and Practice in the United States." *Signs* 10, no. 2: 311–28.

Ferguson, Kathy E. 1984. *The Feminist Case Against Bureaucracy.* Philadelphia: Temple University Press.

Ferguson, Marjorie. 1983. *Forever Feminine.* London: Heinemann.

Fetterly, Judith. 1978. *The Resisting Reader.* Bloomington: Indiana University Press.

Firestone, Shulamith. 1970. *The Dialectic of Sex: The Case for Feminist Revolution.* New York: William Morrow.

Fisher, Sue, and Alexandra Dundas Todd, eds. 1983. *The Social Organization of Doctor-Patient Communication.* Washington, D.C.: Center for Applied Linguistics.

Fishman, Pamela. 1983. "Interaction: The Work Women Do." In *Language, Gender and Society,* ed. Barrie Thorne, Cheris Kramarae, and Nancy Henley. Rowley, Mass.: Newbury House, pp. 89–101.

Fitzgerald, Ann. 1978. "Teaching Interdisciplinary Women's Studies." *Great Lakes Association Faculty Newsletter,* March, pp. 2–3.

Flexner, Eleanor. 1968. *Century of Struggle: The Woman's Rights Movement in the United States.* New York: Atheneum.

Freedman, Estelle. 1982. "Resources for Lesbian History." In *Lesbian Studies: Present and Future,* ed. Margaret Cruikshank. Old Westbury, N.Y.: The Feminist Press, pp. 110–14.

Freedman, Estelle. 1981. *Their Sisters' Keepers: Women and Prison Reform in Nineteenth-Century America.* Ann Arbor: University of Michigan Press.

Freeman, Jo. 1979. "The Feminist Scholar." *Quest* 5, no. 2 (Summer): 26–36.

Freeman, Jo. 1975. *The Politics of Women's Liberation: A Case Study of An Emerging Social Movement and Its Relation to the Policy Process.* New York: David McKay.

Friedan, Betty. 1963. *The Feminine Mystique.* New York: Dell.

Friedl, Ernestine. 1975. *Women and Men: An Anthropologist's View.* New York: Holt, Rinehart and Winston.

Frye, Marilyn. 1983. *The Politics of Reality: Essays in Feminist Theory.* Trumansburg, N.Y.: The Crossing Press.

Gallagher, Margaret. 1985. "Feminism, Communication and the Politics of Knowledge." Paper presented at the annual meeting of the International Communication Association, Honolulu.

Gallop, Jane. 1982a. "Castration, Authority, and the Politics of Writing." Paper presented at the annual meeting of the Modern Language Association, Los Angeles, December.

Gallop, Jane. 1982b. *The Daughter's Seduction: Feminism and Psychoanalysis.* Ithaca: Cornell University Press.

Gallop, Jane. 1985. "Keys to Dora." In *Dora's Case: Freud—Hysteria—Feminism,* ed. Charles Bernheimer and Claire Kahane. New York: Columbia University Press, pp. 200–220.

Garner, Shirley Nelson, Claire Kahane, and Madelon Sprengnether, eds. 1985.

The (M)other Tongue: Essays in Feminist Psychoanalytic Interpretation. Ithaca: Cornell University Press.

Gilbert, Sandra, and Susan Gubar. 1979. *The Madwoman in the Attic: A Study of Women and the Literary Imagination in the Nineteenth Century.* New Haven: Yale University Press.

Gilbert, Sandra, and Susan Gubar. 1985. "Sexual Linguistics: Gender, Language, Sexuality." *New Literary History* 16 (Spring): 515–43.

Gilbert, Sandra Caruso Mortola, and Susan Dreyfuss David Gubar. 1984 "Ceremonies of the Alphabet: Female Grandmatologies and the Female Autograph." In *The Female Autograph,* ed. Domna Stanton. New York: New York Literary Forum, pp. 23–52.

Gilligan, Carol. 1982. *In A Different Voice: Psychological Theory and Women's Development.* Cambridge: Harvard University Press.

Gilman, Charlotte Perkins. 1898. *Women and Economics: A Study of the Economic Relation between Men and Women as a Factor in Social Revolution.* Boston, Mass.: Small Maynard. Rpt. New York: Harper and Row, 1966.

Gilman, Sander L. 1985. "Black Bodies, White Bodies: Toward an Iconography of Female Sexuality in Late Nineteenth-Century Art, Medicine and Literature." *Critical Inquiry* 12, no. 1: 204-42.

Great Lakes Colleges Association Women's Studies Program. 1978–82. Proceedings of the GLCA Women's Studies Conference. Ann Arbor, Mich.: GLCA Women's Studies Program.

Goldman, Emma. 1970. *Living My Life.* New York: Da Capo.

Gordon, Linda. 1975. "A Socialist View of Women's Studies," *Signs* 1, no. 2 (Winter): 559–66.

Gordon, Linda. 1974. *Woman's Body, Woman's Right: A Social History of Birth Control in America.* New York: Penguin.

Grahn, Judy. 1984. *Another Mother Tongue: Gay Words, Gay Worlds.* Boston: Beacon.

Grahn, Judy. 1982. *The Queen of Wands.* Trumansburg, N.Y.: The Crossing Press.

Gray, Francine Du Plessix. 1982. "The Making of a Writer." *New York Times Book Review,* September 12.

Greer, Germaine. 1979. *The Obstacle Race: The Fortunes of Women Painters and Their Work.* New York: Farrar, Straus and Giroux.

Greer, Germaine. 1984. *Sex and Destiny: The Politics of Human Fertility.* New York: Harper and Row.

Grieve, Norma, and Patricia Grimshaw, eds. *Australian Women: Feminist Perspectives.* Melbourne: Oxford University Press.

Griffin, Susan. 1971. "Rape: The All-American Crime." *Ramparts* 10 (September): 26–36.

Griffin, Susan. 1978. *Woman and Nature: The Roaring Inside Her.* New York: Harper and Row.

Gubar, Susan. 1981a. "Blessings in Disguise: Cross-Dressing as Re-dressing for Female Modernists." *Massachusetts Review* (Autumn): 477–508.

Gubar, Susan. 1981b. Cited in *Feminist Readings: French Texts/American Contexts,* ed. Dartmouth College Collective, *Yale French Studies* 62: 10.

Guillaumin, Colette. 1982. "The Question of Difference." *Feminist Issues* 2, no. 1 (Spring): 33–52.

Haile, Berard. 1981. *Women Versus Men: A Conflict of Navajo Emergence.* Lincoln: University of Nebraska Press.

Hale, Beatrice Forbes-Robertson. 1914. *What Women Want: An Interpretation of the Feminist Movement.* New York: Frederick A. Stokes.

Hall, Catherine. 1985. "The Tale of Samuel and Jemima: Gender and Working-Class Culture in Early Nineteenth-Century England." Paper presented at the annual meeting of the International Communication Association, Honolulu.

Hall, Stuart. 1980. "Cultural Studies and the Centre: Some Problematics and Problems." In *Culture, Media, Language,* ed. Stuart Hall et al. London: Hutchinson, pp. 15–47.

Hanisch, Carol. 1969. "The Personal Is Political." In *Feminist Revolution,* ed. Redstockings. New York: Random House, 1975, pp. 204–5.

Haraway, Donna J. 1981. "In the Beginning Was the Word: The Genesis of Biological Theory." *Signs* 6, no. 3: 469–81.

Hartman, Mary, and Lois W. Banner, eds. 1974. *Clio's Consciousness Raised: New Perspectives on the History of Women.* New York: Colophon.

Hartsock, Nancy. 1979. "Feminist Theory and the Development of Revolutionary Strategy." In *Capitalist Patriarchy and the Case for Socialist Feminism,* ed. Zillah R. Eisenstein. New York: Monthly Review Press, pp. 56–77.

Hartsock, Nancy. 1981. *Money, Sex, and Power: An Essay on Domination and Community.* New York: Longman.

Heath, Stephen. 1978. "Difference." *Screen* 19, no. 3: 51–112.

Heath, Stephen. 1982. *The Sexual Fix.* London: Macmillan.

Heilbrun, Carolyn G. 1980. "Androgyny and the Psychology of Sex Differences." In *The Future of Difference,* ed. Hester Eisenstein and Alice Jardine. Boston: G. K. Hall, pp. 258–66.

Henley, Nancy M. 1977. *Body Politics: Power, Sex, and Nonverbal Communication.* New York: Prentice-Hall.

Herschberger, Ruth. 1970. *Adam's Rib.* New York: Pellegrini and Cudahy, 1948. Rpt. New York: Harper and Row.

Hochschild, Arlie Russell. 1983. *The Managed Heart: Commercialization of Human Feeling.* Berkeley: University of California Press.

Hollway, Wendy. 1984. "Gender Difference and the Production of Subjectivity." In *Changing the Subject: Psychology, Social Regulation, and Subjectivity,* by Julian Henriques, Wendy Hollway, Cathy Urwin, Couze Venn, and Valerie Walkerdine. London: Methuen, pp. 227–63.

Hooks, Bell. 1981. *Ain't I a Woman? Black Women and Feminism.* Boston: South End Press.

Hooks, Bell. 1984. *Feminist Theory: From Margin to Center.* Boston: South End Press.

Howe, Florence. 1978. "Breaking the Disciplines." In *The Structure of Knowledge.* Proceedings of the Fourth Annual GLCA Women's Studies Conference (November), pp. 34–37.

Howe, Florence, and Carol Ahlum. 1973. "Women's Studies and Social Change."

In *Academic Women on the Move,* ed. Alice Rossi and Ann Calderwood. New York: Russell Sage, pp. 393–423.

Hrdy, Sarah Blaffer. 1981. *The Woman That Never Evolved.* Cambridge: Harvard University Press.

Hubbard, Ruth. 1981. "The Emperor Doesn't Wear Any Clothes: The Impact of Feminism on Biology." In *Men's Studies Modified,* ed. Dale Spender. London: Pergamon.

Hubbard, Ruth, Mary Sue Henifin, and Barbara Fried. 1979. *Women Look at Biology Looking at Women.* Cambridge: Schenkman.

Huber, Joan, ed. 1973. *Changing Women in a Changing Society.* Chicago: University of Chicago Press.

Hull, Gloria T., and Barbara Smith. 1982. "Introduction: The Politics of Black Women's Studies." In *But Some of Us Are Brave: Black Women's Studies,* ed. Gloria T. Hull, Patricia Bell Scott, and Barbara Smith. Old Westbury, N.Y.: The Feminist Press, pp. xvii–xxxii.

Irigaray, Luce. 1985. *Speculum of the Other Woman.* Trans. Gillian C. Gill. Ithaca: Cornell University Press.

Irigaray, Luce. 1985. *This Sex Which Is Not One.* Trans. Catherine Porter with Carolyn Burke. Ithaca: Cornell University Press.

Irigaray, Luce. 1983. "Veiled Lips." Trans. Sara Speidel. *Mississippi Review* 33: 93–131.

Jacobus, Mary. 1981. "The Question of Language: Men of Maxims and *The Mill on the Floss.*" *Critical Inquiry* 8, no. 2 (Winter): 207–22.

Jacobus, Mary, ed. 1979. *Women Writing and Writing About Women.* New York: Barnes and Noble Books.

Jaggar, Alison M., and Paula S. Rothenberg. 1984. *Feminist Frameworks: Alternative Theoretical Accounts of the Relations Between Women and Men.* 2nd ed. New York: McGraw-Hill.

Janssen-Jurreit, Marie Louise. 1982. *Sexism: The Male Monopoly on History and Thought.* Trans. Verne Moberg. London: Pluto Press.

Janus, Noreene Z. 1977. "Research on Sex-Roles in the Mass Media: Toward a Critical Approach." *The Insurgent Sociologist* 7 (Summer): 19–31.

Jardine, Alice A. 1985. *Gynesis: Configurations of Women and Modernity.* Ithaca: Cornell University Press.

Jehlen, Myra. 1981. "Archimedes and the Paradox of Feminist Criticism." *Signs* 6, no. 4 (Summer): 575–601.

Johnston, Claire. 1978. "*Double Indemnity.*" In *Women in Film Noir,* ed. E. Ann Kaplan. London: British Film Institute, pp. 100–111.

Johnston, Claire. 1980. "The Subject of Feminist Film Theory/Practice." *Screen* 21, no. 2: 27–34.

Johnston, Jill. 1973. *Lesbian Nation: The Feminist Solution.* New York: Simon and Schuster.

Jones, Ann Rosalind. 1981. "Writing the Body: Toward an Understanding of L'Ecriture Feminine." *Feminist Studies* 7, no. 2 (Summer): 247–63.

Jones, Ann Rosalind. 1984. "Julia Kristeva on Femininity: The Limits of a Semiotic Politics." *Feminist Review* 19 (November): 56–73.

Jordan, Brigitte. 1978. *Birth in Four Cultures: A Crosscultural Investigation of*

Childbirth in Yucatan, Holland, Sweden, and the United States. Montreal: Eden Press Women's Publications.

Joseph, Gloria I. 1983. Review of *Women, Race and Class* by Angela Y. Davis. *Signs* 9, no. 1 (Autumn): 134–36.

Kantrowitz, Joanne Spencer. 1981. "Paying Your Dues, Part-Time." In *Rocking the Boat: Academic Women and Academic Processes,* ed. Gloria DeSole and Leonore Hoffmann. New York: Modern Language Association, pp. 15–36.

Kaplan, Cora. 1984. "Wild Nights: Pleasure/Sexuality/Feminism." *Formations of Pleasure.* London: Routledge and Kegan Paul, pp. 15–35.

Keller, Evelyn Fox. 1982. "Feminism and Science." *Signs* 7, no. 3 (Spring): 589–602.

Keller, Evelyn Fox. 1984. *Reflections on Gender and Science.* New Haven: Yale University Press.

Kelly, Joan. 1984. *Women, History, and Theory: The Essays of Joan Kelly.* Chicago: University of Chicago Press.

Kelly, Mary. 1977. "Notes on Reading the Post-Partum Document." *Control Magazine* 10: n.p.

Kelly, Mary. 1981. "Post-Partum Document." *m/f* 5/6: 125–48.

Kelly, Mary. 1983. *Post-Partum Document.* London: Routledge and Kegan Paul.

Kerber, Linda K. 1980. *Women of the Republic: Intellect and Ideology in Revolutionary America.* Chapel Hill: University of North Carolina Press.

King, Katie. 1985. "The Situation of Lesbianism as Feminism's Magical Sign: Contests for Meaning and the U.S. Women's Movement, 1968–72." *Communication* 9, no. 1 (Fall): 65–91. Special issue on Feminist Critiques of Popular Culture, ed. Ellen Wartella and Paula A. Treichler.

Kipp, Rita. 1978. "The Feminist Critique: Plans and Perspectives." In *The Structure of Knowledge.* Proceedings of the Fourth Annual GLCA Women's Studies Conference (November), pp. 49–53.

Klein, Ethel. 1985. *From Consciousness to Mass Politics.* Cambridge: Harvard University Press.

Kleinhaus, Chuck, and Julia Lesage. 1985. "The Politics of Sexual Representation." *Jump Cut* 30: 24–26.

Koedt, Anne, Ellen Levine, and Anita Rapone, eds. 1973. *Radical Feminism.* New York: Quadrangle/New York Times.

Kolodny, Annette. 1980a. "Dancing through the Minefield: Some Observations on the Theory, Practice, and Politics of a Feminist Literary Criticism," *Feminist Studies* 6 (Spring): 1–25.

Kolodny, Annette. 1980b. "A Map for Rereading: Or, Gender and the Interpretation of Literary Texts." *New Literary History* 11: 451–67.

Kramarae, Cheris. 1982. *Women and Men Speaking.* Rowley, Mass.: Newbury House.

Kramarae, Cheris, and Paula A. Treichler. 1983. "Power Relationships and Sex Identity in the Classroom." Paper presented at the Second International Conference of Social Psychology and Language, Bristol, England, July.

Kramarae, Cheris, and Paula A. Treichler. 1985. *A Feminist Dictionary.* With the assistance of Ann Russo. London and Boston: Routledge and Kegan Paul/Pandora.

Kristeva, Julia. 1977. *About Chinese Women.* Trans. Anita Barrows. New York: Urizen.

Kristeva, Julia. 1980. "Motherhood According to Giovanni Bellini." In *Desire in Language: A Semiotic Approach to Literature and Art,* ed. Leon S. Roudiez. Trans. Thomas Gora, Alice Jardine, and Leon S. Roudiez. Oxford: Basil Blackwell, pp. 409–35.

Kristeva, Julia. 1981. "Women's Time." *Signs* 7, no. 1 (Autumn): 13–35.

Kuhn, Annette. 1982. *Women's Pictures: Feminism and Cinema.* London: Routledge and Kegan Paul.

Kuhn, Annette, and AnnMarie Wolpe, eds. 1978. *Feminism and Materialism.* London: Routledge and Kegan Paul.

Kuhn, Thomas 1970. *The Structure of Scientific Revolutions.* 2nd ed. Chicago: University of Chicago Press.

LACW (Latin American and Caribbean Women's Collective). 1977. *Slaves of Slaves: The Challenge of Latin American Women.* London: Zed Press.

Ladner, Joyce A. 1971. "Racism and Tradition: Black Womanhood in Historical Perspective." Rpt. in *Liberating Women's History,* ed. Berenice A. Carroll. Urbana: University of Illinois Press, 1976, pp. 179–93.

LaDuke, Winona. 1983. "They'll Always Come Back." Interview in *Sinister Wisdom* 22/23: 52–57.

Lakoff, Robin. 1975. *Language and Women's Place.* New York: Harper and Row.

Lauter, Estella, and Carol Schreier Rupprecht, eds. 1985. *Feminist Archetypal Theory: Interdisciplinary Re-Visions of Jungian Thought.* Knoxville: University of Tennessee Press.

Law, Sylvia A. "Women in the Constitution." Unpublished manuscript.

Leavitt, Judith Walzer, ed. 1984. *Women and Health in America.* Madison: University of Wisconsin Press.

Lederer, Laura, ed. 1980. *Take Back the Night.* New York: William Morrow.

Le Doeuff, Michèle. 1977. "Women and Philosophy." Trans. Debbie Pope. *Radical Philosophy* 17: 2–11.

Le Doeuff, Michèle. 1984. "The Public Employer." *m/f* 9: 3–17.

Leffler, Ann, Dair L. Gillespie, and Elinor Lerner. 1973. *Academic Feminists and the Women's Movement.* Iowa City, Iowa: AcaFem.

Lerner, Gerda. 1972a. *Black Women in White America: A Documentary History.* New York: Vintage.

Lerner, Gerda. 1969. "New Approaches to the Study of Women in American History." Rpt. in *Liberating Women's History,* ed. Berenice A. Carroll. Urbana: University of Illinois Press, 1976, pp. 349–56.

Lerner, Gerda. 1972b. "On the Teaching and Organization of Feminist Studies." In *Female Studies V,* ed. Rae Lee Siporin. Pittsburgh: KNOW, Inc.

Lesage, Julia. 1979. "Feminist Film Criticism: Theory and Practice." In *Women and Film* nos. 5 and 6: 12–14.

Lewis, Jill, and Gloria I. Joseph. 1981. *Common Differences: Conflicts in Black and White Perspectives.* Garden City, N.Y.: Anchor/Doubleday.

Linden, Robin Ruth, Darlene R. Pagano, Diana E. H. Russell, and Susan Leigh

Star, eds. 1982. *Against Sadomasochism: A Radical Feminist Analysis*. East Palo Alto, Calif.: Frog in the Well.

Lippard, Lucy. 1976. *From the Center: Feminist Essays on Women's Art*. New York: Dutton.

Lorde, Audre. 1980. *The Cancer Journals*. Argyle, N.Y.: Spinsters, Ink.

Lorde, Audre. 1981a. "The Master's Tools Will Never Dismantle the Master's House." In *This Bridge Called My Back*, ed. Cherríe Moraga and Gloria Anzaldúa. Boston: Persephone, pp. 98–101.

Lorde, Audre. 1981b. "The Uses of Anger." *Women's Studies Quarterly* 9, no. 3: 7–10.

Lugones, Maria C., and Elizabeth V. Spelman. 1983. "Have We Got a Theory for You! Feminist Theory, Cultural Imperialism and the Demand for 'The Woman's Voice.'" *Women's Studies International Forum* 6, no. 6: 573–81.

MacKinnon, Catharine A. 1982. "Feminism, Marxism, Method, and the State: An Agenda for Theory." *Signs* 7, no. 3 (Spring): 515–44.

MacKinnon, Catharine A. 1983. "Feminism, Marxism, Method, and the State: Toward Feminist Jurisprudence." *Signs* 8, no. 4 (Summer): 635–58.

MacKinnon, Catharine A. 1979. *The Sexual Harassment of Working Women*. New Haven: Yale University Press.

Makward, Christiane. 1980. "To Be or Not to Be . . . A Feminist Speaker." In *The Future of Difference*, ed. Hester Eisenstein and Alice Jardine. Boston: G. K. Hall, pp. 95–105.

Malos, Ellen, ed. 1980. *The Politics of Housework*. London: Allison and Busby.

Marcus, Jane. 1982. "Storming the Toolshed." *Signs* 7, no. 3 (Spring): 622–40.

Marcus, Jane. 1984. "Still Practice, A/Wrested Alphabet: Toward a Feminist Aesthetic." *Tulsa Studies in Women's Literature* 3, nos. 1/2 (Spring, Fall): 79–97.

Marks, Elaine, and Isabel de Courtivron, eds. 1981. *New French Feminisms*. New York: Schocken.

Martin, Biddy. 1982. "Feminism, Criticism, and Foucault." *New German Critique* 27 (Fall): 3–30.

Martin, Del, and Phyllis Lyon. 1972. *Lesbian/Woman*. San Francisco: Glide.

Martin, Jane Roland. 1984. "Bringing Women into Educational Thought." *Educational Theory* 34, no. 4: 341–53.

Martin, Jane Roland. 1981. "Sophie and Emile: A Case Study of Sex Bias in the History of Educational Thought." *Harvard Educational Review* 51, no. 3 (August): 357–72.

Martyna, Wendy. 1983. "Beyond the He/Man Approach: The Case for Nonsexist Language." In *Language, Gender and Society*, ed. Barrie Thorne, Cheris Kramarae, and Nancy Henley. Rowley, Mass.: Newbury House, pp. 25–37.

McConnell-Ginet, Sally. 1980. "Linguistics and the Feminist Challenge." In *Women and Language in Literature and Society*, ed. Sally McConnell-Ginet, Ruth Borker, and Nelly Furman. New York: Praeger, pp. 3–25.

McConnell-Ginet, Sally. 1984a. "On Saying and Meaning: Radical Pragmatics and the 'Sexist Language' Question." Paper presented to the Linguistic Society of America, Baltimore, December.

McConnell-Ginet, Sally. 1984b. "The Origins of Sexist Language in Discourse." In *Discourses in Reading and Linguistics*, ed. Sheila J. White and Virginia Teller. Annals of the New York Academy of Sciences 433: 123–35.

McConnell-Ginet, Sally. 1983. Review article on language and sex. *Language* 59, no. 2: 373–91.

McConnell-Ginet, Sally, Ruth Borker, and Nelly Furman, eds., 1980. *Women and Language in Literature and Society*. New York: Praeger.

McCormack, Thelma. 1983. "Male Conceptions of Female Audiences: The Case of Soap Operas." In *Mass Communication Review Yearbook*, vol. 4, ed. Ellen Wartella, D. Charles Whitney, and Sven Windahl. Beverly Hills: Sage, pp. 273–83.

McFadden, Maggie. 1984. "Anatomy of Difference: Toward a Classification of Feminist Theory." *Women's Studies International Forum* 7, no. 6: 495–504.

McKluskie, Kate. 1983. "Women's Language and Literature: A Problem in Women's Studies." *Feminist Review* 14 (June): 51–61.

McRobbie, Angela. 1982a. "Jackie: An Ideology of Adolescent Femininity." In *Popular Culture: Past and Present*, ed. Bernard Waites, Tony Bennett, and Graham Martin. London: Croom Helm, pp. 263–83. Rpt. in *Mass Communication Review Yearbook*, vol. 4, ed. Ellen Wartella, D. Charles Whitney, and Sven Windahl. Beverly Hills: Sage, 1983, pp. 251–71.

McRobbie, Angela. 1982b. "The Politics of Feminist Research: Between Talk, Text and Action," *Feminist Review* 12 (October): 46–57.

Merchant, Carolyn. 1980. *The Death of Nature: Women, Ecology, and the Scientific Revolution*. San Francisco: Harper and Row.

Millet, Kate. 1970. *Sexual Politics*. Garden City, N.Y.: Doubleday.

Miller, Jean Baker. 1976. *Toward a New Psychology of Women*. Boston: Beacon.

Millman, Marcia, and Rosabeth Kanter, eds. 1975. *Another Voice: Feminist Perspectives on Social Life and Social Science*. New York: Anchor.

Mitchell, Gillian. 1984. "Women and Lying: A Pragmatic and Semantic Analysis of 'Telling it Slant.'" *Women's Studies International Forum* 7, no. 5: 375–83.

Mitchell, Juliet. 1966. "The Longest Revolution." Rpt. in *The Longest Revolution*. New York: Pantheon, 1984, pp. 17–54.

Mitchell, Juliet. 1974. *Psychoanalysis and Feminism*. London: Allen Lane.

Mitchell, Juliet. 1971. *Woman's Estate*. New York: Vintage.

Mitchell, Juliet, and Ann Oakley, eds. 1976. *The Rights and Wrongs of Women*. Harmondsworth: Penguin.

Mitchell, Juliet, and Jacqueline Rose, eds. 1982. *Feminine Sexuality: Jacques Lacan and the école freudienne*. Trans. Jacqueline Rose. New York: Norton, Pantheon.

Modleski, Tania. 1982. *Loving with a Vengeance: Mass Produced Fantasies for Women*. Hamden, Conn : Archon Books.

Moi, Toril. 1985. *Sexual/Textual Politics: Feminist Literary Theory*. New York: Metheun.

Montrelay, Michèle. 1978. "Inquiry into Femininity." *m/f* 1: 83–101.

Montrelay, Michèle. 1980. "The Story of Louise." In *Returning to Freud: Clinical Psychoanalysis in the School of Lacan,* ed. and trans. Stuart Schneiderman. New Haven: Yale University Press, pp. 75–93.

Mora, Magdalena, and Adelaide R. Del Castillo, eds. 1980. *Mexican Women in the United States.* Los Angeles, Calif.: Chicano Studies Research Center.

Moraga, Cherríe, and Gloria Anzaldúa, eds. 1981. *This Bridge Called My Back: Writings of Radical Women of Color.* Boston: Persephone.

Moreau, Noëlle Bisseret. 1984. "Education, Ideology, and Class/Sex Identity." In *Language and Power,* ed. Cheris Kramarae, Muriel Schulz, and William M. O'Barr. Beverly Hills, Calif.: Sage, pp. 43–61.

Morgan, Robin, ed. 1970. *Sisterhood is Powerful.* New York: Random House.

Morgan, Robin, ed. 1984. *Sisterhood is Global.* New York: Anchor/Doubleday.

Morris, Meaghan. 1982. "A-Mazing Grace: Notes on Mary Daly's Poetics." *Intervention* 16: 70–92.

Moulton, Janice. 1981. "Sex and Reference." In *Sexist Language: A Modern Philosophical Analysis,* ed. Mary Vetterling-Braggin. Totowa, N.J.: Littlefield, Adams, pp. 183–93.

Mullings, Leith. 1983. "Afro-American Women and Occupational Health." Paper presented at Common Differences: Third World Women and Feminist Perspectives, University of Illinois, April.

Mulvey, Laura. 1975. "Visual Pleasure and Narrative Cinema." *Screen* 16, no. 3: 6–18.

Murray, Pauli. 1970. "The Liberation of Black Women." In *Voices of the New Feminism,* ed. Mary Lou Thompson. Boston: Beacon, pp. 87–102.

Nelson, Cary. 1985. "Envoys of Otherness: Difference and Continuity in Feminist Criticism." In *For Alma Mater: Theory and Practice in Feminist Criticism,* ed. Paula A. Treichler, Cheris Kramarae, and Beth Stafford. Urbana: University of Illinois Press, pp. 91–118.

Nichols, Patricia. 1984. "Networks and Hierarchies: Language and Social Stratification." In *Language and Power,* ed. Cheris Kramarae, Muriel Schulz, and William M. O'Barr. Beverly Hills, Calif.: Sage, pp. 23–42.

Nochlin, Linda. 1973. "Why Have There Been No Great Women Artists?" In *Art and Sexual Politics,* ed. Thomas B. Hess and E. Baker. New York: Macmillan, pp. 35–47.

Oakley, Ann. 1981. *Subject Woman.* New York: Pantheon.

Oakley, Ann. 1980. *Woman Confined.* London: Martin Robertson.

O'Brien, Mary. 1981a. "Feminist Theory and Dialectical Logic." *Signs* 7, no. 1: 144–57.

O'Brien, Mary. 1981b. *The Politics of Reproduction.* Boston: Routledge and Kegan Paul.

Ortner, Sherry B. 1974. "Is Female to Male as Nature is to Culture?" In *Woman, Culture, and Society,* ed. Michelle Zimbalist Rosaldo and Louise Lamphere. Stanford: Stanford University Press, pp. 67–87.

Ortner, Sherry, and Harriet Whitehead, eds. 1982. *Sexual Meanings.* New York: Cambridge University Press.

Pajaczkowska, Claire. 1981. "Introduction to Kristeva." *m/f* 5/6: pp. 149–57.

LIBRARY

Parker, Rozsika, and Griselda Pollock. 1981. *Old Mistresses: Women, Art and Ideology.* New York: Pantheon.

Penley, Constance. 1986. "Teaching in Your Sleep: Feminism and Psychoanalysis." In *Theory in the Classroom,* ed. Cary Nelson. Urbana: University of Illinois Press, pp. 129–48.

Piñon, Nélida. 1982. "La Contaminacion de la Lenguaje: Interview with Nélida Piñon." *13th Moon* 6, nos. 1 & 2: 71–75.

Portuges, Catherine. 1985. "The Spectacle of Gender: Cinema and Psyche." In *Gendered Subjects,* ed. Margo Culley and Catherine Portuges. London: Routledge and Kegan Paul, pp. 183–94.

Putnam, Linda L. 1982. "In Search of Gender: A Critique of Communication and Sex-Roles Research." *Women's Studies in Communication* 5, no. 1 (Spring): 1–9.

Pryse, Marjorie, and Hortense Spillers, eds. 1985. *Conjuring: Black Women, Fiction, and Literary Tradition.* Bloomington: Indiana University Press.

Quest Staff and the *Quest* Book Committee, eds. 1981. *Building Feminist Theory: Essays from Quest, A Feminist Quarterly.* New York: Longman.

Radway, Janice A. 1984. *Reading the Romance: Women, Patriarchy, and Popular Literature.* Chapel Hill: University of North Carolina Press.

Radway, Janice A. 1985. "Identifying Ideological Seams: Mass Culture, Analytic Method, and Political Practice." *Communication.* Special issue on Feminist Critiques of Popular Culture, ed. Ellen Wartella and Paula A. Treichler, 9, no. 1 (Fall): 93–123.

Rakow, Lana F. 1985a. "Feminist Approaches to Popular Culture: Giving Patriarchy Its Due." *Communication.* Special issue on Feminist Critiques of Popular Culture, ed. Ellen Wartella and Paula A. Treichler, 9, no. 1 (Fall): 19–42.

Rakow, Lana F. 1985b. "A Paradigm of One's Own: Feminist Ferment in the Field." Paper presented at the annual meeting of the International Communication Association, Honolulu.

Rebolledo, Tey Diana. 1985. "The Maturing of Chicana Poetry: The Quiet Revolution of the 1980s." In *For Alma Mater: Theory and Practice in Feminist Scholarship,* ed. Paula A. Treichler, Cheris Kramarae, and Beth Stafford. Urbana: University of Illinois Press, pp. 143–58.

Reed, Evelyn. 1975. *Woman's Evolution: From Matriarchal Clan to Patriarchal Family.* New York: Pathfinder.

Register, Cheri. 1979. "Brief, A-Mazing Movements: Dealing with Despair in the Women's Studies Classroom." *Women's Studies Newsletter* 7, no. 4 (Fall): 7–10.

Reinharz, Shulamit. 1981. "Experiential Analysis: A Contribution to Feminist Research Methodology." In *Theories of Women's Studies II,* ed. Gloria Bowles and Renate Duelli Klein. Berkeley: University of California Women's Studies, pp. 68–97.

Reiter, Rayna R., ed. 1975. *Toward an Anthropology of Women.* New York: Monthly Review Press.

Rich, Adrienne. 1980. "Compulsive Heterosexuality and Lesbian Existence." *Signs* 5, no. 4 (Summer): 631–60.

Rich, Adrienne. 1976. *Of Woman Born: Motherhood as Experience and Institution.* New York: W. W. Norton.

Rich, Adrienne. 1979. *On Lies, Secrets, and Silence.* New York: W. W. Norton.

Richards, Janice Radcliffe. 1980. *The Sceptical Feminist: A Philosophical Inquiry.* London: Routledge and Kegan Paul.

Richardson, Laurel, and Verta Taylor, eds. 1983. *Feminist Frontiers: Rethinking Sex, Gender and Society.* Reading, Mass.: Addison-Wesley.

Roberts, Helen, ed. 1981a. *Feminist Methodology.* London: Routledge and Kegan Paul.

Roberts, Helen, ed. 1981b. *Women, Health and Reproduction.* London: Routledge and Kegan Paul.

Robinson, Lillian S. 1978. *Sex, Class, and Culture.* Bloomington: Indiana University Press.

Robyns, Janet. 1977. "Reproductive versus Regenerative Education: The Extension of English Education through Reference to Feminism." Unpublished associateship report, University of London Institute of Education.

Rosaldo, Michelle Z., and Louise Lamphere, eds. 1974. *Woman, Culture, and Society.* Stanford: Stanford University Press.

Rose, Hilary. 1983. "Hand, Brain, and Heart: A Feminist Epistemology for the Natural Sciences." *Signs* 9, no. 1 (Autumn): 73–90.

Rose, Jacqueline. 1984. "Femininity and Its Discontents." *Feminist Review* 14 (Summer): 5–21.

Rose, Jacqueline. 1982. Introduction to *Feminine Sexuality: Jacques Lacan and the école freudienne,* ed.Juliet Mitchell and Jacqueline Rose. New York: W. W. Norton.

Rosenberg, Rosalind. 1982. *Beyond Separate Spheres: Intellectual Roots of Modern Feminism.* New Haven: Yale University Press.

Rosenfelt, Deborah Silverton, ed. 1973. *Female Studies 7: Going Strong: New Courses/New Programs.* Old Westbury, N.Y.: The Feminist Press.

Rossiter, Margaret. 1982. *Women Scientists in America.* Baltimore: The Johns Hopkins University Press.

Rothschild, Joan, ed. *Women, Technology and Innovation.* New York: Pergamon.

Rowbotham, Sheila. 1983. *Dreams and Dilemmas.* London: Virago.

Rowbotham, Sheila. 1972. *Women, Resistance, and Revolution.* New York: Pantheon.

Rubin, Gayle. 1984. "Thinking Sex: Notes for a Radical Theory of the Politics of Sexuality." In *Pleasure and Danger: Exploring Female Sexuality,* ed. Carole S. Vance. Boston: Routledge and Kegan Paul, pp. 267–319.

Rubin, Gayle. 1975. "The Traffic in Women: Notes on the 'Political Economy' of Sex." In *Toward an Anthropology of Women,* ed. Rayna R. Reiter, New York: Monthly Review Press, pp. 157–210.

Rubin, Lillian. 1976. *Worlds of Pain: Life in the Working Class Family.* New York: Basic Books.

Ruddick, Sara. 1980. "Maternal Thinking." *Feminist Studies* 6, no. 2 (Summer): 342–67.

Ruether, Rosemary. 1983. *Sexism and God-Talk: Toward a Feminist Theology.* Boston: Beacon Press.

Russ, Joanna. 1983. *How to Suppress Women's Writing.* Austin: University of Texas Press.

Russell, Michelle. 1981. "An Open Letter to the Academy." In *Building Feminist Theory: Essays from Quest, A Feminist Quarterly.* New York: Longman, pp. 101–10.

Ruth, Sheila. 1978. "A Feminist World-view." *Women's Studies International Quarterly* 1, no. 3: 247–54.

Ruthven, K. K. 1984. *Feminist Literary Studies: An Introduction.* Cambridge: Cambridge University Press.

Saadawi, Nawal el. 1982. *The Hidden Face of Eve.* Boston: Beacon.

Salzman-Webb, Marilyn. 1972. "Feminist Studies: Frill or Necessity?" In *Female Studies 5,* ed. Rae Lee Siporin. Pittsburgh: KNOW, Inc., pp. 64–76.

Samois, ed. 1982. *Coming to Power: Writings and Graphics on Lesbian S/M.* Boston: Alyson Publications.

Sanchez, Carol Lee. 1983. "Sex, Class, and Race Intersections: Visions of Women of Color." In *A Gathering of Spirit.* Special issue on North American Indian Women. *Sinister Wisdom* 22/23: 150–54.

Sargent, Lydia, ed. 1980. *Women and Revolution: A Discussion of the Unhappy Marriage of Marxism and Feminism.* Boston: South End Press.

Sayers, Janet. 1982. *Biological Politics: Feminist and Anti-Feminist Perspectives.* London: Tavistock.

Scheman, Naomi. 1980. "Anger and the Politics of Naming." In *Women and Language in Literature and Society,* ed. Sally McConnell-Ginet, Ruth Borker, and Nelly Furman. New York: Praeger, pp. 174–87.

Schreiner, Olive. 1971. *Story of An African Farm.* London: Penguin.

Schulz, Muriel. 1975. "The Semantic Derogation of Women." In *Language and Sex: Difference and Dominance,* ed. Barrie Thorne and Nancy Henley. Rowley, Mass.: Newbury House, pp. 64–73.

Sherfey, Mary Jane. 1973. *The Nature and Evolution of Female Sexuality.* New York: Vintage.

Sherman, Julia, and Evelyn Beck, eds. 1979. *The Prism of Sex: Essays in the Sociology of Knowledge.* Madison: University of Wisconsin Press.

Showalter, Elaine. 1983. "Critical Cross-dressing: Male Feminists and the Woman of the Year." *Raritan: A Quarterly Review* 3, no. 2 (Fall): 130–49.

Showalter, Elaine. 1985. "The Feminist Critical Revolution." In *The New Feminist Criticism,* ed. Elaine Showalter. New York: Pantheon, pp. 3–17.

Showalter, Elaine. 1981. "Feminist Criticism in the Wilderness." *Critical Inquiry* 8, no. 2 (Winter): 179–205.

Showalter, Elaine. 1984. "Women's Time, Women's Space: Writing the History of Feminist Criticism." *Tulsa Studies in Women's Literature* 3, no. 1/2: 29–43.

Smith, Barbara. 1982. "Racism and Women's Studies." In *But Some of Us Are Brave: Black Women's Studies,* ed. Gloria T. Hull, Patricia Bell Scott, and Barbara Smith. Old Westbury, N.Y.: The Feminist Press, pp. 48–51.

Smith, Barbara. 1977. "Toward a Black Feminist Criticism." *Conditions: Two* 1, no. 2 (October): 24–44.

Smith, Dorothy E. 1979. "A Sociology for Women." In *The Prism of Sex: Essays in the Sociology of Knowledge,* ed. Julia A. Sherman and Evelyn Torton Beck. Madison: University of Wisconsin Press. pp. 135–87.

Smith, Hilda. 1976. "Feminism and the Methodology of Women's History." In *Liberating Women's History: Theoretical and Critical Essays,* ed. Berenice A. Carroll. Urbana: University of Illinois Press, pp. 368–84.

Smith, MaryAnn Yodelis. 1983. "Research Retrospective: Feminism and the Media." In *Mass Communication Review Yearbook,* vol. 4, ed. Ellen Wartella, D. Charles Whitney, and Sven Windahl. Beverly Hills Calif.: Sage, pp. 213–28.

Smith, Paul. 1984. "A Question of Feminine Identity." *Notebooks in Cultural Analysis: An Annual Review,* ed. Norman F. Cantor and Nathalia King. Durham: Duke University Press, pp. 82–102.

Smith-Rosenberg, Caroll. 1975. "The Female World of Love and Ritual: Relations between Women in Nineteenth-Century America." *Signs* 1, no. 1 (Autumn): 1–30.

Smith-Rosenberg, Caroll, and Charles Rosenberg. 1973. "The Female Animal: Medical and Biological Views of Woman in Nineteenth-Century America." Rpt. in *Women and Health in America,* ed. Judith Walzer Leavitt. Madison: University of Wisconsin Press, 1984, pp. 12–27.

Snitow, Ann, Christine Stansell, and Sharon Thompson, eds. 1983. *Powers of Desire: The Politics of Sexuality.* New York: Monthly Review Press.

Sofia, Zoë. 1984. "Exterminating Fetuses: Abortion, Disarmament, and the Sexo-Semiotics of Extraterrestrialism," *Diacritics* 14, no. 2 (Summer): 47–59.

Sokoloff, Natalie J. 1980. *Between Money and Love: The Dialectics of Women's Home and Market Work.* New York: Praeger.

Solanas, Valerie. 1968. *Scum Manifesto.* New York: Olympia Press. Rpt. London: The Matriarchy Study Group, 1983.

Solomon, Barbara Miller. 1984. *In the Company of Women: A History of Women and Higher Education in America.* New Haven, Conn.: Yale University Press.

Sontag, Susan. 1973. "The Third World of Women." *Partisan Review* 40, no. 2: 180–206.

Spender, Dale. 1981a. "Education: The Patriarchal Paradigm and the Response to Feminism." In *Men's Studies Modified,* ed. Dale Spender. London: Pergamon, pp. 155–73.

Spender, Dale. 1980. *Man Made Language.* London: Routledge and Kegan Paul.

Spender, Dale. 1981b. "Theorising about Theorising." In *Theories of Women's Studies II,* ed. Gloria Bowles and Renate Duelli Klein. Berkeley: University of California Women's Studies, pp. 119–22.

Spender, Dale. 1982. *Women of Ideas and What Men Have Done to Them, from Aphra Behn to Adrienne Rich.* London: ARK Paperbacks.

Spender, Dale, ed. 1983. *Feminist Theorists: Three Centuries of Key Women Thinkers.* New York: Pantheon.

Spender, Dale, ed., 1981. *Men's Studies Modified.* London: Pergamon.

Spillers, Hortense. 1984. "Interstices: A Small Drama of Words." In *Pleasure and Danger: Exploring Female Sexuality,* ed. Carole S. Vance. Boston: Routledge and Kegan Paul, pp. 73–100.

Spivak, Gayatri Chakravorty. 1983. "Displacement and the Discourse of Woman." In *Displacement: Derrida and After,* ed. Mark Krupnick. Bloomington: Indiana University Press, pp. 169–95.

Spivak, Gayatri Chakravorty. 1985. "Feminism and Critical Theory." In *For Alma Mater: Theory and Practice in Feminist Scholarship,* ed. Paula A. Treichler, Cheris Kramarae, and Beth Stafford. Urbana: University of Illinois Press, pp. 119–42.

Spivak, Gayatri Chakravorty. 1984."Love me, Love My Ombre, Elle." *Diacritics* 14, no. 4 (Winter): 19–36

Spretnak, Charlene, ed. 1982. *The Politics of Women's Spirituality: Essays on the Rise of Spiritual Power within the Feminist Movement.* Garden City, N.Y.: Anchor/Doubleday.

Stacey, Judith, and Barrie Thorne. 1984. "The Missing Feminist Revolution in Sociology." Paper presented to the American Sociological Association, San Antonio, August.

Stack, Carol. 1971. *All Our Kin: Strategies for Survival in a Black Community.* New York: Harper & Row.

Stam, Robert, and Louise Spence. 1983. "Colonialism, Racism, and Representation—An Introduction." *Screen* 24, no. 2 (April): 2–20.

Stanley, Julia Penelope, and Susan J. Wolfe. 1983. "Consciousness as Style: Style as Aesthetic." In *Language, Gender and Society,* ed. Barrie Thorne, Cheris Kramarae, and Nancy Henley. Rowley, Mass.: Newbury House, pp. 125–39.

Stanley, Liz. 1984. "Whales and Minnows: Some Sexual Theorists and Their Followers and How They Contribute to Making Feminism Invisible." *Women's Studies International Forum* 7, no. 1: 53–62.

Stanley, Liz, and Sue Wise. 1983. *Breaking Out: Feminist Consciousness and Feminist Research.* London: Routledge and Kegan Paul.

Stannard, Una. 1977. *Mrs. Man.* San Francisco: Germainbooks.

Stanton, Elizabeth Cady. 1922. "Motherhood." Rpt. in *The Feminist Papers,* ed. Alice Rossi. New York: Bantam, 1973, pp. 396–401.

Stetson, Erlene. 1982. "Black Women In and Out of Print." In *Women in Print I,* ed. Joan E. Hartman and Ellen Messer-Davidow. New York: Modern Language Association, pp. 87–107.

Stimpson, Catharine. 1978. "Women's Studies: An Overview." *Ann Arbor Papers in Women's Studies,* Special Issue (May), pp. 14–26.

Stimpson, Catharine. 1981. "Feminist Criticism and Feminist Critics." In *Feminist Literary Criticism.* Research Triangle Park, N.C.: National Humanities Center, pp. 57–63.

Taylor, Barbara. 1983. *Eve and the New Jerusalem.* New York: Pantheon.

Thompson, Judith Jarvis. 1971. "A Defense of Abortion." *Philosophy and Public Affairs* 1, no. 1 (Fall): 47–69.

Thorne, Barrie. 1983. Feminist Theory Course Syllabus, Stanford University, Spring.

Thorne, Barrie, and Nancy Henley, eds. 1975. *Language and Sex: Difference and Dominance*. Rowley, Mass.: Newbury House.

Thorne, Barrie, Cheris Kramarae, and Nancy Henley, eds. 1983. *Language, Gender and Society*. Rowley, Mass.: Newbury House.

Thorne, Barrie, Virginia Powell, Beverly Purrington, Regi Teasley, and Carol Wharton. 1983. "On Teaching the Sociology of Sex and Gender." Unpublished paper. Michigan State University, East Lansing, Mich.

Thorne, Barrie, with Marilyn Yalom, eds. 1982. *Rethinking the Family: Some Feminist Questions*. New York: Longman.

Tilly, Louise A., and Joan W. Scott. 1978. *Women, Work, and Family*. New York: Holt, Rinehart, and Winston.

Tobach, Ethel, and Betty Rosoff, eds. 1978–83. *Genes and Gender I; Genes and Gender II*, ed. Ruth Hubbard and Marian Lowe, 1979; *Genes and Gender III*, ed. Tobach and Rosoff, 1980; *Genes and Gender IV*, ed. Myra Fooden, Susan Gordon, and Betty Hugley, 1983. Staten Island, N.Y.: Gordian Press.

Trask, Haunani-Kay. "Fighting the Battle of Double Colonization: The View of a Hawaiian Feminist." Undated manuscript.

Treichler, Paula A. 1985. "Alma Mater's Sorority: Women at the University of Illinois 1890–1925." In *For Alma Mater: Theory and Practice in Feminist Scholarship*, ed. Paula A. Treichler, Cheris Kramarae, and Beth Stafford. Urbana: University of Illinois Press, pp. 5–61.

Treichler, Paula A. 1984. "Escaping the Sentence: Diagnosis and Discourse in 'The Yellow Wallpaper.' " *Tulsa Studies in Women's Literature* 3, nos. 1/2 (Spring/Fall): 61–77.

Treichler, Paula A., and Cheris Kramarae. 1983. "Women's Talk in the Ivory Tower." *Communication Quarterly* 31, no. 2 (Spring): 118–32.

Tuchman, Gaye. 1978. "The Symbolic Annihilation of Women by the Mass Media." In *Hearth and Home: Images of Women in the Mass Media*, ed. Gaye Tuchman, Arlene Kaplan Daniels, and James Benet. New York: Oxford University Press, pp. 3–38.

Vance, Carole S., ed. 1984. *Pleasure and Danger: Exploring Female Sexuality*. Boston: Routledge and Kegan Paul.

Vetterling-Braggin, Mary, ed. 1981. *Sexist Language: A Modern Philosophical Analysis*. New York, Totowa, N.J.: Littlefield, Adams.

Vickers, Jill McCalla. 1982. "Memoirs of an Ontological Exile: The Methodological Rebellions of Feminist Research." In *Feminism in Canada: From Pressure to Politics*, ed. Geraldine Finn and Angela Miles. Montreal: Black Rose Books, pp. 27–46.

Walker, Alice. 1982. "One Child of One's Own: A Meaningful Digression within the Work(s)—An Excerpt." In *But Some of Us Are Brave: Black Women's Studies*, ed. Gloria T. Hull, Patricia Bell Scott, and Barbara Smith. Old Westbury, N.Y.: The Feminist Press, pp. 37–44.

Walker, Barbara G. 1983. *The Woman's Encyclopedia of Myths and Secrets*. New York: Harper and Row.

Wallace, Michele. 1979. *Black Macho and the Myth of the Superwoman*. New York: Dial Press.

Walsh, Mary Roth. 1977. *Doctors Wanted, No Women Need Apply: Sexual*

Barriers in the Medical Profession, 1835–1975. New Haven: Yale University Press.

Ware, Celestine. 1970. *Woman Power: The Movement for Women's Liberation.* New York: Tower.

Warren, Mary Anne. 1980. *The Nature of Woman: An Encyclopedia and Guide to the Literature.* Inverness, Calif.: Edgepress.

Wartella, Ellen, and Paula A. Treichler. 1985. Introduction to *Communication* 9, no. 1 (Fall): 1–18. Special issue on Feminist Critiques of Popular Culture.

Washington, Mary Helen. 1985. "How Racial Differences Helped Us Discover Our Common Ground." In *Gendered Subjects,* ed. Margo Culley and Catherine Portuges. London: Routledge and Kegan Paul, pp. 221–29.

Weigle, Marta. 1982. *Spiders and Spinsters: Women and Mythology.* Albuquerque: University of New Mexico Press.

Weir, Angela, and Elizabeth Wilson. 1984. "The British Women's Movement." *New Left Review* 148 (November/December): 74–103.

West, Candace. 1984. *Routine Complications: Troubles with Talk between Doctors and Patients.* Bloomington: Indiana University Press.

Weisstein, Naomi. 1971. "Psychology Constructs the Female." In *Woman in Sexist Society,* ed. Vivian Gornick and Barbara K. Moran. New York: New American Library, pp. 207–24.

Weisstein, Naomi, Virginia Blaisdell, and Jesse Lemisch. 1975. *The Godfathers: Freud, Marx, and the Scientific Protection Societies.* New Haven: Belladonna.

Wenzel, Helene Vivienne. 1981. "An Appreciation of Monique Wittig's Writings in Context." *Feminist Studies* 7, no. 2 (Summer): 264–87.

White, Allon. 1977. "L'éclatement du sujet: The Theoretical Work of Julia Kristeva." Stencilled Occasional Papers. Birmingham, England: Center for Contemporary Cultural Studies.

Whitelegg, Elizabeth, Madeleine Arnot, Else Bartels, Veronica Beechey, Lynda Birke, Susan Himmelweit, Diana Leonard, Sonja Ruehl, and Mary Anne Speakman, eds. 1982. *The Changing Experience of Women.* Oxford: Basil Blackwell in association with the Open University.

Willis, Ellen. 1982. "Toward a Feminist Sexual Revolution." *Social Text* 6 (Fall): 3–21.

Winant, Terry R. 1983. "How Ordinary (Sexist) Discourse Resists Radical (Feminist) Critique." *Women's Studies International Forum* 6, no. 6: 609–20.

Wittig, Monique, and Sande Zeig. 1979. *Lesbian Peoples: Notes for a Dictionary.* New York: Avon.

Wollstonecraft, Mary. 1967. *A Vindication of the Rights of Woman.* New York: W. W. Norton. Originally published 1792.

Woolf, Virginia. 1929. *A Room of One's Own.* New York: Harcourt, Brace and World.

Wynter, Sylvia. 1982. "The Politics of Domination: The Rhetorics of Race." Paper presented at the annual meeting of the Modern Language Association, Los Angeles, December.

Zimmerman, Jan, ed. 1983. *The Technological Woman: Interfacing with Tomorrow.* New York: Praeger.

CONSTANCE PENLEY

Teaching in Your Sleep:
Feminism and Psychoanalysis

The April 5, 1979, issue of the *New York Review of Books* carried this letter from a reader:

> Richard Wollheim ends his informative and challenging article on Jacques Lacan with a polemical aside that leaves me puzzled. He writes: "Lacan's ideas and Lacan's style, yoked in an indissoluble union, represent an invasive tyranny. And it is by a hideous irony that this tyranny should find its recruits among groups that have nothing in common except the sense that they lack a theory worthy of their cause or calling: feminists, *cineastes,* professors of literature."
>
> Would Professor Wollheim care to explain on what evidence he includes feminists in this list? Could he give the names of any individual women or women's groups, here or in France, that have become Lacan's "recruits"? I would certainly be curious to learn how Lacanian theory and feminism manage to coexist.

In his reply Richard Wollheim gives substance to his assertion of the existence of such an unholy alliance by listing several feminist authors and projects that indeed attempt to claim or forge a healthy working relation between feminism and Lacanian psychoanalysis. What this exchange thus serves to indicate in its mutual bafflement is the depth of the present inability to understand what possible interest feminism could have in psychoanalysis, particularly the Lacanian version of it. Haven't feminists themselves, after all, from Betty Friedan to Mary Daly, typically ranged psychoanalysts in the category of men whose job it is to manage and adjust women's minds and bodies in accordance with strictly male standards? And don't feminists frequently expect psychoanalytic theory, in its notorious use of concepts like penis envy and the relative weakness of the feminine superego, to exemplify the worst kind of "scientific" rationalization of women's supposedly inherent inferiority? And wasn't it Jacques Lacan who took more than a little rhetorical pleasure in his notorious suggestion that "Woman does not exist" ("la femme n'existe pas")?

These are some of the symptoms of a general incomprehension that must be met head-on in teaching a course on feminism and psychoanalysis. Yet students readily sign up for such courses. Why? One reason is the renewed academic interest in psychoanalysis (particularly apparent since the time of the *New York Review of Books* letter) that has manifested itself in a flood of conferences, working groups, and special issues of journals on psychoanalytic theory. A second reason is the genuine recognition of the intensity and quality of the work that has come out of the feminist rapprochement with psychoanalysis. Juliet Mitchell's *Psychoanalysis and Feminism* (1974),[1] for example, the first contemporary argument for the feminist use of psychoanalytic theory as a conceptual tool for analyzing the vicissitudes of sexual difference, has been extremely influential and continues to be widely read. But these are positive reasons for taking a course on feminism and psychoanalysis, and students can just as frequently enroll for more negative ones, such as the wish, for example, to validate an already firmly held belief in the fundamental theoretical and political incompatibility of the two areas. In what follows, I want to discuss some of the problems involved in teaching feminism and psychoanalysis *together*. I will not approach these problems directly, say through relating anecdotes of my teaching experiences or offering pedagogical tips, but rather more obliquely, through considering the relation of both feminism and psychoanalysis to *knowledge* and *authority*, an understanding of which seems to me essential to anything one could say about pedagogy. In *The Interpretation of Dreams* Freud said, "When in the course of a piece of scientific work we come upon a problem which is difficult to solve, it is often a good plan to take up a second problem along with the original one—just as it is easier to crack two nuts together rather than each separately."[2] Two tough nuts to crack, then, feminism and psychoanalysis, each in its relation to what might be called an ethics of teaching.

An Analytical Pedagogy?

Psychoanalysis has always had a particularly tenuous and highly fraught relation to pedagogy. Freud himself said very little on the matter, considering teaching to be one of the "impossible professions" (along with governing and healing) and later confessing his ultimate indifference: "I'm leaving all that to Anna," was his attitude.[3] To the perennial question of whether the couch can come to the aid of the blackboard, a recent respondent answers with a strong negative: for Catherine Millot, a French Lacanian analyst and author of *Freud, Anti-pédagogue,*[4] psychoanalysis and pedagogy are *antithetical:* "It seems to me that Freud's own reserve [on the subject of teaching] has its basis in the radical opposition between the analytical process and the pedagogical process" (p. 127). Millot argues that the discoveries of psychoanalysis represent an acute challenge to the assumption that pedagogy can be a science of education. What, then, is the nature of the antithesis? One way to sum it up would be to say that education works on the ego whereas psychoanalysis works on the unconscious. Or that teaching aims to reinforce repression (for social and cultural ends) while psychoanalysis tries to eliminate it as the source of the patient's suffering. The respective methods are no less opposed. Indeed, we could say that there is a fundamental structural contradiction in education which makes it impossible to found an analytical pedagogy. The teacher's main pedagogical tool, for example, is the kind of identification known as transference; in "Some Reflections on Schoolboy Psychology,"[5] Freud offers a striking example of the unconscious and total respect that we accord our teachers:

> As you walked through the streets of Vienna—already a gray-beard and weighed down by all the cares of family life—you might come unexpectedly on some well-preserved, elderly gentleman, and would greet him humbly almost, because you had recognized him as one of your former schoolmasters. But afterwards, you would stop and reflect: "Was that really he? or only someone deceptively like him? How youthful he looks! And how old you yourself have grown! *Can it be possible that the men who used to stand for us as types of adulthood were so little older than we were?*" (P. 241)

Freud proceeds to describe how these teachers become our "substitute fathers" upon whom we fix all the youthful and passionate emotions that were once associated with our parents. Lacan, following Freud, emphasizes that transference, or "the acting out of the reality of the unconscious," can only take place when there is somewhere *a subject supposed to know.*[6] He goes on to stress the direct correspondence between the question of knowledge and the question of love: "Transference *is* love . . . I insist: it is love directed toward, addressed to, knowledge."[7] Teaching proceeds by way of seduction; the student wants to learn because he or she loves the teacher insofar as he or she presumes that the teacher *knows.* Hence the fundamental dilemma in teaching I have already referred to—the teacher, in order to be effective, to be a teacher at all, must fully assume the mantle of the subject supposed to know. To relinquish that imaginary position would be to lose the most important pedagogical tool of all. Psychoanalysis, on the other hand, proceeds in large part through the *analysis of the transference,* its goal being the analysand's understanding of the illusory status of the subject supposed to know, and the fraudulence of absolute or complete knowledge. Whereas analysis asks the patient finally to recognize the reality of his or her own unconscious desires, the educational process requires that the student's desires be those of the teacher—that is, that the student's superego be modelled on that of the teacher. (This same process is manifest in psychoanalytic treatment specifically based on an ego psychology in which the end of analysis is not the destruction of the transference but the final identification of the analysand with the analyst's superego.) In addition to the fact that education cannot take place without transference, the teacher has another reason for not wanting to give up this identificatory power over the students, and that is his or her own narcissistic satisfaction in seeing the students gradually coming to want what he or she wants "for" them. Seen in this light, education is on the side of narcissism and the imaginary, the ideal and "illusion."

Perhaps the difficulty of combining psychoanalysis and education can be seen most strikingly in Anna Freud's version of child analysis-cum-childhood education. She says that it is necessary to *use* the transference to ensure the formation of a parental-type attachment between child and analyst in order to open the door to suggestion. Child analysis, here construed as a kind of analytical education, is thus the opposite of adult analysis because the analyst reinforces the superego while dealing with the drives.

But what about the numerous attempts to reform pedagogy through radical means, many of which claim to found their principles in psychoanalytic insights? Do not these reformist efforts seek to circumvent the very problems we have just been discussing? Millot gives one particularly telling example of a radical educational practice which proposes putting the teacher in the position of the analyst.[8] She cites an exchange which took place between A. S. Neill and one of his students at Summerhill: "Teach me something, I'm bored stiff," demands a little girl who had done no schoolwork in weeks. "Righto!," Neill enthusiastically responds, "What do you want to learn?" "I don't know," she says. "And I don't either," he replies, and walks away. Millot is interested in this conversation because she believes that Neill is doing something psychoanalytically intelligent in his refusal to respond to the girl's demand to tell her what to desire. In analytic treatment such a refusal would serve to leave that demand hanging, so to speak, in the highly charged space between analyst and analysand, so that it could be recognized and seen for what it is (a demand for love, for the desire of the other). Millot, however, makes it quite clear that the teacher is *not* like the analyst, that the teacher is not a smooth mirror in which the student-subject can see the reflected structure of its own demand and desire. This is because the student can always sense the hidden demands of the teacher or parent. The student, like the child with the parent, is almost *clairvoyant* when it comes to understanding the desire of the Other and how best narcissistically to mirror what the Other desires. In A. S. Neill's case, the refusal to respond to the girl's demand clearly hides a demand of his own—that the child, in canonical Summerhill fashion, be autonomous and act according to her own desires. Analytically speaking, the child is already alienated with respect to both language and the desire of its parents. Neill's refusal enacts a comparable alienation in its obfuscation of his demand. All of this leads Millot to the conclusion that the role of the analyst and the teacher cannot be embodied in one and the same person because psychoanalysis and education are fundamentally opposed in their entirely different relations to *knowledge* and *authority*.

Lacan himself scarcely conceals his contempt for the "discourse of the university," assigning it a place between the "discourse of the master" and the "discourse of the hysteric."[9] He characterizes the "discourse of the university" not only by its neglect of the signifier and its obsession with discourse constituted as knowledge, but also by its tendency to ignore questions of subjectivity in favor of knowledge as the ultimate object of desire. But is Freud's and Lacan's highly visible pessimism about the psychoanalytic contribution to education everything that we can learn from them on this matter?

In her discerning essay, "Psychoanalysis and Education: Teaching Terminable and Interminable,"[10] Shoshana Felman strongly disagrees with what she sees as Catherine Millot's "reductive conception" (p. 24) of psychoanalytic thinking about pedagogy. Millot, like many others, is mistaken in referring "exclusively to Lacan's or Freud's explicit *statements* about pedagogy, and thus fails to see the illocutionary force, the didactic function of the *utterance* as opposed to the mere content of the statement" (p. 24). Felman goes on to say that "invariably, all existing psychoanalytically-inspired theories of pedagogy fail to address the question of the pedagogical speech-act of Freud himself, or of Lacan himself: what can be learnt about pedagogy not just from their theories (which only fragmentarily and indirectly deal with the issue of education) but from their way of *teaching* it, from their own practice as teachers, from their own pedagogical performance" (p. 24).

Reading off from the respective teaching *styles* of Freud and Lacan (both of whom she sees as exemplary teachers because they thought of themselves as *students*—Freud of his own unconscious, and Lacan of Freud's writings), Felman redefines psychoanalysis as a pedagogical experience in itself, as a process which provides access to knowledge hitherto denied to consciousness and which therefore affords a lesson in cognition as well as miscognition. Consequently, what is needed is not a conscious *application* of the psychoanalytic process but rather an understanding of its *implications* for teaching. Psychoanalysis, as a means of access to "information hitherto *unlearnable*" (p. 27), demands a new mode of learning, if only because it involves a different temporal experience of learning. It proceeds instead through "breakthroughs, leaps, discontinuities, regressions and deferred action" (p. 27), thus challenging "the traditional pedagogical belief in intellectual perfectibility, the progressive view of learning as a simple one-way road from ignorance to knowledge" (p. 27).

Conversely, the idea of the imperfectibility of knowledge is based on the assumption that the unconscious eludes intentionality and meaning. As Lacan puts it in Seminar XX, "Analysis appears on the scene to announce that there is *knowledge which does not know itself.*"[11] "Ignorance" is not a simple lack of knowledge but is, rather, understood as an integral part of the very structure of knowledge. That is why Lacan opens his seminar entitled *Encore* by announcing that "I am here only to analyze my own 'I don't want to know anything about it' " ("je n'en veux rien savoir," p.9). Thus the material of analysis (or of teaching) is that which *is not remembered,* what will not be memorized. Ignorance is not a passive state but an active *excluding from consciousness* (that is, repression) whatever it does not want to know. "Teaching, like analysis, has to deal not so much with *lack* of knowledge as with *resistances* to knowledge" (p. 30), and an analytically informed pedagogy would have to come to terms with what Lacan called "the passion for ignorance" (p. 110). This refusal, then, is not so much a refusal of information as a refusal to acknowledge *one's own implication* in that information. For Felman, the truly revolutionary insight—from the lesson of Freud's and Lacan's rhetorical styles—consists in showing the ways in which *ignorance itself can teach us something.* But this is an insight with consequences for teachers as well as students, because as Lacan said, "There is no true teaching other than the teaching which succeeds in provoking in those who listen an insistance—this desire to know which can only emerge when they themselves have *taken the measure of ignorance as such*—of ignorance inasmuch as it is, as such, fertile—in the one who teaches as well."[12] Teaching is not therefore the transmission of ready-made knowledge, but the creation of a "new-condition of knowledge—the creation of an original learning-disposition" (p. 31). "What I teach you," says Lacan, "does nothing other than express the *condition* thanks to which what Freud says is possible" (p. 368).

As we have seen, Millot's strongest doubts about the possibility of a psychoanalytically informed pedagogy are rooted in her fundamental mistrust of the pedagogical need to *use* the transference relation to maintain the student's belief in the teacher's knowledge and authority. Neither the teacher nor the teaching institution can afford to question, much less subvert, this belief. Felman, however, argues that the transference relation *can* be put into question and, furthermore, that this *must* be done if any real learning (as opposed to mere indoctrination) is to take place. Taking her lesson again from Lacan, she shows that psychoanalytic learning (which constantly serves as her pedagogical model) is always *dialogic:* "No knowledge," writes Lacan, "can be supported or transported by one alone."[13] In the analytical situation, the analyst listens to and is taught by the analysand's unconscious: "It is by structurally occupying the position of the analysand's unconscious, and by thus making himself a *student of the patient's knowledge,* that the analyst becomes the teacher—makes the patient learn what would otherwise remain forever inaccessible to him" (p. 33). For learning to take place there must always be an Other. Knowledge is what is already there, but always in the Other. Thus it cannot be said that the teacher (or the student) *contains* knowledge, but that it comes about in the intersection of "two partially unconscious speeches which both say more than they know" (p. 33). If we follow out the implications of this unique pedagogical process, the clear-cut opposition between analyst and analysand or between teacher and student disappears. What we finally come to understand is both the psychical necessity and the actual contingency of these shifting and interchangeable positions. The student becomes a teacher when he or she realizes that it is impossible to know everything, that to be a teacher one must never stop being a student. And the teacher can teach nothing other than the *way he or she learns.* For Felman, then, psychoanalytic teaching is pedagogically unique in that it is inherently and interminably self-critical. It is a didactic mode of "self-subversive self-reflection" (p. 39).

In comparing these two arguments—Millot's and Felman's—one pessimistically refuting the idea of an analytical pedagogy and the other polemically claiming psychoanalysis as the only pedagogical practice worthy of the name, we have seen both the problems and the possibilities of a psychoanalytically orientated pedagogy. Keeping in mind the kinds of issues that have been raised concerning the psychoanalytic understanding of knowledge and authority, let us now turn to feminism in its equally precarious relation to institutionalized learning.

A Feminist Pedagogy?

Just as Freud felt compelled to pose the question, "Should psychoanalysis be taught at the university?"[14] feminists, likewise, have wondered if feminism could be taught within the traditional institutions of education. (Freud answered his own question by asserting that the university stood only to gain by the inclusion in its curriculum of the teaching of psychoanalysis; psychoanalysis, however, could dispense entirely with the university without any loss to itself.) In Paula Treichler's comprehensive survey of feminists' attitudes toward teaching feminist theory, as well as their methods ("Teaching Feminist Theory," included in this volume), it is immediately apparent that few feminists see the relation of feminism and traditional pedagogy as an entirely unproblematic one, while they are in essential agreement that feminist teaching methods must accommodate or reflect the political givens of feminism. With respect to feminism's problematic relation to the university, feminists seem to share Freud's cast of mind: they believe that the university can greatly benefit from incorporating feminism into the curriculum but are more dubious about what feminism receives in turn from its new-found academicization. Their doubts, as outlined in Treichler's essay, understandably include the debilitating effects of the continuing entrenched sexism of the university, the loss of feminist theory's political radicalness through the attempt to ensure its academic respectability, and the creation of an "elite" of feminist scholars who take their research cues from the university rather than the movement. But beyond these doubts looms an even larger danger in the incompatability of feminist *ways of teaching* with the more typical pedagogical requirements of exclusiveness, authority, and hierarchy. It is in particular the feminist commitment to "making the personal political" that poses the greatest difficulties for "normal" pedagogical practices. Applying the lessons of the kind of consciousness-raising that grew up with the movement, feminist pedagogy seeks "to restore personal observation and interpretation as trustworthy sources of information about the world" (p. 69). Further, it is often held that feminist theory and its research methods will bring about a new epistemology, one which will challenge the subject/object dichotomies endemic to the "discourse of the university." To give an idea of what these rather general ideas would mean to the feminist classroom, I will cite, as Treichler does, Marilyn J. Boxer's summary of feminism's alternative techniques:

> The double purpose of women's studies—to expose and redress the oppression of women—was reflected in widespread attempts to restructure the classroom experience of students and faculty. Circular arrangements of chairs, periodic small-group sessions, use of first names for instructors as well as students, assignments that required journal keeping, "reflection papers," cooperative projects, and collective modes of teaching with student participation, all sought to transfer to women's studies the contemporary feminist criticism of authority and the validation of every woman's experience. These techniques borrowed from the women's movement also were designed to combat the institutional hierarchy and professional exclusiveness that had been used to shut out women. (P. 69)[15]

Let us now look more closely at the feminist perspective on knowledge and authority that is implied in the very specific pedagogical goals and methods listed above. Since the issue of power and its hierarchized distribution has been of paramount concern to feminists, we shall turn first to the question of authority. The pedagogical techniques typically adopted in the feminist classroom, "use of first names for instructors as well as students," or "collective modes of teaching with student participation," for example, clearly aim toward a dispersal or even elimination of authority. The risk, of course, in aiming toward or claiming the eradication of power relations is that the force and pervasiveness of those relations may be overlooked, "out of sight, out of mind." But can the feminist classroom afford to lose sight of the extreme power of the transferential relation, of the narcissism underlying the demands of both students and teachers, or the basically eroticized nature of learning (the constant appeal for recognition)? I do not want to offer a "wild analysis" of the feminist classroom, but I would like to point to some of the contradictory demands around authority which can be seen there.

A very straightforward example might be found in the role of the teacher in the feminist classroom. Ideally, she carries out a very deliberate self-undermining of her own authority by refusing to be an "authority" at all, or by insisting that the validation of knowledge issue not from her acquired grasp of the material but from the students' own experiences as women and through a collective working-through of the issues raised. Another demand, often just as conscious even when recognized as contradictory, conflicts with the demand that she relinquish her authority. The woman who is a feminist teacher is expected at the very least to be an exemplary feminist, if not a "role model." Much of the effectiveness of the teaching in fact lies in the students' acceptance of her as an appropriate representative of feminism. The teacher, in turn, wants and expects the students to be "like" her insofar as she would rather that they turn out to be feminists than not. It would also be difficult for her not to want the students to accept her idea of feminism (no matter how determinably pluralistic she attempts to be) as feminism *tout court*.

Feminism, then, like psychoanalysis, is characterized by its willful reliance on nonauthoritative knowledge. (The difficulty of separating authority and knowledge is suggested in the spectacle of the discursive ease with which my argument runs one into the other.) Psychoanalysis has recourse to dreams, slips, jokes, and other revelatory "errors" of speech and psyche, while feminism looks beyond the "scientific" certitudes about femininity to what can be learned instead from the personal observations and experiences of women. Psychoanalysis and feminism also share similar ideas about the ambiguous *site* of knowledge. In the analytic situation, as we have seen, knowledge is not contained in the Other, but in the interplay of two partially unconscious speeches, each of which does not (alone) know what it is saying. For feminism, knowledge is likewise unlocalizable, resulting from a collective endeavor which involves retrieving one's own feelings and experiences, and comparing them with those of other women, while working through the material under discussion. There are, however, some important differences. Whereas Freud declared psychoanalysis to be "interminable," feminism, as a political project, necessarily hopes for some sort of termination (a state of achieved sexual equality where feminism would no longer be necessary). Like certain forms of revisionist psychoanalysis (usually the American variety), feminism believes that it cannot function unless it offers the promise of a "cure" (of sexism, of the historical oppression of women). It must therefore promote the possibility of a progressive acquisition of knowledge the mastery of which (when linked to activism) would result in a solution to women's oppression. There is nothing wrong with this idea: it is an absolutely necessary one for any movement seeking to bring about a radical transformation of existing relations (knowledge *is* power).

It is important to recognize, though, that the feminist emphasis on educational democracy, instrumental knowledge, and a common-sense understanding of the world has familiar echoes in the tradition of a distinctively American pedagogy. We should also remind ourselves that the feminist classroom is not an isolated enclave but very much part of the university and hence of the state apparatus, no matter how intentionally "alternative" it might be. John Dewey and others proposed a broad program of American education that stressed the democratic broadening of the constituency and questioned the usefulness of abstractions that may have no useful consequences. The American classroom is therefore geared toward practicality and "learning by doing." In recent years it has become a common-enough claim that the advent of mass culture and the instrumental model of American pedagogy have colluded in producing students who are enslaved to the "concrete" and capable only of the most literal kind of thinking. Reality is dissolved into objecthood; empiricism claims the classroom as its laboratory.[16] Even if one believes that some kind of conceptual or critical thinking still occasionally occurs in the American classroom, the feminist classroom can, ironically, look like the perfect embodiment of a Deweyesque instrumentalism in its demand for practical knowledge stemming from observation and experience rather than useless ("male") abstraction.

Feminism and Psychoanalysis Together?

Is it, then, on the question of empiricism that psychoanalytic and feminist pedagogy are most at odds? As Felman suggested, the didactic mode of psychoanalysis is one of "self-subversive self-reflection." This formula means that the analysand is required not only to recall and speak about past experiences (or dreams or fantasies) but also to *interpret* that speech to see what else might be hidden or contained there. "Experience" is not then a phenomenal reality simply to be retrieved and made "conscious" through language. Rather, the speech that the analysand uses to report or relate that experience is the material for analysis, much more so than the experience "itself." Was it not, indeed, the increasing emphasis in Freud's work on the importance of fantasy to our psychical lives that challenged the very notion of experience "itself"? In his analysis of the Wolf Man, for example, Freud questions whether the events that the Wolf Man recalls (various sexual scenes) ever took place. (He goes on to say, however, that it is not necessary for an event to have occurred for it to have an existence in concrete retrospective effects.) Feminism, by contrast, cannot afford to question either the reality of the woman's experience or the conscious credibility of her speech. This is because feminism's struggle is waged precisely against the historical denial of the value of women's experience as well as the refusal to believe that women are capable of giving a coherent account of that experience.

Clearly it is ironic that feminism should have come to be so closely aligned with empiricism, because feminist thinking, like psychoanalytic theory, constitutes one of the most crucial historical (and political) challenges to empiricism. Feminism shares with psychoanalysis a strong commitment to exposing the "naturally" given or socially self-evident forms of everyday life and language. Through its attention to symptoms, slips of the tongue, and dreams, psychoanalysis radically puts into question empiricism's reliance on observation and experience. Feminism, too, seeks to penetrate beneath the surface of observable phenomena and question not only the presumption of women's "natural" qualities but also the way in which the social system rationalizes those qualities into structures of inequality (sexual division of labor, gender-based wage scales, etc.). The greatest obstacles to the social changes that could be wrought by feminism are in fact those entrenched ideas that are based on "common sense," or that which is "obvious" or "natural" about women.

In a recent article, "Femininity and Its Discontents," Jacqueline Rose offers an example of antiempiricist thinking that shows important links between feminism and psychoanalysis.[17] She first discusses recent work by feminist historians[18] that demonstrates how social policy decisions (such as the Contagious Diseases Act of the 1860s) base themselves on specific qualitative categories of femininity—diseased, degenerate, hysterical, etc.; such women are then claimed to be in need of incarceration, regulation, reproductive restraints, etc. These categories are thus constructed on the basis of that which is "obvious" or "self-evident" about women's nature or anatomy (for example, fragility, underdeveloped sense of morality, sexual prosmiscuity, or an innate tendency toward hysteria). Rose goes on to argue that Freud's contribution to the study of hysteria helped to undermine these social categories of the "visible" which were so detrimental to women. Freud's earliest work on hysteria was under Charcot at the Salpetrière Clinic in Paris, a hospital for women who were considered to be the dregs of society. Charcot's achievement was to rescue hysterics from the closed category of sexual malingerers and to see their condition as a specific and acknowledged disease. The problem with Charcot's approach, however, was that he believed that hysteria was a degenerate, hereditary disease as well as a particular "type"of deviant behavior that was visible to the eye (thus the thousands of notorious Salpetrière photographs of women frozen into "hysterical" poses). Freud's intervention was twofold. First, he questioned the idea that one could recognize a hysteric simply by looking at her body and the visible evidence of her symptoms. Second, he argued that the unconscious mental processes that he himself discovered while studying hysteria (displacement, repression, etc.) were ones to be found in every adult. Freud's approach thus challenged the fixed perception of hysteria as a mode of classifying certain degenerate and isolated individuals, and shifted this category into the center of everybody's psychic experience. Freud's discoveries, of course, are based on assumptions about the fundamental discontinuity of psychic life, assumptions that led him to posit the existence of the unconscious. The difficulty of teaching feminism and psychoanalysis together is that they share the same project of exposing the ideologies of "common sense" and the "visible" only insofar as feminism accepts the idea of the unconscious and seeks to engage in a similar effort of "self-subversive self-reflection." (A discussion of how the latter is and is not like feminist "consciousness-raising" would be too long to include here.) To accept the idea of the unconscious, however, brings with it what many feminists view as unwanted epistemological baggage: the hypotheses of the instability of language and identity, the narcissism underlying all human relations, permanent psychical conflict, infantile sexuality, the pervasiveness and strength of transferential relations, and the links between intellectual activity and infantile sexual investigation, among others. Psychoanalysis is clearly not a "utopianism of the psyche."[19]

Ultimately, however, the greatest obstacle to bringing feminism and psychoanalysis together on any common ground, pedagogical or otherwise, is the very different relation each has to the question of "identity." In order to be either a movement or a discipline, feminism *must* presuppose the category "woman." Although the content of this category may be variously construed according to the aims of the analysis—for example, "victim" of a transhistorical male dominance or "author" of a creative work giving voice to women's concerns—a "feminine identity" has to be presumed even when (necessarily) citing the given historical varieties of "woman," individual women, etc. It is politically necessary to claim that there is a class or group of humans ("women") that is universally oppressed (by "men," "patriarchy," etc.) because no movement can constitute itself without notions of identity and commonality. This clear need, however, conflicts sharply with the refusal of psychoanalysis theoretically to posit a specifically feminine (or masculine) identity. As Freud put it: "In conformity with its peculiar nature, psychoanalysis does not try to describe what a woman is—that would be a task it could scarcely perform— but sets about enquiring how she comes into being."[20] Psychoanalysis does not accept that "men and women, males and females, *exist*,"[21] but rather seeks to describe and analyze the human laws which determine sexual difference. The most striking formulation of psychoanalysis's commitment to antiessentialism can be found in Jacques Lacan's statement that "Woman does not exist" *(la femme n'existe pas)*. Lacan does not mean by this that there are no real women in the world but rather that there is no universal feminine essence, and that what we take to be femininity is only a fantasmatic construction used to support *the very idea of identity as complete and continuous with itself* (the fantasy of wholeness and free access to one's "self"). The distance between the very different theoretical and political needs of psychoanalysis and feminism on the question of identity is perhaps best summed up in the contrast between the notorious bravura of "Woman does not exist" and Sojourner Truth's effectively polemical, "Ain't I a Woman?"[22] We have here, in my rather outrageous juxtaposition of Jacques Lacan and Sojourner Truth, two ideas or strategies that are vitally important to feminism, yet that appear completely at odds. Feminism, like psychoanalysis, must argue against the historical claim that all women are in essence alike, or that femininity is something that is self-evident, because it knows very well the kinds of stereotyped qualities that are invariably attributed to this feminine essence, and always to the detriment of women. It is, however, sometimes politically expedient to make the personal claim that one is a woman, and it is an assertion that can have immediate and concrete political effects. Sojourner Truth's famous declaration disguised as a question, "Ain't I a Woman?" was in response to those who, in fact, refused to say that she was a woman because they refused to include black women in the category of womanhood. Sojourner Truth's femininity or womanness was not at all self-evident to many of those listening to her memorable speech: it was something for which she had to fight, and the establishment of that identity was crucial to her political struggle. Is there, then, any way out of this impasse of radically opposed ideas about the necessity or nonnecessity of an "identity"?

One of the paradoxes of feminism has been the strength of its assertion of an identity for women at precisely the historical moment when such accounts of individual subjectivity are being radically called into question by Lacan, Althusser, Derrida, and Foucault, among others. But in these new accounts of identity and individual subjectivity, feminism may discover ways to rethink the question of identity that not only acknowledges the absolute political necessity of *an identity* for women (a political one) but also maintains the equal necessity of examining "identity" (or "femininity") as an epistemological, metaphysical, or ideological category. These new accounts often argue that each individual comprises several "identities." One's identity, for example, as a legal subject does not always coincide with one's identity as a sexual or medical subject. Each individual "exists" only as a nexus of various and *sometimes contradictory* subjectivities which are legislated or assumed, either consciously or unconsciously. This allows us to support a more complex working definition of subjectivity as well as a firmer understanding of the conflicts and contradictions at work in our social and psychical makeup. Like the psychoanalytical emphasis on the importance of the unconscious and fantasy in our lives, this approach goes beyond those easy claims for conscious, controlled, or deliberate political action. But in its acknowledged political success and longstanding pledge to the idea that "the personal is political," it is perhaps feminism that can most productively incorporate these newer and more complex notions of subjectivity without succumbing to any political fatalism.

144

Another way to avoid the absolute opposition between an empirical subject and a psychical subject, and again to argue for a notion of multiple identities, is to acknowledge that political struggles (here, specifically, women's struggles) develop on all fronts (economic, ideological, political). These conditions often require the preservation, for longer or shorter periods, of presuppositions (like "woman" or "femininity") that will have to be questioned later or from someplace other than the point of actual, daily confrontation. It has to be accepted, moreover, that these presuppositions must and will be challenged because they are ideas that belong so solidly to the structures that are under attack: "Woman" or "Femininity" as the major allegory of Truth in western discourse, or as the fantasmatic other of its supposed complement, "masculinity." It is psychoanalysis, of course, which first provided the concept of the "split subject" (a subject divided against itself in its conflicting desires and conflictual responses to demands) that has become so crucial to these newer approaches to the question of subjectivity. Although there is an obvious tension or difference between the notions of identity found in psychoanalysis and feminism, it is through teaching them together that we can begin to fully determine what might now be gained from acknowledging or incorporating these more complex ideas about subjectivity at the very moment that feminism continues its necessary effort to forge a new identity for women.

In my discussion of the problems of teaching feminism and psychoanalysis together, I have neglected the difficulties that are specific to teaching psychoanalysis in relation to a progressive political movement such as feminism *in America today*. There are some very real and important reasons why American feminism has rejected psychoanalysis, reasons that can help us to understand why we do not have in America the kind of serious debate about feminism and psychoanalysis that is presently taking place in other countries like England and France; perhaps, for the same reasons, American students experience difficulties in grasping the relation between feminism and psychoanalysis. In its move to America, psychoanalysis underwent both a theoretical retreat from the more radical of Freud's discoveries as well as an atrophication of its own institutional structures. The turn toward an adjustment-oriented ego psychology and the medicalization of the profession, with the consequent exclusion of women, was largely the result of the conservatism forced upon the emigré analysts (many of whom had been very active in European leftist politics) seeking respectibility in an America that valued "professionalism" above all else.[23] Psychoanalysis in this country is an admittedly conservative institution. In Britain, by contrast, psychoanalysis is still considered socially and professionally "marginal," and since (following Freud's suggestion) analysts are not required to be doctors, there are many lay practitioners. In addition, much of the most important psychoanalytic work in England has been carried out by women like Anna Freud, Melanie Klein, Joan Rivière, Susan Isaacs, Paula Heimann, and, more recently, Juliet Mitchell.[24] French psychoanalysis has of course been marked by the iconoclastic presence of Lacan's anti-institutionalism, which encouraged would-be analysts to decide for themselves when they were ready to practice and whose teachings have been readily assimilated to leftist politics.[25] Similarly, the names of certain women analysts are central to French psychoanalytic theory and its politics—Julia Kristeva, Catherine Clément, Luce Irigaray, Michèle Montrelay, and Eugènie Lemoine-Luccioni, among others. Thus in a very practical way it is important in a course on feminism and psychoanalysis to get across to the students the idea that "psychoanalysis" is not a homogeneous institution, nor does it exist solely in the politically and culturally impoverished version of it familiar to us in America, which has been so rightfully criticized by feminists.

In looking at the intertwined pedagogical and theoretical difficulties of teaching a course on feminism and psychoanalysis, I hope I have shown not only that it is *not* an "impossible" task, but also that teaching them together is perhaps the most productive way of teaching either feminism or psychoanalysis on its own. It is not a question of what feminism holds out for psychoanalysis or what psychoanalysis has to offer feminism, but how each invites the other to examine its relation to knowledge and authority as well as its understanding of identity and sexual difference.

NOTES

1. Juliet Mitchell, *Psychoanalysis and Feminism* (New York: Vintage Books, 1975).

2. Sigmund Freud, *The Interpretation of Dreams,* in *The Standard*

Edition of the Complete Psychological Works of Sigmund Freud (hereafter abbreviated *S.E.*), trans. and ed. James Strachey *et al.*, 24 vols. (London: Hogarth Press, 1953–64), 5: 135–36.

3. Sigmund Freud, "Explanations and Applications, " in *New Introductory Lectures on Psychoanalysis, S.E.* 22: 146–47: "[With respect to] the application of psychoanalysis to education . . . I am glad that I am at least able to say that my daughter, Anna Freud, has made this study her life-work and has in that way compensated for my neglect."

4. Catherine Millot, *Freud, Anti-pédagogue* (Paris: Editions du Seuil, 1979–La Bibliothèque d'*Ornicar?*).

5. Sigmund Freud, "Some Reflections on Schoolboy Psychology," *S.E.* 13: 241–44.

6. Jacques Lacan, *The Four Fundamental Concepts of Psychoanalysis* (New York: W. W. Norton, 1981), pp. 174, 267.

7. Jacques Lacan, *Scilicet* V, p. 16.

8. Millot, *Freud*, p. 162.

9. For a concise discussion of Lacan's "four discourses," which were introduced in his 1969–70 seminar, *L'envers de la psychanalyse* (XVIII), see Jacqueline Rose, *Feminine Sexuality: Jacques Lacan and the Ecole freudienne*, ed. Juliet Mitchell and Jacqueline Rose (London: Macmillan, 1982), pp. 160–61.

10. Shoshana Felman, "Psychoanalysis and Education: Teaching Terminable and Interminable," *Yale French Studies* 63 (1982): 21–44.

11. Jacques Lacan, Seminar XX, *Encore* (Paris: Editions du Seuil, 1975), p. 88.

12. Jacques Lacan, Seminar II, *Le moi dans la théorie de Freud et dans la technique de la psychanalyse* (Paris: Editions du Seuil, 1978), p. 242.

13. Lacan, *Scilicet* I, p. 59.

14. "Should Psychoanalysis Be Taught at the University?" is the original title of a paper Freud published in a Hungarian translation. The *Standard Edition* title is "On the Teaching of Psychoanalysis in Universities" 17: 171–73.

15. For another comprehensive survey of feminist pedagogical theory and techniques, see *Learning Our Way: Essays in Feminist Education*, ed. Charlotte Bunch and Sandra Pollack (Trumansburg, N. Y.: The Crossing Press, 1983).

16. For example, see Stanley Aronowitz's "Mass Culture and the Eclipse of Reason," in his *The Crisis in Historical Materialism*, (New York: Praeger, 1981).

17. Jacqueline Rose, "Femininity and Its Discontents," *Feminist Review* 14 (Summer 1983): 5–21. My discussion of the feminist alliance with anti-empiricism is indebted to Rose's argument in this essay.

18. For example, Carol Dyhouse, *Girls Growing Up in Late Victorian England* (London: Routledge and Kegan Paul, 1981) and Judith Walkowitz, *Prostitution and Victorian Society; Women, Class and the State* (Cambridge: Cambridge University Press, 1980).

19. Rose, "Femininity and Its Discontents," p. 18.

20. Freud, "Femininity," *S.E.* 22: 116.

21. Juliet Mitchell, *Feminine Sexuality,* p. 23. As opposed to Kleinian and non-Kleinian object-relations theorists for whom "the distinction between the sexes is not the result of a division but a fact that is already given, men and women, males and females, *exist.*"

22. Sojourner Truth's famous speech can be found in *Ain't I a Woman?,* a book on black women and feminism by Bell Hooks (Boston: South End Press, 1981).

23. For a history of the political consequences of the American "professionalization" of psychoanalysis, see Russell Jacoby, *The Repression of Psychoanalysis: Otto Fenichel and the Political Freudians* (New York: Basic Books, 1983).

24. This same point is made by Rose, "Femininity and Its Discontents," p. 6.

25. See Sherry Turkle, *Psychoanalytic Politics: Freud's French Revolution* (Cambridge, Mass.: The MIT Press, 1981).

S. P. MOHANTY

Radical Teaching, Radical Theory: The Ambiguous Politics of Meaning

The ideas of the ruling class are in every epoch the ruling ideas, i.e., the class which is the ruling material force of society is at the same time its ruling intellectual force.
— K. Marx & F. Engels, *The German Ideology*

All *pedagogic action* is, objectively, symbolic violence insofar as it is the imposition of a cultural arbitrary by an arbitrary power.
— Pierre Bourdieu and Jean-Claude Passeron,
Reproduction in Education, Society and Culture

If, as Richard Rorty suggests, American literary criticism since World War II has increasingly compensated for the "professionalization" of philosophy and its withdrawal into purely technical and academic concerns, then modern "criticism" is not merely a discipline but rather a larger social phenomenon, supplanting history, philosophy, or religion as the site of cultural and moral pedagogy *par excellence*.[1] The renaissance of "theory" in the American literary academy since the early seventies may, however, suggest a significantly different cultural prospect. The development of highly specialized languages of critical practice, the assumption of the inherent superiority of matters of theory beyond the immediate questions of textual interpretation, the particular combination of the prophetic tone with the desire for scientificity and rigor—all these point to a substantial change in the cultural role and function of contemporary literary criticism. Less a culturally effective discourse than a specialized set of language games,

149

contemporary criticism may indeed resemble academic philosophy in its most technical modes, appealing to a trained coterie.

From the outside, it is possible to lament this truncation of the public functions of criticism. Edward Said, whose career straddles—uncomfortably, but with a great deal of courage—both high theory and the popular, cultural critical modes, recently attacked much of contemporary theory on the grounds of its political ineffectuality. By implicit contrast to the very critics Rorty would identify as the previous generation's culture heroes (Lionel Trilling, Edmund Wilson, etc.), Said chides even contemporary Marxist critics for their apparent contentment with the discursive contexts of academic institutions.[2] For anyone concerned with the politics of culture, this is a significant charge and needs, certainly, to be thought through. There are institutional pressures towards insularity and irrelevance: it is safer for an American cultural critic today to write about theories of ideology than to analyze, say, Reaganism's hidden racist agenda and its implications for immediate educational and cultural issues.[3] But Said may be too hasty in assuming that critics like Paul de Man and Harold Bloom are ineffectual angels. In conferences on literary criticism as well as in course readings of young scholar-teachers all over the country, the growing influence of the new theory may be easily seen. The American literary academy may well be entering a long period of theoretical emphasis and debate. Many of the major critics are influential in the way their students extend and disseminate their ideas in classroom and colloquium alike, and it is already evident that even the national magazines are buzzing about "deconstruction" and "semiology." We may be at the beginning of a larger movement where the college literature classroom is the register of fundamentally new aesthetic-cultural ideologies. The death of the author; the valorization of *jouissance*, not pleasure; the text, not the work; the play of mobile signifiers, not the search for determinable meaning—the slogans point to the possibility of a systemic and a basic change that touches our discourses of society as well as of art. Such a phenomenon requires at least an intrinsic theoretical critique, not a purely sociological diagnosis.

I want, then, to engage the current polemical context of theoretical discussion by offering reinterpretations of a number of assumed alliances and oppositions. I will look at an issue of *Yale*

French Studies and, in some detail, at the work of Paul de Man. Finally I will address the pedagogical scene, in part as an attempt to locate the discussion of theory, laden as it is these days with charges of privilege and irrelevance on the one hand and of a nihilistic antihumanism on the other, in a context that makes the delineation of theoretical issues more precise by clarifying their immediate "practical" dimension. The pedagogical context is for me the instance of the everyday and the contingent, but it is also the challenge of the need to *think* the institutional limits of the discursive. As such, it allows us to deetherealize the claims of theory while offering the possibility of situating it in its network of determined relations.

The recent issue of *Yale French Studies* titled *The Pedagogical Imperative: Teaching as a Literary Genre* may be in this instance an ideally representative text.[4] Its emphasis on teaching—the theater, the politics, the discourses—grounds its theoretical discussion in a context all of us are familiar with. Some of the essays are in the form of manifestoes (Paul de Man's, for instance, or the editor's preface), and are thus easier to analyze theoretically. Others provide detailed textual analyses that enable the authors to generalize about text, genre, social context, and their ideological interpenetrations (see, for example, Richard Terdiman's "Structures of Initiation: On Semiotic Education and its Contradictions in Balzac"). Several of the other essays remain models of witty, *nouvelle vague* criticism of individual texts with a desire to recapture itinerant meanings and impulses, plays of power and desire (Jane Gallop and Neil Hertz are the best examples here). In addition, there are short extracts from Jacques Derrida and Jean-Francois Lyotard and essays by, among others, Barbara Johnson, Andrew McKenna, and Michael Ryan. At the heart of the volume, however, is Shoshana Felman's provocative essay, "Psychoanalysis and Education: Teaching Terminable and Interminable," which formulates and clarifies the central implication of the title of the collection. Given the obviously rich diversity of the volume and the significance of its subject, it may be useful for an ideological analysis to begin here. It is in these meditations on teaching that the larger politics of contemporary theorizing about literature becomes evident, and it is possible here to analyze in detail *both* the politics and the theory. What follows is merely propaedeutic to such work, and my emphasis on Paul de Man, as will soon be obvious, is primarily due to his exemplary status and his influence within contemporary theory.

Let me begin by quoting from two of the essays in the first section of the volume: "Whenever the autonomous potential of language can be revealed by analysis, we are dealing with literariness . . ." (p. 10). "One cannot determine the function of language in literature . . . without taking into account the political and economic functions of language" (p. 55). For the liberal "pluralist" in the cultural politics of American criticism, there would be in this volume (to judge by the above) a basic schism in methodology or approach. On the one hand there would appear to be something like an *intrinsic* approach in literary matters, an approach that would respect the internal dynamism of texts, of language and literature. This would appear to be the common characteristic of the essays by de Man, Barbara Johnson, Joan de Jean, and others. On the other hand would be the Marxists, stressing that language and literature are defined in their "political and economic functions and uses." Such writers as Ryan and Terdiman, it would seem at first glance, stress the extrinsic, the sociological dimension, remaining basically opposed to the earlier writers. This division between the extrinsic and the intrinsic is, however, fundamentally misleading, particularly when we encounter a collection of essays such as this. Much of the radical basis of contemporary theory—psychoanalytic, Marxist, or what is loosely called poststructuralist[5]—suggests that there is a fundamental commonality here. Any understanding of American literary criticism today needs to start from an acknowledgment of this shared basis, this common ground that it does not share with the theoretical foundations of, say, New Criticism. This common idea is evident in claims about the text (and textuality), about language, about literature and literariness, about notions of context and history—in short in every major idea or term that is being debated in literary critical journals these days. For the sake of convenience, let me call this a debate about "meaning," about what it is that texts and contexts do when they are said to mean something. What guided much of the older debate about meaning was a concern for validity and correctness: is this what this passage from *Finnegans Wake* or *The Faerie Queene* means? Under what conditions, with what guarantee, will we know what the limits of its meaning are? History, in these views, is either the (inert) context that needs to be recovered to clarify and instruct us in our search, or (as with the New Critics) a covertly installed myth of literary and cultural history that sanctions "purely immanent" textual analysis and evaluation.[6] In this general context, then, we need to be clear about what is being represented and about what is the representation. The new view of meaning renders many of these questions obsolete. Now, the discussion is not about the *what* of meaning, but rather the *how*. A text is considered to be less a self-evident object to be analyzed, with strata or levels to be unearthed, than a dynamic intertextual *process;* and the death of meaning is heralded and sung because it is not the stable embodiment of meaning that critics choose to analyze but rather its discursive mobility.

The political basis of this new emphasis can only be understood when we realize that particular meanings are conventional and cultural, "ideological" in their apparent naturalness. To attempt to deny meaning in theory, then, is to attempt to suspend the transmission of culturally dominant ideas in the natural course of things: teaching our English 101 students to valorize "Order," for instance, is not an innocent teaching of *Troilus and Cressida;* it is a specific form of acculturation. To oppose order to chaos, form (and culture) to nature, method to madness, is to be complicit with the transmission of political *doxa,*[7] to aid in the reproduction of ethical binarisms or ideologically coded hierarchies. Against this background, the new theory's para-doxical teaching is that meanings do not exist as such, but are produced; what we thought we knew was an illusion of meaning—an effect of our subjective desires or our (political) positionings.

At their best, many of the essays in *The Pedagogical Imperative* (no matter what their methodology or ideological tag) display this concern implicitly. Paul de Man, for instance, rejects traditional aesthetic categories on the ground that they conjure up in one form or another a prediscursive connectedness of word and thing, valuing an ideal notion of experience and meaning over the instability of linguistic processes. For de Man, this instability is "literariness," revealed in the "figurality" of language. Barbara Johnson, in much the same spirit, would see the "pedagogical moment" as best represented by a "blank" space, for it inherently seeks to transmit and codify that which cannot be known. In her essay on Moliere's *L'École des femmes,* she substantiates this idea much along the lines discussed above: "The question of education, in both Moliere and Plato, is the question not of how to transmit but of how to *suspend* knowledge. In a negative sense, not knowing results from repression, whether conscious or unconscious. Such negative ignorance may be the necessary by-product—or even the precondition—of any education whatsoever. But positive ignorance, the pursuit of what is forever in the act of escaping, the inhabiting of that space where knowledge becomes the obstacle to knowing—*that* is the pedagogical imperative we can neither fulfill nor disobey" (p. 182). The ideal, then, is to "suspend knowledge," not to "transmit" it, to foster a "positive ignorance" of that which is culturally coded and determined. As in the case of de Man, Johnson sees the role of literature as constitutive in this process: literature is structured aporia, and literariness the self-deconstructing play of language over and within the discourses of the conventional and the ideological. Jane Gallop reads Sade's *Philosophy in the Bedroom* as precisely a celebration of an "irrational bodily materiality" which subverts "rational order," the guarantor of cultural meaning. Michael Ryan, enlarging the analysis to what we more familiarly call "institutions" (such as the university), considers the institutional codedness of knowledges and values. The assumption of objectivity in teaching, Ryan argues, operates on the basis of an exclusion of what cannot be thought within the institutional power hierarchies; the norms of "propriety" and "integrity" can be deconstructed to show how they guarantee the persistence of existing power relations. It follows from all these accounts, then, that meanings are highly charged *values,* not innocent counters of literary-critical discourse. The repudiation of meaning is based on the recognition of its implication in politics: to suspend it is to enable us to progress from coded knowledges to positive and liberating "ignorance." Thus, this new emphasis within criticism registers a wide range of cultural and political issues that may well be central to contemporary intellectual culture.

The general critique of meaning can be understood at another theoretical level. This is a point often made by contemporary Marxism, by psychoanalysis (especially after Lacan), and by post-Saussurean philosophies of language. There is a common and far-reaching assertion that "meaning" must be attacked in its superficial homogeneity, its ideality, because it always implies the corresponding categories of consciousness and self-present expe-rience. The speciousness of such categories is shown in the context of the "Copernican" discoveries specific to our times: the radical alterity of the unconscious in psychoanalytic theory, not as the unplumbed depths of consciousness but as its unrepresentable blank edge; the Althusserian thesis, in Marxism, that history is not inert context or linear narrative but a text that can only be grasped in the symptomatic gaps and dehiscences within our dis-courses; and, finally, the (post)modernist claim that language is not so much a human *instrument* as the very index of our finitude, speaking its own alien history and density in the very cadences we utter. The central lesson is that the mastery of the human subject over its meanings and its consciousness is rendered uncertain and spurious. True knowledge is, in this case, less a substance to be learned or transmitted than what Shoshana Felman (in her essay in *The Pedagogical Imperative*) calls a veritable "structure of ad-dress," an acknowledgment of the complex transsubjective play of our positionings within desire and ideology, ignorance and in-sight. Pedagogy, particularly in the realm of culture, needs then to face the fundamental challenge to escape both the transmission of coded knowledge and the coded transmission of knowledge: it must seek to suspend the process of this continuity, to question the self-evidence of meanings by invoking the radical—but deter-mining—alterities that disrupt our flawless discourses of knowl-edge. In a valuable discussion of psychoanalysis as a pedagogic process, Felman is able to conclude that pedagogy is itself a sit-uation akin to the psychoanalytic one: "Teaching, like analysis, has to deal not so much with *lack* of knowledge as with *resistances* to knowledge. Ignorance, suggests Lacan, is a 'passion'. . . . Ig-norance, in other words, is nothing other than a *desire to ignore:* its nature is less cognitive than performative; . . . it is not a simple lack of information but the incapacity—or the refusal—to ac-knowledge *one's own implication* in the information" (p. 30). Learning is dialogic, but not in the traditional Socratic sense. It involves a necessary implication in the radical alterity of the un-known, in the desire(s) not to know, in the process of this unre-solvable dialectic. Teaching "meanings" is a fundamentally ideo-logical act: it ignores the ruses and ruptures of politics and desire in favor of self-evident knowledges, of what Pierre Bourdieu and Jean-Claude Passeron would call "cultural arbitraries."

It is in this general context, then, that we need to understand the polemics about language or textuality. When the deconstructionist wants to put the text *en abîme,* to show how the tropics of discourse unravel the sutured text and reveal an imbricated intertextuality, we need at least to appreciate the politics of the gesture. Meanings, structures, totalities are revealed in their pure conventionality—declared to be provisional and produced. It is in this sense that the politics of Paul de Man's influential work is best appreciated. De Man is one of the most influential theorists today; his work commands respect even where it is not widely read or directly grappled with. However, this influence and prestige are not, as may be suspected, a purely "theoretical" matter. The appeal of "de Manism"—for it is indeed a theory which is also an ideology, implicated and defined in its contexts—derives as much from its combination of a certain lucidity with a certain kind of rigor as it does from what Frank Lentricchia identifies as the "rhetoric of authority."[8] The political edge of the theory is seen clearly in its deconstructive relationship to the history of criticism and philosophy. But that is not the only source of its power. For de Man, as I shall argue here, may indeed have completed the formalist cycle, capturing and negating the "world" in one sweep of the linguistic wand. And this, in contemporary literary critical culture, is an immensely attractive option. It makes possible a radicalism without the messy implications of *engagement;* the rarefied rigors of such "textuality" obviate the need for con-textual contaminations. It is this dual appeal—of the radicality of a meta-critique and the transcendental purity of its location—that we need to discuss to understand adequately what much of "theory" is doing in our classrooms today.

De Man's contribution to *The Pedagogical Imperative,* "The Resistance to Theory," is almost a manifesto, and may thus be an opportune place to locate our analysis.[9] The essay was originally commissioned by the Committee on the Research Activities of the Modern Language Association of America for a volume entitled *Introduction to Scholarship in Modern Languages and Literatures* but was, as de Man tells us himself, subsequently rejected by the editors. The reason may not be too difficult to assess: de Man, who was supposed to write on the state of the art of research in literary theory, chose to emphasize the general (unscholarly?) de Manian thesis that the "main theoretical interest of literary theory consists in the impossibility of its definition," and to support this claim by stressing the unstable basis of any scholarly field that has as its focus language or literature. Much of this may seem fair, and even teasingly disruptive. As we go on, however, problems begin to arise. What purported to be a survey of the field turns out to be a peculiarly de Manian version of things: "The resistance to theory is a resistance to the rhetorical or tropological dimension of language, a dimension which is perhaps more explicitly in the foreground in literature (broadly conceived) than in other verbal manifestations . . ." (p. 17). Elsewhere in the essay we have been told that "literariness" is revealed when we are dealing with the "autonomous potential" of language, when we move beyond naive conceptions of language (such as, say, Cratylism) in which expression and the phenomenon, the name and the thing named, are primordially linked. The critique of reductionist philosophies of language forms the basis of de Man's thought; much of his work is intended to displace our notions of reference or expression as the constitutive bases of linguistic processes and meaning production. Hence de Man's insistent emphasis on the tropological dimension, on language as unstable and (more importantly) self-deconstructing play. Powerful and strategic as this view may be in contemporary literary theoretical debates, this is only *one* view, and an E. D. Hirsch or an Edward Said may have considerable difficulty accepting this as the constitutive claim of contemporary theory. It is easier now to understand the hesitation of the editors who rejected the essay; but its open biases may make the piece all that much more valuable for our discussion.

De Man's theory necessarily builds upon an initial rejection of all those theories of language that would deny its material density or its autonomously productive nature. Whether it be the legacy of phenomenology or hermeneutics on the one hand or the residual phenomenalism of some versions of semiotics on the other, what de Man's critique seeks to displace and problematize is the source and locus of semantic categories. As such, his main targets of attack are those theories that short-circuit the aleatory dynamics of language by a hasty assimilation of these processes into uncritical notions of the phenomenal world as the source and the guarantor of the linguistic. The problem with de Man, however, is that he moves too hastily from a rejection of, say, the referential fallacy to a full-blown theory of language (and literature) as primarily figural, defined in this indeterminable rhetorical play that subverts the security of any meaning. As a negative gesture, rhetoric is powerfully deconstructive, and literariness a valuable political slogan. However, when rhetoric itself is hypostatized as the ineluctable process of language, a new essentialism emerges. Meanings are no longer insistently derived from the "world," but they are negated with a similar insistence, invoking an unchanging machinery of tropical self-dissolution. The main issue that is elided in this context is one that contemporary semioticians (Umberto Eco in particular) identify as the "problem" of the referent. If we refuse to consider the referent as a "real object" guaranteeing the artificial circumscription of every semiotic operation and providing a theological security to interpretation, then *referentiality* suggests a larger question, one that deals with the *social determination* of signifying practices, linguistic or otherwise. This question opens out onto an entire problematic, one which preoccupied such founders of our intellectual modernity as Marx and Freud (witness, for instance, the close connection between the two in the transposed history of the concept of "overdetermination" borrowed from *The Interpretation of Dreams* by the Marxist philosopher Louis Althusser[10]), as well as such radical thinkers as Derrida, whose "grammatological" project would seek to pose, in (re-)considering the "problems of critical reading, . . . the question of the text, its historical status, its proper time and space."[11] In this context, I would argue that de Man, emphasizing the "autonomy" of language, is unable to see the relationship between such autonomy and (social) determination as anything but purely oppositional. The reason is that for de Man determination can only be conceived in the form of referential or expressive myths of the functioning of linguistic signs.

De Man's criticism is most powerful when we treat its hypotheses about language and literature as purely heuristic. In *Blindness and Insight,* for instance, he declares his intention to examine the constitutive problem of all criticism as the "necessary immanence of the [critical] reading in relation to the [literary] text" (*BI,* p. 110); his interest is thus in the "cognitive status" of "the language of criticism in general" (p. 119). In examining the works of such critics as Georg Lukács, Georges Poulet, and even Derrida, de Man's concern is to delineate the gap between their "method" and their "insight" (*BI,* p. 106), and in this the uneasy encounter between the critic and the (literary) text is crucial: it is not symptomatic but constitutive. In a similar way, *Allegories of Reading* deconstructs the totalizations of meaning that inhere in critical methods (e.g., semiology) as well as philosophical and aesthetic concepts (e.g., the classical notion of trope, or the coherence of logic). The value of such readings for literary criticism becomes even clearer in de Man's most recent collection, *The Rhetoric of Romanticism,* where the period concept of "Romanticism" is shown, through a series of readings of Wordsworth, Shelley, Hölderlin, or Kleist, to have no more than a fictional coherence, unable to sustain a viable literary history. De Man's readings are, then, critiques of critique; but as meta- or para-criticism such readings are the most effective only to the extent that they take the literary text (i.e., that in relation to which the original critic's language has an "immanent" existence) as a contingent unknown, as the model of the unformulatable Other that exists defined only as an intertextuality manifested in the critic's discourse. The *positive* status of the literary needs, then, to be an open—and variable—question, to be "read" rather than determined in advance. It ought to be approached asymptotically in the interplay of blindness and insight in specific critical texts, in critical readings themselves considered as ideologies of reading, of the text, indeed of the literary itself.

The uncompromisingly critical nature of de Man's project depends, then, on its radicalization of *reading:* insofar as it is irreducibly paratextual or interstitial, its deconstructive movement keeps metaphysics at bay. But underlying de Man's criticism there has also been a theory of language (and a related notion of literariness) that renders such radical reading impossible. For in all his works, there has always been the assertion that it is a certain property of *language* which *performs* the deconstruction of critical and other tertiary discourses. In the opening essay of *Allegories of Reading* "rhetoric" or the "figural potentiality of language" is equated with "literature itself" (*AR,* p. 10). Hence, "Poetic writing is the most advanced and refined mode of deconstruction; it may differ from critical or discursive writing in the economy of its articulation, but not in kind" (*AR,* p. 17). "Literariness" performs the most rigorous criticism, and in his own critical work, de Man claims, he is only "trying to come closer to being as rigorous a reader as the author had to be in order to write the [text] in the first place" (*AR*, p. 17). No simple intentional fallacy is involved here, of course: in "The Rhetoric of Blindness" de Man had disclaimed any such notion, pointing rather to the "knowledge that [Rousseau's] language, *as language*, conveys about itself, thereby asserting the priority of the category of language over that of presence" (*BI*, p. 119, emphasis added). This characteristic of Rousseau's language, i.e., its knowledge of itself, is what distinguishes it as literary. What is even more fundamental here is that this definition of the literary is predicated on a prior understanding of all language as primarily figural. For like music, language is a "diachronic system of relationships" (*BI*, p. 128), but essentially—again by analogy—"a mere structure because it is hollow at the core" (*BI*, p. 128). (This is the insight of Rousseau's that de Man chastises Derrida for being blind to.) The metaphoricity that exists as the "origin" of all languages has no "literal referent: . . . Its only referent is 'le neant des choses humaines' " (*BI*, p. 135).

It is this thesis about language that is never challenged in de Man's work. Indeed, many of the details of his entire critical project depend on such an understanding of language and the related thesis about literature as that language which "implicitly or explicitly signifies its own rhetorical mode" (*BI*, p. 136). In *Allegories of Reading* the chapter on "Metaphor," which also deals with Rousseau, makes the underlying theory of language even clearer: "All language is language about denomination, that is, a conceptual, figural, metaphorical metalanguage. As such, it partakes of the blindness of metaphor when metaphor literalizes its referential indetermination into a specific unit of meaning. . . . If all language is about language, then the paradigmatic linguistic model is that of an entity that confronts itself" (*AR*, p. 153). At the heart of language, "first of all," is a "wild spontaneous metaphor which is, to some degree, aberrant" (*AR*, p. 153). But it is "not intentional, because it does not involve the interests of the subject in any way" (*AR*, p. 154): the aberration "results exclusively from a formal, rhetorical potential of the language" (*AR*, p. 154). The "wild" origin is then what makes the entire theory of language and literature possible in de Man's work.[12] And it is this thesis that subtends (and explains) the necessary "blindness" of the critical texts de Man reads: in one way or another, these works misread—in a manner they cannot avoid, since it is constitutive of their implication in the "literary" text—the more "enlightened" texts de Man would call "literary."[13] The "light" that is the property of literary texts is one that reveals less and blinds us all the more because of its abyssal vision of the "nothingness" ("le neant") we glimpsed earlier. If aberration is constitutive of metaphoricity, so, it must be stressed here, is its wildness and its "spontaneous" springing forth. This is where, in de Man's theory, we can *read* no further. True, this may not always be formulated as a secure ontological truth, but its instability can be localized *and yet not submitted to a further reading*. At this point, every critical reading can, a priori, be translated as a vain attempt at mastery, and deconstructed by Language.

This "Language" is, then, no longer an unknown, for it performs, outside any system of its possible relationships, a relentless deconstruction of all systems. It has been constituted outside of all readings and the very idea of relationships which reading inevitably implies. "Spontaneous" in its origin as aberration, this Language can no longer be language, no longer quite what de Man had earlier called a "diachronic system of *relationships*" (BI, p. 131, my emphasis). Before we have considered any determinate signifying function, indeed outside any system of its functioning, language has been determined as Language, its nature formulated, its "center" granted privileged residence *elsewhere*. The possibility of any articulation of such a cataclysmic origin with the history of metaphysics (or with metaphysics as history) is not raised; the issue remains foreclosed. Here, in this absolute gesture, we encounter the (metaphysical) unthought of de Manian theory.

What remains unthought, or at least inadequately thought here is, however, an issue that is central to de Man's problematic. It concerns the figural productivity of language, the index of its autonomous functioning. The Nietzschean understanding of language as the co-implication of truth and "metaphor" at least offered one solution here, but that is not one that de Man can accept. For Nietzsche, truth is, as we know from that oft-quoted passage, "a moving army of metaphors, metonymies and anthropomorphisms, in short a sum of human relationships that are being poetically and rhetorically sublimated. . . ."[14] The question of Truth remains, for Nietzsche, dependent on the formulation of "truths," and the text(ure) of such truths is essentially metaphorical, engaged in the deepest activities of living and "lying" in order to live. The fabric of language, "ideological" in the Althusserian sense of the word, is woven out of human relationships, enabling—and con-stituting—the irreducible complexities of social existence. The ef-fect of defining language outside this network of determinations is to define it in essentialist terms, not to guarantee its "unlimited semiosis" (Charles Sanders Peirce's phrase, which de Man cites), but to predetermine its nature outside of any possible *human* con-text.

Peirce is the obvious figure who comes to mind here, because it is his major contribution to a theory of semiosis that provides what is probably the most detailed account of the autonomous yet decentered productivity that constitutes linguistic processes. Peirce insisted on the constitutive function of the interpretant in all sig-nification: "A sign stands *for* something *to* the idea which it pro-duces, or modifies. . . . That for which it stands is called its *object;* that which it conveys, its *meaning;* and the idea to which it gives rise, its *interpretant.*"[15] The interpretant is not, however, another interpreter, but itself a sign, dependent on the *cultural* space in which signification occurs. As Eco points out, in one of the best studies informed by and building on Peirce's work, what we need to consider in the context of any signification is the *dynamics* of reference, not the referent as a mere object or thing:

> Let us try to understand the nature of the object that corresponds to an expression. Take the term /dog/. The referent will certainly not be the dog *x* standing by me while I am pronouncing the word. For anyone who holds to the doctrine of the referent, the referent, in such a case, will be all existing dogs (and also all past and future dogs). But "all existing dogs" is not an object which can be perceived with the senses. It is a set, a class. . . . *Every attempt to establish what the referent of a sign is forces us to define the referent in terms of an abstract entity which moreover is only a cultural convention.* . . . What, then, is the meaning of a term? From a semiotic point of view it can only be a *cultural unit.* . . . [S]ignification (as well as communication), by means of continual shiftings which refer a sign back to another sign or string of signs, circumscribes cultural units in an asymptotic fashion, without ever allowing one to touch them directly. . . . *Semiosis explains itself by itself;* this continual circularity is the normal condition of signification.[16]

For contemporary semiotics, the Peircean notion of the interpre-tant opens up referentiality as a genuine problem, and it becomes an index of the determined cultural textuality of human signification. Thus, linguistic production cannot be considered outside the network that constitutes the social text. De Man refers to Peirce in his discussion of rhetoricity in *Allegories of Reading,* but the passage is a curious one, revealing no real contact with the theoretical implications of the notion of "unlimited semiosis," which should be so significant to de Man's own project:

> Charles Sanders Peirce, who, with Nietzsche and Saussure, laid the philosophical foundation for modern semiology, stressed the distinction between grammar and rhetoric in his celebrated and so suggestively unfathomable definition of the sign. He insists, as is well known, on the necessary presence of a third element, called the interpretant, within any relationship that the sign entertains with its object. . . . The interpretation of the sign is not, for Peirce, a meaning but another sign; it is a reading, not a decodage, and this reading has, in its turn, to be interpreted into another sign, and so on *ad infinitum.* Peirce calls this process by means of which "one sign gives birth to another" pure rhetoric, as distinguished from pure grammar which postulates the possibility of unproblematic, dyadic meaning, and pure logic, which postulates the possibility of the universal truth of meanings. Only if the sign engendered meaning in the same way that the object engenders the sign, that is, by representation, would there be no need to distinguish between grammar and rhetoric. (*AR,* pp. 8–9)

The citation may do, at a very simple level, what de Man wants it to do—i.e., it may help him reestablish the distinction between semiology (in the model of a grammar) and rhetoric. But it brings with it more problems than it is worth. For there is a significant and necessary misreading of Peirce here.[17] How, for instance, does the *object* "engender the sign"? What exactly does the answer de Man takes for granted ("by representation") mean in a Peircean context? Peirce's claim about the relationship between sign, object, and interpretant seems to be that it is *irreducibly a triadic relation.* This is what Peirce goes on to assert immediately after the passage de Man is most probably alluding to: "A *Sign,* or *Representamen,* is a First which stands in such a genuine triadic relation to a Second, called its *Object,* as to be capable of determining a Third, called its *Interpretant,* to assume the same triadic relation to its Object in which it stands itself to the same Object. The triadic relation is *genuine*—that is, its three members are bound together by it in a way that does not consist in any complexus of dyadic relations."[18]

De Man, on the other hand, privileges the relationship between the sign and the interpretant (another sign) over what he considers to be the unproblematical relationship between the object and the sign. This can only be because he sees the Peircean "object" as merely the "given"— an observable fact, it is of no great significance in the processes of sign production. But for Peirce, "[t]he object of representation can be nothing but a representation of which the first representation is the interpretant."[19] Thus, the relationship between the sign and the interpretant can only be seen *in the context of the object that they "interpret" together.* The relationship of the sign or the interpretant to the "object" is not a formal one: it is not purely internal to the sign but is based, as another recent commentator argues, agreeing implicitly with Eco's account, on such "collateral information" as an "insistent environment common to all three terms."[20] Such environment cannot by definition be purely intrinsic to the sign; the sign has no pure interior as its defining characteristic. The obdurate *facticity* of the object needs to be understood as a constitutive *semiotic* fact in order for us to appreciate the material *autonomy* of the sign. The refractory at the heart of semiotic processes is what we saw in Eco's definition of the referent as a "cultural convention," and it suggests that such notions of process as de Man seems to suggest (rhetoric: pure generation of signs) are fundamentally misleading. Signifying processes can only be understood in their relationality, and the "insistent environment" that ties together sign, object, and interpretant does so only to make it possible for them (as terms of analysis) to come into existence in the first place. The "purity" of the pure logic, grammar, and rhetoric de Man alludes to can only asphyxiate the semiosis that Peirce sees as the basis of language and signification.

In this case, then, the problem of "determination"—i.e., the ways in which signifying processes are both limited and shaped by their contexts—remains one that any theory of language or literature must inevitably face. In this essay I have used the term *referentiality* to designate a problem which is evaded at a significant cost by de Manian literary theory precisely because it is named and circumscribed as the fallacy of simple referential determination. It goes without saying that such a notion of reference underlies not only simplistic varieties of historical and political criticism but also, more significantly, those kinds of semiotics which would valorize literature as a purely nonreferential discourse. The constitutive metaphysical idea in both theoretical positions is the same: the referent is the real world, available in some ultimately unproblematical way. For a traditional historical criticism, for instance, or for what is called "vulgar Marxism," the nonsemiotic stability of "the real world" makes possible the security of a certain kind of meaning, and the dynamics of textual process need not be considered as anything but epiphenomenal. But a formalist definition of the literary as purely nonreferential would also be dependent on a prior understanding of reference in reductionist terms. Much of de Manian theory may appear to fall into this second kind of position, since "Literature" has been defined in its capacity for self-knowledge or its figural auto-referentiality. But the conflation of de Man's entire theory with a formalist paradigm would be both unfair and misleading. De Man's notion of figurality, especially in the essays in and after *Allegories of Reading,* suggests a more complex performative paradigm. It is a paradigm that would undo, as de Man puts it himself in his essay on Michael Riffaterre, "the distinction between reference and signification."[21] It is "poetry" which, in this essay at least, "smuggles the wiles of rhetoric into the hygienic clarity of [Riffaterre's model of] semiotics," putting into question the method's claim to rigor, complicating the status of its very insights into literary processes. De Man's critique of Riffaterre is essentially that the latter's definition of the literary in nonreferential terms is untenable, because literary signification requires a referential axis. However, it must be remembered that de Man does not argue with Riffaterre's simplistic notion of reference; rather, his critical move consists mainly in exposing the limits of Riffaterre's formalist *definitions*. De Man's own theory of textuality also depends on an understanding of referential processes not too different from Riffaterre's. The notion of the "text," for de Man, is formulated in terms of the "figural dimension of language," but this figurality is predicated on the discomfiting realization of a "divergence between grammar and referential meaning."[22] The referential meaning invoked here is determined at the simplest level of self-evidence, as that derived from the unproblematical reality of the real world. There is no notion of determination here except in the most obvious and reductive form, and referentiality cannot involve a consideration of any of the problems we discussed earlier. Reference becomes interesting for de Man only in its most brutal conception, and with such a concept he can go only in a certain direction. The theology of Language needs such a metaphysics of the referent. Thus, Peircean semiotics cannot be encountered in any serious form: since we cannot accuse it of a "hygienic clarity," its specific challenges in the general context of cultural determination cannot be faced. For if "semiosis" is, as Eco argues, irreducibly cultural and yet it "explains itself by itself," the referent, caught in the network of figurality, can also be culturally determined and determinable. As such, it must guide and control our "interpretation" of the "purely" linguistic. To summarize, then: in de Manian theory the linguistic is too hastily opposed to the real world; what is elided in this process is the possibility that there could be discursive determinants of linguistic play that are simultaneously cultural ("Real"[23]). A more adequate theory of referentiality, such as we see in the works of Peirce or Eco, would suggest that linguistic play is determined even in its freedom. Readings and interpretations, then, need to take into account what Tzvetan Todorov calls the "discursivity" of language, i.e., the contextual implications of what may appear as purely autonomous. De Manian literary theory moves too easily from a rejection of an extrinsic notion of determination (as in the referential fallacy) to a hypostatization of certain notions of the linguistic ("rhetoricity," "figurality") as essential and constitutive features of language and literature. Consequently, the danger of this new system is that the reading of texts can take on a mechanical form; at a certain point, "reading" congeals into "Reading": beneath the text (or within or alongside it, as the metaphors go) is the tropological substratum that ultimately needs to be revealed. In the classroom this can devolve into a predictable maneuver: text after text would be revealed in its subtextual play of emptiness, for an unceasing and unchanging allegory of textuality always "Reads" itself to reveal the hand of the new God in all Its creation. "The task of literary criticism in the coming years," writes de Man with the assured tone of both prophecy and power, will be such a predictable operation. In this oft-cited passage from the opening essay of *Allegories of Reading,* after a reading of a Proust passage, we conclude with a characteristic vision of the "whole of literature" being read in a similar way. There is only the *minor* qualification that "the techniques and the patterns would have to vary considerably . . . from author to author. But there is absolutely no reason," de Man asserts, "why analyses of the kind here suggested for Proust would not be applicable, with proper modifications of technique, to Milton or to Dante or to Hölderlin" (*AR,* pp. 16–17).

In sharp opposition to this view, a criticism that would seek to deal with the specificity of the "literary" would have to take *reading* more seriously. It would need to face squarely the question of the referent and the complex dynamics of cultural production and consumption. It would deal with the unlimited semiosis of linguistic play and the shifting but provisionally localizable determinations of meaning and code. Building on Peirce, Saussure, and Eco's recent development of their ideas, such criticism would make contact with theories of ideology and cultural representation as they have been formulated in (post)Althusserian Marxisms.[24]

In a wishful moment quite characteristic of his most recent work, de Man seems to suggest that his version of literary theory will lead us from text to larger, institutional—para-textual or con-textual—levels: "What is it about literary theory that is so threatening that it provokes such strong resistances and attack? It upsets rooted ideologies by revealing the mechanics of their workings; it goes against a powerful philosophical tradition of which aesthetics is a prominent part; it upsets the established canon of literary works and blurs the borderlines between literary and non-literary discourse. By implication, it may also reveal the links between ideologies and philosophy . . ." (*TPI,* pp. 11–12). But de Man himself rarely ventured beyond the canonical texts, whether in literature or in philosophy.[25] Unlike Derrida, for instance, whose work with GREPH has had more direct political content, or whose recent analyses of the university or even such local institutions as the signature or the copyright law connect the deconstruction of texts to the power situations they are imbricated in,[26] de Manian literary theory has seemed content with many of the limits of its own institutional definitions. Its claims to radicality are absolute and transcendent; freed from any compromising determinations, "Language" sanctions a "Reading" which is itself "forever impossible to read" (*AR,* p. 77). The problem is that in the semi-pastoral world of American liberal arts colleges, images of absolute radicality attract all too easily, for they provide an other-worldly Archimedean point for criticism or politics. What such theory needs to examine is the extent to which the inflation of aporias is tied to their consequent devaluation. For if meanings are ideological, so is their insistent negation; what we need to develop, rather, is a sense of the profound contextuality of meanings in their play and their ideological effects. Without such a sense of the determined and determining sense of culture and language, the strongest version of American deconstruction runs the risk of easy assimilation into the existing power hierarchies. Radicalism has always been, in our times at least, an infinitely cooptable commodity.

The criticism I am making originates from a recognition of the significance of Paul de Man's theoretical work; my suggestion is that an examination of its (contextual) limits and effects can only enable us to elaborate it in the ways in which it can be politically and pedagogically the most valuable. What is at stake here is not, to be sure, the future of our planet, or even the rise or fall of the new militarism. But de Man and contemporary theory are part of a larger cultural politics, and as such are most effective not only in the rarefied world of high theory but mainly in the ideological disseminations in the university classrooms. These may well be the orthodoxies of tomorrow's literary criticism: "theory" is often accompanied (as in this case) by ideologies that determine the shape of the undergraduate teaching of literature. It is both as a theoretical practice and as sociological fact (i.e., with specific effects) that contemporary literary theory in general needs to be recognized. A theory's positive political gains need to be appreciated for us to understand the necessary occultations of its practice. Particularly in the pedagogic situation, "theory" is not an innocent will to know but an effective intersection of knowledge and power. It is with this recognition that we need to approach teaching theory or to theorize teaching.

In the light of the issues raised by de Manian literary theory, it is the pedagogic situation which foregrounds most dramatically for us the challenge of accepting—and thinking—its irreducible *contingency*. Inescapably contextual, open and variable, teaching poses for (literary) theory not simply the pragmatic questions of its effectiveness (as communication), but rather the basic problem involving the theory's conditions of intelligibility, i.e., its self-constitution in the contexts of its institutional existence. To what extent can *literary* theory (a theory of "Literature" in de Man's sense) raise the question of (its own) institutionality? The general issue involved here deals with the dependency and mutual conditioning that exist between discourses and the institutional contexts they inhabit. Whereas Derrida's work has increasingly concerned itself with an explicit consideration of the significance of institutions and determinate forms of power as they shape the "propriety" of knowledges and meanings, the dominant form of American deconstruction remains indifferent to the subject. Here, perhaps, the notion of Language performing radical deconstructions is singularly debilitating. If the contexts of specific literary and critical texts can be thus sublimated, and if the only concern should be with the mere "modifications of technique" of our (meta)critical operations, then our theoretical position is *transcendent*. The role of such mediating instances as the university, the publishing industry, or the ethos of the star system, can be commented on in passing, as a more or less "sociological" perception or insight, but need not be considered in any detail for it is not determining. The teaching of literary theory can continue in its search for the transcendentally aporetic only insofar as it does not confront, *within itself,* the specific conditions of its own production, elaboration, and transmission. Let us reconsider, for example, a rather basic perception that is rarely taken to be theoretically interesting. "Theory" is formulated at the "core," the "metropoles" in the geopolitics of the American university system (the privately owned schools, especially the Eastern ones) and is disseminated elsewhere, in the "peripheral" world where students learn the now canonized ideas as the new frontiers of literary-critical knowledge. When this perception is used to somehow *prove* the social irrelevance of such theory, the point is silly and ultimately inconsequential. However, the pedagogic situation raises this issue to the status of a paradigmatic theoretical problem. In the classroom, as in the analogous world of Barthesian textuality, "performance" is all; the "substance" of theory is subsumed into the exigencies of the situation, i.e., the situatedness of communication and the relationships it renders visible or invisible. This much at least we learned from the discussion of teaching in the essays by Barbara Johnson and Shoshana Felman in the volume we started by considering. The main reason literary theory must consider as theoretically problematical what I called its geopolitics is that theoretical propositions do not travel too well: aporetic insights become specific knowledges, indices of particular situations and relationships, and must live, overdetermined, in the contexts of their new emphases and valorizations.

With the shrinking job market, for instance, and the near-absolute division between literature departments that expect their students to teach only freshman composition in college and those that hope their students will be able to deal with "literary matters" in their classes, theory, in its transmission to all departments, needs to resolutely guard the purity of its insights. To the extent that it must be transmissible, it must be codifiable, made simpler perhaps, and purer. Here the transcendental status of the "literary" (no matter how negative a vision it purports to be) is both attractive and functional. Its unchanging tropical dissolution of *all* ideologies ensures that institutional pedagogy can go on unhindered. *Literature* can be taught to the extent that "literariness" has been defined outside any specific context of teaching, of the production or consumption of specific "literatures" and literary texts—in short, outside any cultural relation. Thus the ideologization of the "literary" ensures the teaching of "Literature" which, in turn, is predicated on a fundamental blindness to the institutional functioning of pedagogy—its hierarchies, its recodification of knowledges. In this sense, such "theory" is inherently contextual. And the pedagogic situation is a powerful model of the uneven development constitutive of the state of (the) culture, or rather, more specifically, of the culture of the State. By this I am not merely suggesting that what de Man calls literary theory is related to the culture at large, but rather that the conditions of production and consumption of such theory are constitutive of all theory *as* theory. Teaching theory in our literature classes can teach us, in its turn, to the extent that we will allow it to do so, the political allegory of its own *situation:* "The Outside Is the Inside."[27]

At this point, it may be worth our while to return in some detail to the volume on pedagogy with which I started. To juxtapose knowledge and power, as I have been trying to suggest, to read theory through the lenses of politics, need not be an unfair reduction of criticism to the merely sociological (i.e., the extrinsic). For power lies inscribed *within* knowledge, and what Richard Terdiman in his essay in *The Pedagogical Imperative* calls the social "structure of initiation" is visible not only in the discrete content (the meanings) we teach our students but also in the "structure of

170

regulatedness which sustains [such meanings], reinforcing the systematicity of the social whole." This systematicity, Terdiman goes on to argue, drawing on the work of Bourdieu and Passeron, is "never abstract, but . . . 'oriented': partisan, exploitative, consonant with certain social interests, structures, positions. As such, it constitutes the constraints of a *regime de sens,* of a system governing meaning, whose operation is the more binding on account of its transparency" (*TPI,* p. 223).

This transparency is what contemporary theory, at its most powerful, destroys; this is indeed what we as teachers need to foreground as the unrecognized "content" of the forms (in) which we teach. Between the harsher connotations of Althusser's characterization of the modern university as an "Ideological State Apparatus" and the less tangible ecologies of the individual classroom, we need to formulate our understanding of the politics that inhere in teaching (literature) in contemporary America. Any notion of "radical" teaching will always have to be developed on the basis of the specific ideologies that inhere in these specific contexts. For teaching—like language—is not only a *process* but also, inescapably, a *relation;* and if pedagogy is a "literary genre" as the subtitle of *The Pedagogical Imperative* suggests, it must remain a radically insecure one, open to the imperatives of history.

NOTES

1. See Richard Rorty, "Professionalized Philosophy and Transcendentalist Culture," in his *Consequences of Pragmatism* (Minneapolis: University of Minnesota Press, 1982), pp. 60–71. The literary critic Harold Bloom stresses the responsibility that the teacher of literature now has for a general moral pedagogy. We may or may not respond to the plaintive tone in which Bloom asserts this, particularly in the following passage cited by Rorty, but it identifies a phenomenon both Rorty and Bloom describe in the same general terms. Bloom: "The teacher of literature now in America, far more than the teacher of history or philosophy or religion, is condemned to teach the presentness of the past, because history, philosophy and religion have withdrawn as agents from the Scene of Instruction," cited in Rorty, p. 68.

2. See Edward W. Said, "Reflections on American 'Left' Criticism," in his *The World, the Text, and the Critic* (Cambridge, Mass.: Harvard University Press, 1983), pp. 158–79; and "Opponents, Audiences, Con-

stituencies, and Community" in *Critical Inquiry* 9:1 (special issue on "The Politics of Interpretation").

3. I borrow the phrase from David Edgar (cf. "Reagan's Hidden Agenda: Racism and the New American Right," *Race and Class* 22:3 [Winter 1981]: 221–38).

4. *The Pedagogical Imperative: Teaching as a Literary Genre*, special issue of *Yale French Studies* 63 (1982). Subsequent quotations from this volume will, whenever necessary, be followed by the abbreviation *TPI* and the page number(s) in parentheses.

5. Considering the general nature of this essay, I have found it useful to retain these terms for the sake of convenience. For a valuable and timely critique of at least the terms *poststructuralism* and *deconstruction* as they are used in the U.S., see Philip Lewis, "The Post-Structuralist Condition," *Diacritics* 12:1 (Spring 1982): 2–24.

6. Cf. Fredric Jameson's comment on New Criticism made in the context of his general discussion of "theories of history":

> . . . The New Critics—long thought by themselves as well as by others to be resolutely ahistorical—in reality devoted significant energies to the construction of historical paradigms: the dissociation of sensibility from Donne to Shelley, the reconquest of style and image from Swinburne to Yeats; such characteristic frameworks for analysis amount to Hegelian models of literary change. . . . Indeed . . . the individual analysis projects its own diachronic framework, it could not have been otherwise. Only this model now tries to pass itself off as a theory of history in its own right, and at once the characteristic marks of pseudohistory appear: the obsession with historical rise and decline, the never-ending search for the date of the fall and the name of the serpent. . . . Such false problems . . . are in turn pressed into ideological service, in which an eschatological framework helps conservative politics masquerade as ethics in an ostensibly aesthetic enterprise. *Marxism and Form* (Princeton: Princeton University Press, 1971), pp. 323–24.

7. A coincidence as insistent as it is familiar: as I revise an early draft of this essay, Reagan announces the invasion of Grenada on national television. The second of his "reasons" for sending in the Marines, he states paternalistically, was to "forestall chaos" in that "Marxist country."

8. Frank Lentricchia, *After the New Criticism* (Chicago: University of Chicago Press, 1980), pp. 282–317. It is interesting that Jonathan Culler, who is clearly more sympathetic to de Man's project than Lentricchia is, acknowledges the same characteristic of de Man's writing: "De Man's . . . writings . . . frequently assert, with authoritative confidence, claims that require demonstration but instead are simply adduced in order to move on to more 'advanced' reflections. His essays often assure the reader that demonstration of these points would not be difficult, only cumbersome, and they do provide much detailed argument

and exegesis, but these gaps in argumentation may be quite striking" (*On Deconstruction* [Ithaca: Cornell University Press, 1982], p. 229). But Culler seems to also consider this a "strategy": "Though most critical prose seeks to suggest such authority, de Man's writing is special—and often especially annoying—in its strategy of omitting crucial demonstrations in order to put readers in a position where they cannot profit from his analyses without according belief to what seems implausible or at least unproven. As de Man says of Riffaterre's 'dogmatic assertions,' 'by stating them as he does, in the blandest and most apodictic of terms, he makes their heuristic function evident' " (p. 229). As will be evident from my own account of de Man in this essay, I find it hard to accept that we could consider several of his basic claims about language or literature as "heuristic." Their status as the *unthought* within de Man's own critical paradigm is what needs to be examined in some detail, perhaps through a comparison between his work and Derrida's. This essay is intended to suggest some significant points of difference between the two, and my claims here can be extended (obviously in a much longer study) by inquiring into the roles (philosophical) propositions as such (e.g., specific theses about, say, the "nature" of language) play in their respective works.

This may also be the place to indicate the main reason I find Lentricchia's critique of de Man not entirely convincing. It is not because Lentricchia reads de Man (as Culler puts it) "as an existentialist," but because I find that after accepting the "necess[ity] to agree" with de Man's theoretical arguments, Lentricchia falls back on the familiar "But what about politics?" kind of criticism. The following passage shows the inadequacy of Lentricchia's critique; we accept the necessity of the aporetic within an insular "wall-to-wall discourse," but "we must resist" it: "Where has de Man left things? Even should we agree that in the world of wall-to-wall discourse the *aporia* is inevitable—and I believe it is necessary to agree to this and to the poststructuralist problematic upon which the idea rests—we must resist being pushed there, unless we wish to find ourselves with de Man and other avant-garde critics in the realm of the thoroughly predictable linguistic transcendental, where all literature speaks synchronically and endlessly the same tale. . . . In this realm the discourse of literature would suppress the powerfully situating and coercive discourses of politics, economics, and other languages of social manipulation" (Lentricchia, p. 317). One of my implicit claims in this essay is that to want to "resist" the cogency of "wall-to-wall discourse" is to have misconceived the issues from the start; any perspective that is insular cannot be significantly analyzed by merely stressing that the world "outside" exists, and that it would be healthy to acknowledge it. Rather, an adequate critique must expose the complicity between the insular "inside" with its domesticated notion of the "outside."

9. In addition to this essay, I shall be referring to the following books by de Man: *Blindness and Insight,* 2nd ed. rev. (Minneapolis: University of Minnesota Press, 1983), *Allegories of Reading* (New Haven: Yale University Press, 1979), and *The Rhetoric of Romanticism* (New York: Columbia University Press, 1984). These will henceforth be cited as *BI, AR,* and *RR* respectively, with page numbers provided in parentheses in the body of the essay.

10. See particularly "Contradiction and Overdetermination" in Louis Althusser, *For Marx,* trans. Ben Brewster (New York: Pantheon Books, 1969), pp. 87–128. Althusser's essay on Lacan may also be of interest in this context: cf. "Freud and Lacan," in *Lenin and Philosophy,* trans. Ben Brewster (New York and London: Monthly Review Press, 1971), pp. 189–219.

11. Jacques Derrida, *Of Grammatology,* trans. Gayatri C. Spivak (Baltimore: Johns Hopkins University Press, 1976), p. lxxxix. But though Derrida asserts that "the science of writing—*grammatology*—shows signs of liberation all over the world," he must be cautious: to think *history* (or the "text's historical status") is a problem that is far from being simple, and needs, first of all, to be *posed.* The question can be posed only if it recognizes its dependence on a complex network of determinations: "The idea of science and the idea of writing—therefore also of the science of writing—is meaningful for us only in terms of an origin and within a world to which a certain concept of the sign . . . and a certain concept of the relationships between speech and writing, have *already* been assigned. A most determined relationship, in spite of its privilege, its necessity . . ." (p. 4).

12. It should be clear that I am suggesting that there is a fundamental continuity between de Man's early work (*Blindness and Insight,* in particular) and the later essays collected in *Allegories of Reading.* This is an issue that has been the subject of the most fruitful debate surrounding de Man's work; the two best essays I have read on de Man are sharply opposed on this question. See Rodolphe Gasché, " 'Setzung' and 'Übersetzung': Notes on Paul de Man," *Diacritics* 11: 4 (Winter 1981): 36–57, and Suzanne Gearhart, "Philosophy *Before* Literature: Deconstruction, Historicity, and the Work of Paul de Man," *Diacritics* 13: 4 (Winter 1983): 63–81. On the whole, my position here is closer to Gearhart's.

13. Rousseau, for de Man, is a "non-blinded author" whose "first readers" are always "blinded": "These blinded first readers . . . then need, in turn, a critical reader who reverses the tradition [of their misreadings] and momentarily takes us closer to the original insight. The existence of a particularly rich aberrant tradition in the case of the writers who can legitimately be called the most enlightened is therefore no accident, but a constitutive part of all literature . . ." (*BI,* p. 141).

14. Here is the passage in its entirety: "What therefore is truth? A mobile army of metaphors, metonymies, anthropomorphisms: in short a sum of human relations which became poetically and rhetorically intensified, metamorphosed, adorned, and after long usage seems to a nation fixed, canonic, and binding; truths are illusions of which one has forgotten that they *are* illusions; worn out metaphors which have become powerless to affect the senses; coins which have their obverse effaced and now are no longer of account as coins but merely as metal," from "Truth and Falsity in an Ultramoral Sense." The entire essay has been conveniently anthologized in *The Philosophy of Nietzsche*, edited with an introduction by Geoffrey Clive (New York: New American Library, 1965). The translation is the one used in the eighteen-volume Oscar Levy edition.

In both the places where de Man deals directly with this passage (*AR*, chapter 5, and *RR*, chapter 9), the emphasis of his analysis overlooks a significant part of the passage. In fact, in the later essay de Man's quote stops exactly where we find Nietzsche explicitly explaining "metaphors, metonymies, anthropomorphisms" as "a sum of human relations." This equation is cited but never really dealt with in the essay in *Allegories of Reading*.

15. Charles Sanders Peirce, "Thirdness," *Collected Papers* (Cambridge, Mass.: Harvard University Press, 1931), I: 171.

16. Umberto Eco, *A Theory of Semiotics* (Bloomington and London: Indiana University Press, 1979), pp. 66–67, 71.

17. Here is the passage from Pierce de Man probably has in mind:

> In consequence of every representamen being thus connected with three things, the ground, the object, and the interpretant, the science of semiotic has three branches. The first is called by Duns Scotus *grammatica speculativa*. We may term it *pure grammar*. It has for its task to ascertain what must be true of the representamen used by every scientific intelligence in order that they may embody any *meaning*. The second is logic proper. It is the science of what is quasi-necessarily true of the representamina of any scientific intelligence in order that they may hold good of any *object,* that is, may be true. Or say, logic proper is the formal science of the conditions of the truth of representations. The truth, in imitation of Kant's fashion of preserving old associations of words in finding nomenclature for new conceptions, I call *pure rhetoric*. Its task is to ascertain the laws by which in every scientific intelligence one sign gives birth to another, and especially one thought brings forth another. ("Logic as Semiotic: The Theory of Signs," *Philosophical Writings of Peirce*, selected and edited by J. Buchler [New York: Dover, 1955], p. 99.

This is also the passage Derrida cites in the *Grammatology*.

18. *Philosophical Writings of Peirce*, pp. 99–100.

19. Peirce, cited in Eco, *A Theory of Semiotics*, p. 69.

20. David Savan, *An Introduction to C. S. Peirce's Semiotics, Part 1* (Toronto: Toronto Semiotic Circle Monograph no. 1, 1976), p. 55.

21. Paul de Man, "Hypogram and Inscription: Michael Riffaterre's Poetics of Reading," *Diacritics* 11: 4 (Winter 1981): 34.

22. I am quoting from the famous passage in *Allegories of Reading* where de Man gives his definition of the text: "The divergence between grammar and referential meaning is what we call the figural dimension of language. This dimension accounts for the fact that two enunciations that are lexicographically and grammatically identical can, regardless of context, have two entirely divergent meanings. . . . We call *text* any entity that can be considered from such a double perspective . . ." (*AR,* p. 270).

23. Barthes's brief gloss on the distinction between "reality" and the Lacanian "Real" is helpful here: "one is displayed, the other demonstrated" ("From Work to Text," in *Textual Strategies* ed. Josué Harrari [Ithaca: Cornell University Press, 1979], p. 74.)

24. An excellent essay which begins to do this is Thomas E. Lewis, "Notes toward a Theory of the Referent," *PMLA* 94: 3 (May 1979): 459–75. My essay has benefitted immensely from Lewis's discussion of the relationship between contemporary semiotics and Althusserian theory.

25. The one essay where de Man comes closest to considering the political relationship between "ideologies and philosophy" is the enigmatic last essay in *The Rhetoric of Romanticism*. This brooding piece, which critiques Schillerian "aesthetic education" by exposing it as an ideology that "succeeds all too well, to the point of hiding the violence that makes [the education] possible" (*RR*, p. 289), may suggest, for many readers, a significant turning point.

26. It may be worthwhile to (re)read at least the Derrida-Searle debate (*Glyph* 1 and 2) with this focus in mind. See Jacques Derrida, "Signature Event Context," and John R. Searle, "Reiterating the Differences: A Reply to Derrida," *Glyph* 1 (1977): 172–97 and 198–208, as well as Derrida, "Limited Inc.," *Glyph* 2 (1977): 162–254. Gayatri Spivak's "Revolutions That (As Yet) Have No Model: Derrida's *Limited Inc*," (*Diacritics* 10: 4 [Winter 1980]: 29–49) provides a valuable political commentary. This general aspect of Derrida's work has been becoming clearer in his most recent lectures and essays. One particularly explicit piece is the lecture Derrida gave at Cornell as A. D. White Visiting Professor in 1983; it appeared in print as "The Principle of Reason: The University in the Eyes of Its Pupils" (*Diacritics* 13: 3 [Fall 1983]: 3–20).

27. The quote is, of course, from *Of Grammatology* (p. 44); its value as a political slogan is perhaps what we need to consider in some more detail.

LAWRENCE GROSSBERG

Teaching the Popular

In a 1979 *Rolling Stone* interview Susan Sontag commented that one of the reasons she left academia was that her
colleagues could not accept the intersection of serious scholarship
(and politics) with the pleasure of the popular.[1] More, perhaps,
than other cultural domains, the popular demands pleasure before
understanding. Critical theory in the United States has too often
avoided confronting this reality, one that certainly dominates the
lives of our students if not our own. Instead, academic criticism
has typically dealt with popular culture by way of value systems
and classifications that simultaneously protect professorial authority and deny the popular its specificity: mass culture, mass
communication, media studies, or formularized genres.

There are in fact a number of similarities between popular
culture and teaching. Both exist outside the idealized forms of
academic discourse. Popular culture is what remains of culture
after subtracting the part that is worthy of serious critical consideration ("high culture"); teaching, that transitory form of academic talk in which concessions must be made to popular taste,
is what is left of academic discourse when publication is subtracted.
There is a radical disjuncture between both the way we construct
the "aesthetic object" and the "popular object" and the way we
construct the "theoretical object" and the "pedagogical object."[2]
Both popular culture and teaching appear rather mundane in their
concreteness, although academics have often constructed an im-
possibly idealized image (e.g., the Socratic) of teaching. On this
point I agree with Paul de Man that teaching is not an intersubjective relationship but rather a discursive practice in which our
subjectivities are only marginally implicated.[3] Yet both popular
culture and teaching are important sites of cultural struggle.

Finally, while both are structured around alternating moments of pleasure and pain, neither offers the totally exhilarating joy of transcendence. The conclusion I wish to draw from these similarities is that the study of popular culture may provide us with a unique perspective on a more modest Socratic insight: that the theoretical and pedagogical moments are often already implicated in each other.

It is not enough, however, to point out that these discursive practices intersect; we must try to specify how teaching and theory are mutually determined. We are, by now, aware that theories are never simply applied but always worked out in a confrontation with particular texts. Similarly, texts are never read free of all theoretical entanglements. If there is a similar economy of exchange between pedagogy and theory, it has been protected from critical scrutiny by our power to dictate apparently "natural" pedagogical practices. Demystifying this economy would politicize both theory and pedagogy and the relations between them. This project, most powerfully embodied in contemporary feminism and poststructuralism, places the theoretical and the pedagogical object in a larger social and cultural context.[4] The politics of the popular, on the other hand, differs from that of the two intellectual movements with which I have compared it; the popular implicitly challenges the aestheticization of politics in deconstruction and the personalization of politics in the feminisms of the 1970s. The popular places us instead within the economy of the politics of everyday life.

I would like to examine this economy concretely by describing my own attempts to teach and write about contemporary popular music. I will present a theory of "the popular" as well as some suggestions for a theory of interpretation (or analysis) as these have developed out of my own teaching and research. Finally I will use my work on rock and roll to illustrate certain pedagogical and interpretive strategies.

Rock and Roll: From Pedagogy to Theory

For the past five years, I have been teaching courses in the cultural history of rock-and-roll and youth cultures.[5] From the outset this placed me in a double bind: If I positioned myself as a scholar and cultural critic, I lost my credibility as a "fan" and the students in my class became suspicious and skeptical. Moreover, I knew that my pleasure in the music offered a simple but privileged access to the phenomenology of the music and its culture. But to speak with the voice of a fan was to relinquish my position as a critic and professor. Further, my colleagues charged that to speak as a fan was to sacrifice interpretation and critique in favor of celebration, and they challenged rock and roll's right to be included within the university curriculum. As one put it to me, "How can you intellectualize about the insignificant and trivial?"

The students, on the other hand, jealously guarded their music, claiming that, in the very attempt to dismantle and interpret its significance, I not only demonstrated my lack of understanding but also betrayed the music by contributing to rock and roll's unwanted legitimation. I must admit to having found this accusation both troubling and somewhat incomprehensible. After all, the academy's power to legitimate rock and roll is trivial compared to the legitimacy which time, the economy, and the mass media have already conferred on it. Yet I nonetheless felt that my students were mounting a valid challenge to my interpretive apparatus. Their voices might ultimately be closer to the voices of the music itself. Increasingly, I turned my attention to the significance of this double bind, attempting to read rock and roll in terms of the demands which its culture placed upon my own critical discourses.

In a sense, the classroom became my critical laboratory, the object of my interpretive gaze. The students claimed their right to speak as "experts" or at least as privileged witnesses, offering me the opportunity as a teacher to dismantle and challenge at least a part of the self-assuredness of their judgments and self-posturings. But my own biases were equally visible, compelling me to acknowledge them publicly and to include them as a part of the textual history I was trying to interpret. My interpretation of rock and roll was itself a trace of what I was trying to describe: the place of rock and roll in contemporary culture.

But if my reading of the music was a measure of my own social and cultural history, it was also the site of an intersection between my interest in cultural theory and my attempt to articulate that theory through practical analysis. Three problems I had been working on found their material embodiment in the ways in which rock-and-roll fans respond to the music: (1) rock-and-roll fans interpret and use the same music in different ways; (2) they relate to and use rock-and-roll songs through larger "assemblages" of musical and cultural events; and (3) they relate to and use the music at levels other than the signifying or representational.

There is clearly a complex and apparently uncoded heterogeneity to interpretations of musical events (songs, genres, performances). Contrary to what most cultural critics think, even among fans there are often contradictory readings of rock-and-roll texts. While critics of popular culture generally ignore this multiplicity of readings, the existence of multiple readings is a generally acknowledged issue elsewhere in critical theory. Some critics have resigned themselves to it, others have celebrated its liberating possibilities, and still others have desperately sought to tame the "monster of undecideability."[6] For the student of popular culture and its effects, the multiplicity of readings is an interpretive crisis.

This crisis threatens to break cultural criticism's connection to everyday life, relegating it to the gaps between semiotics and social psychology. There it would merely seek more refined ways to analyze the correlations between the processes of encoding and decoding culture.[7] But those correlations can rarely be established. The critic is usually left with two irreconcilable readings: a reading of the alternative possibilities coded into the text and their relations to the institutions producing them, a description of audience interpretations and how they relate to the social positions of the interpreters. Such analyses merely reproduce the traditional dichotomy of production and consumption; they cannot locate the concrete moment when the text enters into the material life of its consumers within a larger social context.

It is necessary to question whether such texts construct their own meanings, meanings we can decipher and use to account for audiences' actual responses. That means challenging the basis of both semiotic and hermeneutic interpretation. When teaching, I found that my attempts to "read" texts as if they had an inside that, when deciphered properly, would account for peoples' responses remained unconvincing. It was apparent that the text's meaning was not inherent in the text itself. As Stuart Hall has argued, "The meaning of a cultural form and its place or position in the cultural field is not inscribed inside its forms. . . . The meaning of a cultural symbol is given in part by the social field into which it is incorporated, the practices with which it articulates and is made to resonate."[8] Here one is treading on dangerous ground: without claiming that the actual construction and sound of the songs (a product of musical, linguistic, and technological devices) are unimportant, one needs to argue that they cannot be directly interpreted to explain the effects of the music.

One of the demands that rock and roll placed on me as an interpreter was that I take seriously the notion of overdetermination—i.e., that the effects of a text are not internally determined, nor even necessarily limited by a text's internal constitution. The meaning of a text is to be found in the concrete context in which it is momentarily located and rearticulated. But how does one interpret a text when its significance is the complex product of all its relationships? The problem is further complicated because every element of the context is similarly overdetermined; no element has an identity that can be isolated and taken for granted. My problem was to describe the contexts within which rock and roll emerged (and reemerges) and to elaborate its local effects.

This led me to a second feature of rock-and-roll fans' responses: they often treat a musical text as "hollow" and superficial. Not only does popular culture seem to deny its own existence as a series of independent aesthetic texts or objects, its impact does not come from claims for textual self-sufficiency or meaningfulness. Thus it is largely irrelevant either to idealize or to deconstruct popular culture. The students in my course could neither hear nor see meaning that seemed obvious to me, as both a critic and member of a different generation of the rock-and-roll culture. Even when they acceded to my readings, this had little impact on their responses to the music. In part this is because they respond not merely to particular songs but also to larger structures through which songs are "articulated." This larger apparatus is historically produced; it includes not only the "acceptable" music (defining both synchronic and diachronic "cartographies of taste") but also a range of related institutional and cultural practices and media representations. The relationship between specific musical texts and the larger apparatus is similar to Foucault's description of the relationship between the existence of a "statement" and its place within a larger "discursive regime."[9] In the case of rock and roll, the larger apparatus is an important part of the social formation of postwar American youth culture.

For all these reasons I realized that it was not useful to proceed by analyzing the textual structures and signifying relations of rock and roll. These observations were reinforced by a third feature of fans' responses: similar interpretations do not guarantee similar uses. Although individual fans sometimes treat the music as a representation of nonmusical experiences, I try instead to direct my analysis toward the ways in which rock and roll is empowered by and empowers particular fractions of its audience. This is not, however, a matter of asking how individuals consciously use the music. It is rather a matter of asking what possibilities are opened up by and for the rock-and-roll apparatus.

This leads to a particularly difficult issue in contemporary cultural theory. It is often quite obvious that popular culture is ideologically oppressive (who would deny rock and roll's complicity in the reproduction of patriarchal gender categories?). Yet critics too often assume that fans of popular culture are "ideological dupes" who cannot recognize the texts' biases. On the other hand, as Michele Mattelart has suggested (about women viewers of soaps), "What is disturbing is the exhilaration that these tales continue to give spectators who are critically aware of how alienating they are and who have located the mechanisms through which their nefarious work is carried on. We cannot simply ignore the question of taste, of the pleasure (albeit a bitter one when it goes hand in hand with a developed consciousness) produced by these fictional products of the cultural industry."[10]

The current tendency of cultural theory to limit criticism to analyses of ideological effects prevents us from acknowledging the affective power of the popular. Indeed, any exclusive emphasis on analyzing meaning undercuts our ability to describe, for example, the immediate sensuous relation to the popular and to the everyday, both of which are organized around the body. I believe our complex affective relations to daily life provide ways of resisting the ideological message of popular culture.[11] In the next section, I shall develop this general view of an affective politics of the popular, returning thereafter to its implications for a strategy of interpretation and pedagogy.

Defining "the Popular"

Studies of popular culture typically begin by defining their subject matter rather than by trying to describe and understand it. This usually means applying categories developed for use in other cultural areas. Popular culture has been defined formally (as formularized), aesthetically (as opposed to high culture), quantitatively (as mass culture), sociologically (as the everyday culture of "the people") and politically (as "folk culture": "the cultures of those oppressed groups or classes held to constitute the site upon which the imaginative resistances to the socially dominant culture and ideology cluster or develop").[12] Stuart Hall offers a revised model of the political definition built on the idea of marginality: "the structuring principle of the popular in this sense is the tensions and oppositions between what belongs to the central domain of elite or dominant culture, and the culture of the periphery."[13] Yet it seems odd to describe youth culture as peripheral in America, or to imply that there is no popular culture at the center.

It is not enough, however, to correct these theories by pointing out that the relations between different cultural domains are continually being redefined and challenged. Certainly, the boundaries of the popular are fluid; as Tony Bennett argues, culture is a shifting noun and the "popular" is a shifting qualifier.[14] The question is what is involved in the assumption that the qualifier always modifies the particular noun. We can also agree that the popular is the site of a struggle, but that does not automatically tell us what we are struggling over and what the weapons are.

I would propose that we describe how the popular functions by demonstrating how its fans' responses describe and circumscribe the genre. Rock-and-roll fans have two evaluative scales: they discriminate between good and bad music, and they distinguish authentic from coopted music. By coopted music I mean music that fans exclude from the genre because it does not function effectively within their lives. There is apparently no way to code this changing boundary. There are a wide variety of reasons that may be given for excluding music from the genre. Moreover, anything can become rock and roll; anything can be excluded from the category. The boundary that encircles and celebrates rock and roll's status as popular is constituted from within the rock-and-roll culture rather than merely by hegemonous processes of production and representation. It is not only the existence of such a boundary but its nature that gives us a clue to the workings of the popular, for the boundary is always an affective one: it signals a highly charged emotive relation to the rock-and-roll apparatus and to everyday life, one structured by pleasure and pain, by desire.

Although there is considerable debate about how music works to organize emotion, it is clear that the musical environment has real power in our lives.[15] Music has a direct and material relation to the body: its sensual effects are, to some extent, unmediated. At the simplest level, the body vibrates with sound, and that vibration can be articulated with other practices and events to produce complex effects. The physicality of music gives it its affective power to translate individuals (an ideological construct) into bodies.[16] My claim, then, is that the popularity of rock and roll is rooted in the music's relationship to a material body which is already worked over by lines of desire; this body is surprisingly able to resist hegemonic attempts to regulate its desire.

In order to put this claim into practice, I will need to make some modifications in contemporary culture theory and its use of the concept of hegemony. Contemporary cultural theory most often sees culture as an ideological practice—i.e., as a set of signifying forms and practices that represents our relationship to reality and makes the representation seem natural.[17] Ideology produces experience and substitutes it for reality. But ideology is never singular; there are always competing and local ideologies. Thus ideology never produces a single coherent representation of the world. This is the critical thrust of the concept of hegemony: hegemony reveals ideology to be the site of an ongoing struggle between competing realities. Yet individuals are not always aware of these competing realities. The theory of hegemony, in short, fails to explain how particular realities can sometimes seem to exhaust the limits of common sense. How is our experience given this relative stability?

This stability comes from the relationship between ideology and subjectivity: ideology positions the individual as a subject, placing the individual in a mediated relation to the object world.[18] Of course the subject is also multiple and fluid, defined by its complex and often contradictory place within various social registers (economic, educational, familial, legal, political). Yet ideology provides a medium in which our multiple subjectivities are represented as a unified subject. The totalizing power of ideology rests, then, upon its production of a totalized subjectivity.

In order to understand the relation of this totalized subject to reality it is necessary to recognize that the world is affectively as well as semantically structured.[19] I am using the term *affect* to refer to the intensity or desire with which we invest the world and our relations to it. Desire, however, cannot be limited to sexual energy. This affective production is organized within and circulates around the body, understood as more than simply a semantic space and less than a unity defining our identity. The body is placed into an apparently immediate relation to the world through its affective investments. Such investments are always fragmented, connecting partial objects: moments of the individual's reality are set in relation to isolated fragments of the world.[20] Yet this process of affective investment (through which the body is inserted into its physical and social environment) results in the very possibility of a totalized sense of reality. Just as social life is built on totalizing the subject, it also rests on the projection of a totalized affective structure. This struggle over our affective investments defines "the popular."

The popular circumscribes reality; its geography of desire marks the existence of the boundaries of reality without necessarily defining them.[21] By structuring our multiple affective investments, the popular opens up the very space of the phenomenological, the space within which meaning and subjectivity operate. The popular produces our internal and external horizon.

This analysis of the power of the popular is made possible by a somewhat artifical separation between ideology and the structure of our affective investments. We need to remember, however, that they readily interpenetrate one another; their actual condition is a mixture of radical complicity and conflict.[22] In rock and roll, the two are often in contradiction: while rock and roll can produce a "politics of pleasure" that opposes the dominant culture, it often articulates a conservative sexual ideology. It is helpful to conceptualize this relationship as a struggle to define the nature of desire and to realize that the popular carries on this power struggle within the larger process of hegemony. The hegemony tries not only to win people to its view of reality but also to regiment desire. By fixing the lines of desire, by closing off its possibilities, the structuring power of affective investments can be both oppressive and revolutionary.

Finally, it is important to place the popular in its current context—within postmodern culture in late capitalism. I do not want to argue, as many others have, that our period displays a radical rupture with the past, but there are real differences in our historical moment. For the study of popular culture, the important differences include a changing experience of time and history, new distributions of knowledge, and new forms of reflexivity. As a result, the popular now undergoes constant redistribution and re-alignment. Although its function remains the same, the popular can no longer be counted on to project a stable and unified affective horizon. Instead the popular works by producing temporary "affective alliances."

A comparison with an older form of the popular—religion— will help make the difference clear. For many generations religion served not as an exact body of knowledge but as an affective structure, one that helped produce the feeling that the world was a totality, that life must have a meaning. The nature of that meaning was less important, perhaps, than the confidence that the world, despite its contradictions, still made sense. The popular can still serve that function, but it cannot do so by producing a stable and enduring affective horizon. In part this change reflects the fact that our affective relation to the world has become increasingly fragile and momentary. No doubt this also helps explain the sense that the popular is so easily manipulated.

The project of the popular has not changed, but the conditions and modes of its possibility have. Unlike more stable affective structures, affective alliances work by making whatever is incorporated into their space pleasurable. Thus the fragments linked together need not in any sense be pleasurable outside of that space. It is their location within a particular alliance that empowers them in concrete ways. It is as if affective alliances do not allow themselves a vertical anchor in the real and, instead, operate entirely horizontally. They thus deny themselves the stability necessary to oppose the dominant affective structurations successfully.[23] At the same time, they attack the possibility of any stable affective structuration. But since this assumption is a condition of the existence of hegemonic power, affective alliances define themselves within a paradoxical position of resistance. Insofar as they constitute moments of resistance, they are always local, fragile, hesitant, and temporary, waging a kind of guerrilla warfare with little or no organizational support.[24]

Teaching a Popular Genre: Rock and Roll

We need to develop an interpretive strategy that helps us describe how a genre functions affectively—as the production of local "formations of pleasure." Such a strategy must also respond to three other issues: (1) overdetermination; (2) the affirmation of real effects beyond signification; and (3) the determination of the genre within the "apparatus."[25]

Accepting the full consequences of overdetermination threatens to make all interpretation futile: Imagine you are confronted with a box with the pieces of an undisclosed number of jigsaw puzzles. All of the original boxes are lost so you don't know what the puzzles are supposed to look like. It is also possible that the same piece will fit in several different puzzles. Thus each piece is defined only by its place in the picture-contexts constructed around it. The place of any one piece is only partly determined by its shape and appearance. A blue piece might serve as part of a sky, an ocean, or a blue thunderbird. Thus you cannot name a piece or describe its contribution before the puzzle itself is assembled. No meaning can be taken for granted, and in the end the significance of any piece—its possibilities for serving a range of functions—can never be exhausted.

Applied to interpretation, this parable suggests that, while historical events do exist, we cannot recover them. Interpretation does not reconstruct the historical contexts in which cultural texts emerge with particular meanings and effects; it fabricates them. Interpretation is a struggle for the power to identify and define a text's effects.

Yet while there is no necessary correspondence between the surface signifiers of the text and any signified, the surface is never blank or innocent. It is scarred by traces of its history, a history of functions and effects that mark its emergence and survival. Read as signifying practice, any piece can be related to any other piece. Read alternatively as a function that allows and is allowed by particular connections, interpretation is a process of mapping the vectors of effects that traverse and encircle a text. The metaphor of a jigsaw puzzle, which too easily suggests a static representation of a real situation, needs to be replaced with a more active and multidimensional one: a functioning apparatus.

The notion of an apparatus, however, brings more with it than just these two features. It also suggests an organization or structure. This third characteristic is crucial if interpretation is to mean more than juxtaposing myriad cultural events and themes. Fabricating contexts requires as well the identification of effects and determinations, the concrete empowering relations that give texts their historical identities. Furthermore, as the jigsaw puzzle metaphor suggests, interpreters need a principle that helps them select the "pertinent" sets of possible relations. Elaborating this interpretive strategy will bring me back to the pedagogical context with which I began this essay, a context within which pedagogy, theory, and interpretation interrogate and implicate each other.

Most attempts to interpret rock and roll locate it as entertainment (for the masses) or culture (for particular subsets of the population). Either approach seems to condemn it to powerlessness—if not insignificance—except in economic terms. Those who argue for its status as entertainment see it, at best, as a form of youthful irresponsibility that can be condoned, a kind of symbolic play outside the restraints of adult social roles. At worst, as entertainment, it is the ideological reproduction of sterotypical representations of reality. Those who focus on the economic implications of entertainment often condemn it for substituting commodities for culture and for furthering the reduction of human subjects to consumers: passive, acritical, and unable to oppose the existing political and ideological institutions.

On the other hand, a number of more sympathetic critics have read rock and roll as a cultural text that, at moments, exists at the site of real ideological struggle. Building on the suggestion that rock and roll represents the psychological, cultural, economic, and political experiences of youth, they read the history of rock and roll as a repeating cycle of coopted entertainment and ideological opposition—the particular moment is usually taken to be determined by the music's economic complicity with corporate capitalism.[26] Still others have attacked the cultural politics of rock and roll by locating its origins within a socially determined textual history. Its authenticity is located in the original moment, defined alternately as black rhythm and blues, or as working-class (and usually southern) culture. In either case, the entire history of rock and roll becomes a "rip-off" and a "watering down" of authentic popular music.

Such views do not deal with the ways in which rock and roll works in everyday life. And they are unable to account for the diversity of concrete responses to and interpretations of the music. In fact, any reading of rock and roll as only a musical text or an economic practice will, as I have argued, find itself caught between encoding and decoding, between production and consumption. Furthermore, while such perspectives have often been applied pedagogically, they force a wedge between the student and the music.

The students in my class resisted my attempts to describe rock and roll in terms foreign to rock-and-roll culture. They also refused my attempts to begin with an established set of texts. Neither rock and roll as a general category, nor its specific texts, provided an acceptable object for interpretation if I wanted to uncover its power and popularity. What was available to me as a resource and topic for interpretation was their experience of the music as fans. What had to be read, then, was the structure of their responses to rock and roll.

Defining a consistent pedagogical practice out of this situation posed some unique problems, especially when joined with my theoretical assumptions. The traditional resources of interpretation—either an intertextually defined canon or some other isolatable set of objects—simply were unavailable. Further, if nothing's identity and significance could be taken for granted, then the potential field of analysis would have to remain uncircumscribed. If I did not want to privilege their responses to the music as self-sufficient, and they would not let me treat the texts as such, then both the musical practices and the audiences' relations to them had to be treated as historically situated cultural productions. My task became one of developing a rhetorical criticism to describe the relations between text, audience, and daily life in nonphenomenological terms.

I devised a three-stage teaching strategy: The first stage is to describe the structures of response. This is essentially a phenomenology of rock-and-roll fans' responses—not merely their obvious conscious attitudes but rather the constitutive relations of their experience. While the fact of experience must be taken for granted, the subject's knowledge of it cannot be. The surface of experience is not disrupted by such investigation, but its lines are traced out more clearly in terms of the relations between subjectivity and textuality. Such experiences are not directly available for the entire history of rock and roll; they must often be constructed from a variety of sources and documents.

But phenomenology can only be the starting point because it fails to recognize that the poles of subjectivity and textuality, the very structures of phenomenological response, are themselves the product of social and historical determinations. The second stage, then, is to "deconstruct" the fan's phenomenological relation to rock and roll, to "excavate" the social structures of response. This demonstrates that the experience of rock and roll is neither merely a product of each fan's particular subjective history nor the outgrowth of some communicated message inherent in the music itself. The third stage involves fabricating the contexts within which the relations between fans and music acquire affective and political functions. If the first two define the functions of the rock-and-roll apparatus, the last locates its realizations at moments in the history of rock and roll.

This strategy does not deny the need for various kinds of interpretive practices. But it does suggest that the kind of interpretation required is to be determined within the particular analysis. Textual analysis, for example, becomes necessary when locating particular structures of functions and effects. The appropriate sites for different interpretive practices are themselves defined by the continuous struggle to describe specific empowering and empowered relations of rock and roll.

However, as soon as one approaches the demands of concrete analysis, the fragility of this theory of interpretation becomes all too visible, for both its practice and its conclusions are, in a real sense, unteachable. In the end, the actual historical functioning of the music cannot be described while remaining within its concrete context. Its affective power can only be invoked, situated in the intersticies between the bricolage of contexts fabricated around music and audience and the apparatus defining the relation between postwar popular music and youth.

This assemblage gets its unity from what I have called the "rock-and-roll apparatus," which organizes the seemingly random collection of cultural events that interpenetrate the rock-and-roll culture. For the emergence of rock and roll in the mid-fifties, one would want to draw the connection between the music, its fans, and their responses to the following dispersed events: literature (e.g., *Catcher in the Rye, On the Road,* as well as Roth and Bellows), art and fashion, movies (*Rebel Without a Cause, The Wild One, Blackboard Jungle* as well as more mainstream features and the early rock-and-roll films), television, the musical hit parade, the range of rock-and-roll styles, the fact of the baby boom, everyday cultural practices, diversions and fads, politics (Eisenhower, McCarthy, the Cold War), economic trends, the enduring impact of major historical events such as World War II and the atomic bomb, intellectual discourses emerging at the time, the response to rock and roll and its emerging culture, dance styles, sexual mores, child-rearing and educational practices, and race relations.

However, this moment of bricolage is useful only if it is brought into relation to the interpretive strategy outlined above. Analyzed as an "apparatus" it will have to show the music's relation to these events and demonstrate how the music is empowered by and for its fans.

We can quite safely observe, for example, that rock and roll was both vehemently attacked and celebrated. Furthermore, although both sides made distinctions between acceptable and unacceptable music, the two systems of classification did not correspond. Quite often, the fans' response was predicated on the assumption that (1) its attackers simply could not understand why the music was important and why particular music was to be appreciated and that (2) nevertheless the celebration of the music was to flaunt precisely those features that elicited the attacks. For the fans, one of the primary functions of the music was to create boundaries separating "them" from "us"—i.e., constituting difference.

Both sides took their positions in response to structures of action and physical response evoked by the music and its culture, not on the basis of the meaning of messages communicated. For both sides, the issue was an apparently uncontrolled celebration of bodily pleasures, movements, and styles. The ways in which rock-and-roll fans enacted their relation to the music, as well as the criteria they used to differentiate "authentic" from "inauthentic" rock and roll, suggests that underlying such issues as musical construction or mode of production was a more powerful phenomenological need to escape boredom. Boredom was associated with both adulthood and the world it constructed. The celebration of pleasure and the body functioned to reinforce and redefine the separation of "them" and "us."

Finally, one needs to recognize the size and diversity of the rock-and-roll audience (including musicians) in the fifties. Despite differences of class, race, gender, and social geography, there was a common allegiance to the music. Of course such sociological differences produced different responses to and uses of the music. But the commitment to difference and pleasure was mounted in opposition to a common sense of frustration and futility. It is difficult to define that common response to "postmodernity," but it is fair to say that rock-and-roll fans saw themselves confronting a historically unique world and occupying a unique position within it. At times, this was an exhilarating and optimistic vision, at others, a terrifying and pessimistic one. Rock and roll worked for a generation that found itself celebrating the present; whatever the future, it was excluded from consideration within the culture itself.

It will not suffice to argue that such patterns of behavior and commitment typify the transition from childhood to adulthood, from leisure to work, from the lack to the fullness of responsibility. It is within the rock-and-roll culture that such terms have been interpreted for postwar America. Nor are these three structures unique to the emergence of rock and roll in the fifties. I have several times said that the students in my class forced me to revise my own analysis. Let me give an example of this that will also demonstrate the importance of these structures of relation between rock and roll and its fans.

Heavy metal is a subgenre of rock and roll that emerged, as a musical form, at the end of the counterculture. Building on the guitar-dominated sound of the early Who and later acid rock groups like Cream and Jimi Hendrix and drawing on the violence and sexuality of groups like the Doors, it also returned to the blues sources of rock and roll. Groups such as Led Zeppelin, Grand Funk Railroad, and Black Sabbath created a loud, apolitical celebration of music, youth, and sexuality. Using extremely powerful amplification and courting the dissonant sounds produced by feedback, heavy metal is a sometimes slow but always pounding version of rock and roll; it appeals primarily to an audience too young to have participated in the counterculture. Since the seventies, such groups have had a major presence in the charts. In the mid-seventies, some bands took on a particular image and set of themes:

they sang about sex and violence, and they appeared on stage (both in costumes and actions) in ways that earned the genre the name "cockrock." It was a celebration of adolescent male sexual fantasies, often including violent hostility toward women. Through the seventies other variations have appeared, including groups trying to wed the genre to more artistic pretensions or to other genres of rock and roll (such as punk and noise music) and mellower groups who substituted romance for violence and used a high, piercing male vocal lead. But the macho image was consistently maintained, even by those women who entered into the genre and worked to define an image of "female macho."

Heavy metal is typically interpreted as a rather perverted adolescent form of rock and roll that celebrates a macho violence and masculinity without considering the place of women in its own culture. I was quite willing to dismiss it as a rather unimportant moment in the history of rock and roll, one with no claim for affective political opposition. I found, however, that many of the students in my classes were fans of this music. Indeed the Midwest is considered one of the centers of heavy metal, in terms of both its production and audience. The students demanded that I look past my own interpretations of the music (loud, using unpleasant feedback and distortion, sexist, violent) and consider how it functioned for them. They pointed out that heavy metal has many female fans and, unless I was willing to take the rather patronizing position that I could judge them to be pawns in a patriarchal game of chess, I had to look at the ways they used the music and at the particular ways in which the musicians' images functioned for them.

They did not identify directly with the macho images of the musicians but used them rather as absurd stereotypes of their own fantasies and of the social world in which they found themselves. Moreover, they did not respond directly to the lyrics and often claimed not to listen to them. What, then, are the functions of such music? What is its appeal to this largely middle- and lower-middle-class white audience, predominantly midwestern, who begin as fans in high school but who often continue to be fans as they enter college or seek (and even find) employment? These fans come from suburbs, small towns, and farms where life is, above all for them, boring, partially because there are few places and activities designed for their pleasure.[27] The music celebrates their right to pleasure. Furthermore, because it is music that attacks and segregates itself from other genres of rock and roll, it apparently functions to define its fans' difference, not only from the adult world, but also from other styles of youth that have no place in the Midwest of the seventies. Heavy metal is, above all, a rejection of the naivité and optimism of the counterculture and of the sophisticated artistic styles of urban rock and roll. It works to find ways of outraging those generations of rock-and-roll fans who came before it, just as it continues to seek ways of outraging, and hence differentiating itself, from those that have come since. Finally, it appeared at a moment when the promise of the future that had been crucial to the counterculture had collapsed. It appealed to generations who saw a world in which progress appeared to be a myth and insanity appeared to be the order of the day. It is music for adolescents who are afraid to contemplate their own future. Thus it reproduces for its fans, albeit in different forms, the very same structures that defined the power of rock and roll in the fifties.

If we return now to the elements defining the context of rock and roll in the fifties, we can understand why interpreting rock and roll means organizing the relations among these elements according to the power of the rock-and-roll apparatus to produce an affective alliance—i.e., a universe structured by the three planes I have identified: youth as difference; pleasure and the body; and a particular historical relation to the future. We could then examine each of the events and locate its relation to rock and roll in terms of its place within the larger structured context centered about the rock-and-roll apparatus.

My claim, then, is that the rock-and-roll apparatus is both empowered by and empowers its fans in specific ways, by drawing connections with certain domains of everyday life. The power of this apparatus lies, not only in these connections, but even more importantly, in its foregrounding and production of particular organizations within and between these domains. This popular apparatus, then, organizes the social space of its fans according to three planes: (1) the social differences of generations multiplied and inscribed on the field of social relations; (2) the celebration of pleasure inscribed on the site of the body; and (3) the structure of uncertainty inscribed on the circuit of history and meaning. The rock-and-roll apparatus organizes its fans' lives according to the structures of youth, pleasure, and postmodernity. This structuration, which I referred to as an "affective alliance," constitutes particular "formations of pleasure." The forms that these planes take, as well as their structures, may change (and be influenced by other social domains). Thus the politics of pleasure of a particular moment of rock and roll can only be contextually described and evaluated. For example, in the late fifties, youth was constructed, not only as difference, but with a particular identity as well—that of the teenager. Because it went beyond difference, the position could be taken up and exploited by those outside of the apparatus itself. Similarly, pleasure was constructed as sexuality (although by the end of the decade, this was balanced by a concern for the pleasure of romance and dancing itself), and the future, while not dismissed as meaningless, was simply bracketed as irrelevant. (Again, by the end of the decade, this was balanced by a concern with the future as a time of almost mythical legitimation of youth's concerns and feelings).

Nevertheless, the limits of rock and roll as a popular genre are precisely articulated by the contours of this affective production.[28] This dialectic of apparently stable limits and unstable realizations defines the existence of the popular as an affective politics and the possibilities of interpretation as invocation. This is not, however, identical to a dialectic of the theoretical and the pedagogical objects, nor can it be reduced to the dimension of general versus concrete, for this is always an arbitrary decision: any description is already concrete and can be made more so. In fact, I would like to conclude by suggesting that the theoretical object is nothing more than a set of strategies or tools available to the teacher and critic. Its "truth" is the place of those techniques within an entire economy of social and cultural practices, political and economic institution, and the discursive boundaries of knowledge. Its "truth" is the measure of the possibilities it opens for us as critics and teachers.

NOTES

1. Jonathan Cott, "Susan Sontag: The Rolling Stone Interview," *Rolling Stone,* October 4, 1979, pp. 46–53. I want to thank Cary Nelson for the detailed suggestions he made in the course of revising this essay.

Teaching the Popular

2. Tony Bennett, "Popular Culture: A 'Teaching Object,'" *Screen Education* 34 (1980): 18–29. See also Iain Chambers, "Rethinking 'Popular Culture,'" *Screen Education* 36 (1980):113–17.

3. Paul de Man, "The Resistance to Theory," *Yale French Studies* 63 (1982): 3.

4. See, for example, Michèle Barrett, *Women's Oppression Today: Problems in Marxist Feminist Analysis* (London: Verso, 1980); Mary Daly, *Gyn/ecology: The Metaethics of Radical Feminism* (Boston: Beacon, 1978); and Roland Barthes, "Lecture," *Oxford Literary Review* 4 (1979): 31–44.

5. See my reading of rock and roll in "The Politics of Youth Culture: Some Observations on Rock and Roll in American Culture," *Social Text* 8 (Winter 1983/84): 104–126; "Another Boring Day in Paradise: Rock and Roll and the Empowerment of Everyday Life," *Popular Music* 4 (1984): 225–58; "Is There Rock after Punk?" *Critical Studies in Mass Communication,* in press; and " 'I'd Rather Feel Bad Than Not Feel Anything at All': Rock and Roll, Pleasure and Power," *Enclitic* 8 1/2 (1984): 94–111.

6. Cary Nelson, "Reading Criticism," *PMLA* 91 (October 1976): 801–15.

7. David Morley, " 'The Nationwide Audience'—A Critical Postscript," *Screen Education* 39 (1981): 3–14.

8. Stuart Hall, "Notes on Deconstructing 'the Popular'," in *People's History and Socialist Theory* ed. Raphael Samuel (London: Routledge and Kegan Paul, 1981), p. 235.

9. Michel Foucault, *The Archeology of Knowledge,* trans. A. M. Sheridan Smith (New York: Pantheon, 1972).

10. Michèle Mattelart, "Women and the Cultural Industries," *Media, Culture, and Society* 4 (1982): 141.

11. See Gilles Deleuze and Felix Gauttari, *Anti-Oedipus: Capitalism and Schizophrenia,* trans. Robert Hurley, Mark Seem, and Helen R. Lane (New York: Viking, 1977).

12. Bennett, "Popular Culture," p. 22.

13. Hall, "Deconstructing 'the Popular'," p. 234.

14. Bennett, "Popular Culture," p. 20.

15. Because of music's problematic relation to meaning, it foregrounds the affective resources of the popular. This is evidenced not only in the multiple ways in which various forms of popular music have functioned in third-world struggles against imperialism but also in the unique importance of locally produced music in the international recording industry. Larry Shore, "The Crossroads of Business and Music: The Music Industry in the United States and Internationally (unpublished manuscript, 1983).

16. Dick Hebdige, oral communication, 1983. See his "Posing . . . Threats, Striking . . . Poses: Youth, Surveillance and Display," *Sub-Stance* 37/38 (1983): 68–88. This is not to deny that even the sonorial is culturally coded but rather to question the ways in which such codings are effective.

17. See my "Cultural Studies Revisited and Revised," in *Communications in Transition* ed. Mary Mander (New York: Praeger, 1983), pp. 39–70, and "Strategies of Marxist Cultural Interpretation," *Critical Studies in Mass Communication* 1 (1984): 392–421.

18. This mediation is accomplished by placing the individual within the signifying chain as the author and authorization of particular meanings. See Louis Althusser, "Ideology and Ideological State Apparatuses," in *Lenin and Philosophy,* trans. Ben Brewster (New York: Monthly Review Press, 1971), pp. 127–86. For a discussion of the hierarchical structure of this ideologically totalized subject, see my "Ideology of Communication: Poststructuralism and the Limits of Communication," *Man and World* 15 (1982): 83–101.

19. My claim that affective totalizations are not necessarily mediated by structures of meaning can be seen in relation to a number of theoretical projects: Alfred Schutz's attempt to account for the coherence amongst the multiple realities, each with its own structure of meaning and accent or feeling of reality, that enables us to live in and move between them ("On Multiple Realities," in *Collected Papers,* vol. 1, *The Problem of Social Reality* ed. Maurice Natanson [The Hague: Martinus Nijhoff, 1971], pp. 207–59); Martin Heidegger's argument that we find ourselves in a "mood" that defines the possibilities of our interpretations of reality (*Being and Time,* trans. John Macquarrie and Edward Robinson [New York: Harper and Row, 1961]); and contemporary feminist claims that sexuality cannot be reduced to gender and that its construction involves more than ideological processes (Ellen Willis, "Toward a Feminist Sexual Revolution," *Social Text* 6 (1982): 3–21.) The claim that hegemony involves more than processes of signification—e.g., political, economic, and affective practices—does not deny that all practices are articulated by the ideological (Stuart Hall, "The Problem of Ideology—Marxism Without Guarantees," in *Marx 100 Years On,* ed. Betty Matthews [London: Lawrence & Wishart, 1983], pp. 57–85).

20. Gilles Deleuze and Felix Guattari propose that desire be understood as "desiring production," which is materially structured by "asignifying practices." The breaks and flows of desire cannot be reduced to the reenactment of ideologically produced fantasies upon the stage of the unconscious. Nor is desire merely an explosive interruption of the power of ideological significations. See my "Experience, Signification and Reality: The Boundaries of Cultural Semiotics," *Semiotica* 41 (1982):

73–106. My own position is that "formations of pleasure" are always the product of both ideological and affective practices.

21. The distinction between the popular and entertainment (musical "pop") is not intrinsic to the texts but is rather a function of the relationship between the audience and the texts. Pop is what rock-and-roll fans describe as "coopted"; while such texts may elicit affective responses and even momentarily resonate with the affective structures of the audience's daily life, they fail to find a place within the project of affective totalization. One must be careful to differentiate between texts within a hegemonic popular, those which, attempting to function oppositionally, fail for that particular audience, and those which are tolerated as effectively popular for another audience.

22. The fact that particular practices may participate in or be appropriated into both productions raises a number of questions. First, the relations between the two hegemonic processes need to be explored concretely. For example, rock and roll exists within an ideological field which struggles to articulate its affective opposition into hegemonic terms. Second, we need to investigate the use of signification in popular texts where it may function to evoke desire rather than to represent reality. For example, while it is certainly true that many rock-and-roll fans find identity in the musical apparatus, it does not follow that the music constructs particular subject-positions for them. Finally, we need to explore the general relations between these two processes. Foucault, for example argues that the project of the contemporary hegemony is to appropriate materiality and affect into the representation of subjectivity as the unconscious (*The History of Sexuality: An Introduction*, trans. Robert Hurley [New York: Pantheon, 1978]).

23. As a student in my class said, "Even if there were a meaning to life, I probably would not agree with it."

24. They produce a "simulacrum" that displaces the materiality of their own affective investments. Thus, their politics is built upon alliances of exteriority, encapsulating audiences within their spaces without necessarily giving them meaning or identity. The power of affective alliances is the power of difference. See Jean Baudrillard, "Forgetting Foucault," *Humanities in Society* 3 (1980): 87–111.

25. Michel Foucault, "Two Lectures," in *Power/Knowledge: Selected Interviews and Other Writings 1972–1977*, ed. Colin Gordon (New York: Pantheon, 1980), pp. 78–108, and "Questions of Method: An Interview," *I & C* 8 (1981): 3–14. See also Gilles Deleuze and Felix Guattari, "Rhizome," *I & C* 8 (1981): 49–71.

26. The most sympathetic and elaborate reading of rock and roll is Simon Frith's *Sound Effects: Youth, Leisure and the Politics of Rock 'n' Roll* (New York: Pantheon, 1981). According to Frith, rock and roll

offers a "politics of leisure" that celebrates leisure in the dream of a life without work. While this is characteristic of many forms of American popular music, rock and roll locates it within a unique sociotextual coding of the relations, images, and fantasies about and between street and suburban forms of postwar youth and culture. I have four objections to this reading. First, this is only one of the ways in which rock and roll has organized and presented itself. Second, such images have been consistently mediated through the ideological system of the various cultural industries. Third, by relying upon preconstituted functional categories (leisure versus work), Frith takes for granted not only interpretations of the musical texts but also a description of youth's social reality. It seems odd to claim that youth's daily lives are dominated by concerns with "work." Finally, Frith acknowledges but marginalizes questions of the materiality and pleasure of the music.

27. This is by no means a complete or adequate analysis of heavy metal. I have chosen to ignore not only significant differences within this audience over time but also, more importantly, the second major audience of heavy metal: an urban working-class audience, largely white and male, located primarily in the industrial northeast. This audience fraction has a different age range, with a significantly larger proportion of older fans. It tends to prefer the harder, louder, more violent, and often more blatantly sexist end of the musical spectrum. It also has a distinctive, visible subcultural style: it has appropriated the biker style of leather, denim, studs, boots, military insignia, etc., as well as certain countercultural signifiers of rebellion like long hair. This subculture is often thought of as conservative and even "redneck" by other rock-and-roll fans (including many midwest heavy metal fans), although this image is not necessarily valid. While the midwest audience tends to eschew style (favoring simply jean and T-shirts), the two factions do share some important practices: both associate the music with images taken from a particularly mythic and science fiction rhetoric; both have made the old rock-and-roll ritual of "air guitar playing" central; both have altered the form of rock-and-roll dancing (either rejecting it entirely or reducing it to a pre–"slam dance" version often described as "headbanging"); both tend to replace the countercultural drugs with alcohol and downers. Furthermore, the more subculturally defined heavy metal audience also exists in the Midwest, and certain fractions of the midwest audience (especially some high school males and those who immediately enter the labor market upon graduation) share more of its musical preferences and stylistic challenges. Nevertheless, I do not think we can assume that these two audiences use the music in the same ways, nor do I think that these differences can be explained by any simple set of sociological characteristics (e.g., as working class versus middle class). Also, I have not attempted to explore the

relations of female fans, in either of these groups, to the music. One needs to inquire into the ways which the music empowers and is empowered by its different female fans. Finally, I have not discussed the significance of the differences within the musical genre itself, and their complex relations to the various economic and media institutions. Answering all these questions would require constructing the specific affective alliances within which the music functions and which it functions to produce, and their relations to each other and to non-heavy-metal rock-and-roll alliances. I would like to thank Dave Marsh for his suggestions and criticisms on this issue.

28. See my "If Rock and Roll Communicates, Why Is It So Noisy?" a paper delivered at the meeting of the International Association for the Study of Popular Music, Reggio Emilio, Italy, September, 1983, forthcoming in *Popular Music Perspectives* 2.

ALBERT D. HUTTER

Literature, Writing, and Psychoanalysis: A Reciprocity of Influence

For Peter Loewenberg

In psychoanalysis there has existed from the very first an inseparable bond between cure and research. . . . Our analytic procedure is the only one in which this precious conjunction is assured.
　—Sigmund Freud

Whether he be original or a plagiarist, man is the Novelist of himself.
　—Jose Ortega y Gasset

From 1972 through 1978 I studied psychoanalysis at the Southern California Psychoanalytic Institute. My fellow students ("clinical associates") were all medically qualified psychiatrists, some beginning their pychoanalytic studies after many years of private practice. Almost all of them had come to accept as fact the biases of their training, particularly the conviction that all other fields, certainly any form of psychoanalytic practice and theory, must be viewed within the determining framework and assumptions of medical science. If psychiatry is now one of many possible medical specialties, then psychoanalysis (particularly in America) is the medical specialist's specialty, the most carefully restricted of medical fraternities.

My orientation on joining the Southern California Institute was equally biased; but the biases were very different, based on the rites of graduate education in the humanities. The perspectives of that training were in fact so different, particularly in the ways I had been taught to "read" subjects, human as well as literary, that I found my own training immediately tested, used, and altered;

I also began, simultaneously, a radically new form of *experiential* education, based on clinical observation, analyzing patients under regular supervision while also experiencing that same process in reverse, as analysand. From the start, theory and practice were played off against one another, constantly challenging and changing my perspective on the analytic process as a whole.

Having used my Ph.D. as the necessary credential for "certification," I first practiced the relatively harmless subspecialty of English professor—a profession historically infamous for offering few cures of any kind. I had taught myself psychoanalytic theory haphazardly during graduate school, attending some classes when I could, but following no systematic program. Like most academics, characteristically, I had simply wanted to learn just enough about psychoanalysis to solve specific literary problems. I hoped, once I had a university appointment, to expand this random study of psychoanalysis systematically in order to teach and publish in what seemed to be emerging as an especially exciting, if demanding, interdisciplinary field.

But the unexpected opportunity for full psychoanalytic training (including all aspects of clinical training) was unique;[1] it was also perfectly suited to my sense from first beginning my readings in psychoanalysis that the absence of any clinical experience was the most serious handicap for the thorough—balanced—understanding I sought. I had plunged randomly into my graduate reading in psychoanalysis in part because I saw that I could not logically "read up on"—much less master, however diligently I worked—a field based on treatment; I could not "get up" psychoanalysis in the way I might have mastered, on my own, Victorian history or Georgian architecture.

Unlike contemporary historical theories about an earlier age or its art, and unlike most literary theory, psychoanalytic theory is the direct and necessary product of psychoanalytic practice. It is, first of all, a skill developed in and for treatment. Its theories are like tools for the fine tuning of a delicate musical instrument, which then allows the skilled practitioner to perform with greater expertise. Similarly, modifications, alterations, or repudiations of that theory usually derive from persistent clinical problems not satisfactorily solved through the use of current theories, from discoveries made in the course of treatment itself, or from observational research. For instance, the innovative studies of children in

England and America over the past thirty years have so altered psychoanalytic theories of development that they are generally felt to have shifted the bedrock of psychoanalysis itself, moving its foundations deeper, or earlier, in time and making the pre-Oedipal period the most significant developmentally—a stage which not only subordinates the Oedipal phase but, to a large extent, also determines its nature and outcome.

Modifications in theory may originate in the evolution of competing theoretical approaches, but such competition always shares a common goal: to achieve a more complete and efficacious cure. Most practicing analysts must regularly modify and, in important ways, balance their sense of theory against a sense of its usefulness and pliability, of how the theory "works out" and how flexible it is in the face of ever-changing presenting problems and the variety of personalities who "present."

I now understand psychoanalysis in an altogether different way, and this change occurred as soon as clinical experience began to modify what earlier had often seemed theoretically rigid. As a result, I also began to perceive how most academic applications of analysis were based on the same doctrinaire readings of theory: identical psychoanalytic texts seemed to me misunderstood by my colleagues, sometimes by misreadings of major concepts, which these colleagues then misapplied to literary texts. This led, all too often, to a reductionist literary criticism.

In regularly putting their theoretical training to the test, most practicing analysts find that rules are made, if not to be broken, then at least to be modified and questioned, that no one practices "by the book" any more than a touring pianist plays every work in the same style and the same key. Yet we continue applying the same overused assumptions about psychoanalysis in thousands of publications in "applied psychoanalysis," half of them reducing every literary work to a version of "the primal scene." In 1926, in his defense of "lay analysis," Freud described the unique and "inseparable bond between cure and research. Knowledge brought therapeutic success. It was impossible to treat a patient without learning something new; it was impossible to gain fresh insight without perceiving its beneficial results. Our analytic procedure is the only one in which this precious conjunction is assured."[2] It was this experience of "procedure," of an ongoing exchange between theoretical and clinical knowledge, which altered my own view of psychoanalysis and of most contemporary writings in "applied psychoanalysis."

In a short space of time the scholar of English literature may learn a great deal of important "experiential" data which will affect the way he or she subsequently understands and applies psychoanalytic theories. Indeed, both fields need an exchange of knowledge and experience; each offers a uniquely important perspective on the other. But the different kinds of training generated by graduate schools on the one hand and analytic institutes on the other, combined with the unusually strict, institutional isolation of exclusively medical psychoanalytic training in America, have, until recently, made this reciprocal exchange virtually impossible.

Rigorous and lengthy, psychoanalytic training itself demands a minimum of four to six years of formal seminars; its candidates must conduct a specified number of different "training cases" (at least one of which, in the unfortunate diction analysts employ to describe their own profession, must be "terminated"); in turn, each training case demands long-term supervision (one meeting per week with a senior analyst for each week of a candidate's work with a patient); finally, and it is usually considered the most demanding requirement of all, every would-be analyst must undergo his or her own "training analysis" with one of the elite—a designated, institute-approved "training analyst." And, assuming he or she is gifted or lucky enough to be admitted to an institute, the candidate may embark on all of these new training requirements only *after* completing medical school, internship, residency, and specialized training in psychiatry.

"Learning by doing," learning psychoanalysis by analyzing several patients under close supervision while simultaneously experiencing analysis "from the couch" (candidates' training analyses typically continue through much, if not all, of their candidacy), seems unusually demanding and as alien to the experience of most academics as working only at the level of abstract theory seems to the practicing psychoanalyst. In general, when psychoanalysis is "applied to" other fields nonanalytic authors assume no responsibility for what they do not know; they dismiss "practice" altogether, in effect bypassing the practical foundation of the field and equating "psychoanalysis" with psychoanalytic theory, usually only with the theoretical approach of a single school. In the most common approach to the application of psychoanalysis to literature (or to any field), analytic theory is entirely divorced from its clinical context. Moreover, this approach is addressed to a nonanalytic audience so thoroughly imbued with the same assumptions that even a simple acknowledgment is rarely made to what, a priori, introduces such distortion, dividing psychoanalysis in half before using it.

Even without the problems inherent in trying to separate theory from clinical practice, competing psychoanalytic theories have grown so wide-ranging and complex, beginning with the twenty-four volumes of Freud's *Standard Edition,* that even most analysts find their own field, in its entirety, arcane, Byzantine, or just plain unmanageable. As a result they, too, may be tempted to isolate theory from their daily practice. In what remains the most modern and detailed study of *The Technique and Practice of Psychoanalysis,* Ralph Greenson begins with a review of what he considers basic to "the psychoanalytic point of view." He stresses the necessity for "a reciprocal relationship between theory and practice. Clinical findings can lead to new theoretical formulations, which in turn can sharpen one's perceptiveness and technique so that new clinical insights may be obtained. . . . Whenever there is a lack of integration between theory and technique, both aspects are likely to suffer." And he concludes this introductory section by arguing that "our greatest hope for progress in technique lies in a better integration of clinical, technical, and theoretical knowledge."[3]

The various practical demands and limitations of current psychoanalysis are regularly combined with related confusions contributed by other fields and then exacerbated by adoption of any partial psychoanalytic explanation that seems useful. The majority of those who apply psychoanalysis are often drawn to it as the most convenient field from which to pick explanatory concepts to support their own preconceptions—presented, of course, as the conclusive products of an "objectively applied" psychoanalytic criticism.[4]

Psychoanalytic institutes across the country are regularly inspected and certified by their aptly named "parent" institute, the American Psychoanalytic Association. After careful screening, including individual interviews of candidates by senior analysts, affiliated institutes accept each year a select group of psychiatrists for training, though outside the small psychoanalytic community itself most people are inclined to view the processes of acceptance and training as a peculiar version of fraternal initiation.[5] In the eyes of the general public, including its more widely read representatives like academicians, the actual training of a psychoanalyst is so far removed from any familiar form of graduate or postdoctoral education that it seems to encourage needless misperception. Both by their wish for autonomy and by their training requirements, psychoanalysts bear considerable responsibility for their public self-definition and, consequently, for the ways in which they are misunderstood or in which they ritualistically misuse their own field by becoming clinically inflexible. "If students [clinical associates] are submitted to a fixed ritual of education," wrote Edward Glover some thirty years ago, "it is only natural that they should unconsciously seek to get their own back by overemphasizing their own rituals."[6]

To the nonanalytic world, clinical associates appear to be joining the most highly educated and sophisticated group of "medicine men" ever to practice in western society. But for all of their presumed sophistication psychoanalysts are especially vulnerable to dismissive labels. Thus they are favorite targets for name-calling at high professional levels: "shrinks" and even "psychological witch-doctors."[7] It has become not only an "impossible" profession but, in its application to other fields, among the most distorted and disliked of interdisciplinary subjects because it is commonly separated into theory and practice from the outset, and also because "theory" so frequently stands for all analytic theories when in fact it is derived from only one of many "schools" or self-explanatory hypotheses ("theory" referring here to any tentative explanation for the continually changing clinical experience of analysis).

At the same time, psychoanalysis may well be the most universally discussed discipline, a field in which everyone is an expert. "If you raise a question in physics or chemistry," Freud complained, "anyone who knows he possesses no 'technical knowledge' will hold his tongue. But if you venture upon a psychological assertion, you must be prepared to meet judgements and contradictions from every quarter. In this field, apparently, there is no 'technical knowledge.' Everyone has a mental life, so everyone regards himself as a psychologist."[8] And it is often on these grounds that psychoanalysis is appropriated and "applied" by writers from every discipline.[9] Finally, most applied psychoanalysis assumes that it is applying not only a single, unified discipline, but one that is understood and accepted as clearly by the audience as by the author.[10]

If the clinical rites of psychoanalysis seem vague to most academics interested in the field, its emotional impact is usually clear. To the layman, undergoing an analysis is made to sound as demanding as analytic training itself, except that it is now conducted in a manner the analysand must always find mysterious, arbitrary, and, if at all successful, wrenching. Its success is understood to be in direct proportion to the degree of anxiety and regression produced in the analysand, to the pain rediscovered in early repressed memories and emotions, or in the most terrifying self-discoveries and humiliating personal disclosures. From the layman's point of view, during this entire process the analyst is believed to impose arbitrarily a series of unexpected and frightening demands.

Throughout his career, in various papers on technique and clinical recommendations, Freud also regularly used words like *mysterious* and *magical* to describe one's impression on first analyzing a patient and employing the seemingly impossible techniques of analysis, like "free association," the cornerstone of what is referred to as "the fundamental rule" of psychoanalytic practice, but which, in spite of its theoretical and clinical centrality, is virtually impossible to describe in abstract terms alone.

"Free association" is oversimplified because, like so much of psychoanalysis, its importance derives from the peculiar and subtle ways in which it must be further defined by practice. Indeed, it is perhaps the clearest example of how an analytic term may be totally skewed, without any deliberate misreading of theory by critics, unless they also have some way of comprehending its clinical functions. What is demanded, and made to sound plausible, in theory, is literally—and deliberately—made impossible in practice. "The fundamental rule" implies several basic principles which structure the entire course of an analysis. The patient is first asked to free associate: "to try, to the best of his ability, to let things come up and to say them without regard for logic or order; he is to report things even if they seem trivial, shameful, or impolite."[11] But when that patient, however committed to the process, tries to free associate, the task will prove impossible; and through this impossible demand the nature of the patient's specific resistances and neuroses is revealed, leading to the analyst's subsequent interpretations, the patient's reactions, and thus the basis for transference and the analytic process in general.

Often the analyst's interpretations take the form of noting a "failure" to observe the request for free association. But the patient is bound to fail, even by "overcompliance"—for example, using an incomprehensible string of words and images: free association rendered as primary process. Although such freedom to regress to, and express, primary process thinking is in one sense desired, in another it offers an especially effective defense, since it simultaneously "expresses" the inexpressible by an *unintelligible* communication of unwanted, shameful feelings which the process of association has indeed made conscious, but opaque. More typically, however, the "failure" is a conscious one: the resistances of silence, or avoidance, or dismissal by the patient of a subject he or she decides unilaterally to be too trivial, boring, or repetitious. Indeed in every imaginable way this apparently simple request imposes its inherent contradictions on patients by requiring simultaneously that they "let go" and allow the unconscious to surface and express itself while it also assumes that any conscious expression of such "letting go" will be made intelligible to another—to the analyst—as well as to oneself. And in order for a reasonably clear communication to occur, linguistic rules must transform primary process thinking into secondary process expression so that a purely "free" set of associations is either useless or impossible. We might say that the cornerstone of psychoanalysis is a seemingly simple but ultimately unachievable, in fact, impossible, demand, and that progress in therapy occurs whenever that demand is *not* met.[12]

Greenson puts the case in a typically dramatic and humorous fashion: "We ask the patient to let himself be carried away by his emotions in the analytic hour so that he can feel the experience as genuine. But we do not wish him to become unintelligible or disoriented. At the end of the analytic hour we expect him to drive home without killing anyone" (p. 362). What the English and American writers on technique, like Glover and Greenson, treat clearly but usually with a wry pragmatism, the French tend to press to their outer limits, extracting from a constantly changing technique all its possible implications—and their implicitly contradictory demands on the patient. Thus J. Laplanche and J.-B. Pontalis note that "the fundamental rule [of analysis] has a number of consequences," among them that "as the subject . . . gradually submits" to such demands "he becomes committed to saying everything and *only* to saying it: his emotions, bodily impressions, ideas, memories—all are channelled into language." This makes of the rule "more than a technique for investigation—this is the sense in which it can be described as fundamental, despite the fact that it is not the only component of a situation where other factors, especially the neutrality of the analyst—play decisive parts."[13]

Laplanche and Pontalis conclude by emphasizing Lacan's similar understanding of this demand to establish the purely linguistic nature of analytic work: "The fundamental rule contributes to the establishment of the intersubjective relationship between analyst and analysand as a *linguistic relation*" (p. 179). In their careful and lengthy definition they have in effect limited analysis to an enterprise based only on language, opposing it to "unanalytic" (that is, nonverbal) resistances, like "acting out," elsewhere defined by them as "an impulsive aspect, relatively out of harmony with the subject's usual motivational patterns" (p. 4). They conclude their equally detailed definition of acting out by reiterating the emphasis on language and the desire to place everything which is not linguistic outside the realm of analysis proper:

> One of the outstanding tasks of psycho-analysis is to ground the distinction between transference and acting out on criteria other than purely technical ones—or even mere considerations of locale. . . . This task presupposes a reformulation of *action* and *actualization* and a fresh definition of the different modalities of *communication*.
>
> Only when the relations between acting out and the analytic transference have been theoretically clarified will it be possible to see whether the structures thus exposed can be extrapolated from the frame of reference of the treatment—to decide, in other words, whether light can be shed on the impulsive acts of everyday life by linking them to relationships of the transference type.[14]

But as Greenson's comic example implies, acting out suggests two distinct concepts: an action that occurs during the session ("acting in"!) and an action taken independently by the patient *outside* the treatment situation. The former is usually considered more productive than the latter, often providing a form of unconscious *re*-enactment of repressed memories which allows the analyst an unusual, nonverbal glimpse of the patient's unconscious. When a patient chooses to act out by an unconscious and defensive, or oppositional, behavior to ward off the powerful feelings generated within the sessions and by the transference, it is far more problematic.

A typical example of this defensive *re*-action might be an impulsive, unannounced marriage, unconsciously protecting the patient against overwhelming transference feelings toward the analyst; the best-known example is Dora's unilateral termination of her treatment, an acting out which resulted in Freud's somewhat belated discovery of the transference and its powerful consequences for the patient—both in and out of the office. By definition, acting out refers to an *action* in opposition to *words;* Greenson claims it is also defined in opposition to memories and affects. He goes on to illustrate "one simple kind of acting out that frequently occurs early in the course of analysis [which] is the patient's talking about the material from the analytic session *outside* [my italics] of the analytic hour to someone other than the analyst."[15]

In their different ways, Greenson on the one hand and Laplanche and Pontalis on the other define terms polemically, Greenson in particular oversimplifying a concept which is perhaps the most confused term in psychoanalysis. In their 1973 study, *The Patient and the Analyst: The Basis of the Psychoanalytic Process,* three British analysts provide the most objective and comprehensive account of this concept, concluding at one point that "the only common denominator" to emerge from so many different uses of the same term is "that the particular action referred to as 'acting out' has unconscious determinants."[16] This bland and all-inclusive definition is, in analytic thinking, a virtual truism and, hence, meaningless. They go on to trace "part of the present confusion" to Freud's original use, in 1901, of the colloquial *Handeln,* which they translate as *to act;* and they then discuss Freud's use of *Agieren* in the (1905) Dora case, which they call "less colloquial"; although it has a similar meaning of *to act* it has as well "a slightly more emphatic connotation" (presumably emphasizing action itself, taking action), and they argue that the word is here used by Freud "in a particular technical sense." *Agieren* was translated into English as *acting out* and, as they note, the preposition created many of our subsequent difficulties with the concept as a whole. Freud typically saw, and tried to resolve, these difficulties by multiplying and elaborating on his distinctions and by further redefining his now various definitional subcategories: "Freud distinguishes between acting out *within* the analytic situation and acting out *outside* the analysis. Both forms are regarded as a consequence of the analytic work and the treatment situation. Within analysis, the transference provides the vehicle for acting out, and this may be the only way in which repressed memories may initially find their way to the surface. Acting out outside the analysis carries with it potential dangers to the treatment and to the patient, but it is often impossible to prevent."[17]

Although it further complicates an already confusing concept, it is essential to note the more subtly disguised bias of the French perspective, presented as an objective, detailed, and factual definition. Thus Laplanche and Pontalis begin their definition by noting only the term *Agieren* and claiming that it was "not a part of German common usage." This is quite true, but then few Freudian terms were ever part of German common usage. In *Returning to Freud*—that is, resolving for him Freud's own presumed confusions and then "properly" using what they believe he must have meant— they first note the Latin origin of *Agieren* and then claim that "for referring to action or acting German prefers such words as *'die Tat', 'Tun', 'die Wirkung'* etc." But while the first point is both self-evident and in no way conclusive (a Latinate origin does not automatically exclude a word from usage), the second point is more slippery, switching the noun-agent of the sentence to "German" in place of "Freud" and, more important, omitting Freud's earlier use, as noted above, of *Handeln*.

By their initial and seemingly objective "translation," they are then able to argue their own specific concerns: "The term 'acting out' enshrines an ambiguity that is actually intrinsic to Freud's thinking here: he fails to distinguish the element of *actualisation* in the transference from the resort to *motor action*—which the transference (q.v.) does not necessarily entail." Through this subtly misread and, I believe, mistaken critique of Freud's "failure to distinguish," Laplanche and Pontalis entitle themselves to speak for Freud, limiting the concept of transference itself, like all of analysis, to *language*.[18]

When an occasional and unusually gifted writer succeeds in describing analytic work lucidly enough even for the uninitiated, the complications are necessarily oversimplified so that the analytic process then appears to be, more directly and persuasively, impossible. Janet Malcolm's *Psychoanalysis: The Impossible Profession* draws its title directly from Freud's 1937 paper on "Analysis Terminable and Interminable," where Freud had labelled analysis one of those "impossible professions in which one can be sure beforehand of achieving unsatisfying results."[19] Malcolm's study of analytic practice is the most vivid description of this process from the point of view of the outsider, noting "its radical unlikeness to any other human relationship, its purposeful renunciation of the niceties and decencies of ordinary human intercourse, its awesome abnormality, contradictoriness, and strain."[20]

For the privilege of practicing such a profession, initiation is extraordinarily expensive and lengthy: a training analysis, annual tuition, and supervisory fees alone now total well over $100,000, and few clinical associates graduate within less than six or seven years of beginning their training. In addition to charging impossibly high fees to train an elect few in the impossible techniques of an impossible profession, the institutes insist on four or five years of "theory courses" so that their students may begin to master the complex theories engendered by varying practices—even among the most "orthodox" forms of current psychoanalysis.

By simple good fortune my first teaching position (at UCLA in 1970) coincided with the Southern California Psychoanalytic Institute's formal commitment to an unusual—and still very controversial—admissions policy: it violated what most people, including most M.D.s, had assumed to be by then an unquestioned prerequisite for anyone applying for admission as a clinical associate. The debate over "lay analysis" was thought to have been resolved almost from the beginning of the psychoanalytic movement in America.

Established in 1911, the American Psychoanalytic Association had, within twelve years, aligned itself with the powerful and highly respected American Medical Association, thereby conferring an almost instant legitimacy on this new and, certainly in America, often suspect field. By contrast, many European associations continued, and continue, to accept and train lay analysts as a matter of course, making no formal distinction between medical and nonmedical practitioners. Freud had not only argued in favor of lay analysis but he had gone to some trouble to refute, quite explicitly, "the bluntest rejection" which had been "expressed by our American colleagues." In their desire immediately to distinguish themselves from the enormous number of "quack analysts" found in America, Freud argued, the American Psychoanalytic Association had developed something like a group symptom, a "resistance" which *seemed* to have been "derived wholly from practical factors. . . . The resolution passed by our American colleagues against lay analysts, based as it essentially is upon practical reasons, appears to me nevertheless to be unpractical. . . . It amounts more or less to an attempt at repression."[21] One immediate impractical result of this "repression" was its automatic exclusion of many highly qualified candidates who were, by necessity, obliged to join and train with one of the "quack" groups, or to practice without proper training and accreditation, or simply to give up any hope of gaining full training in psychoanalysis.

A striking—and moving—example of this last choice is described by Talcott Parsons, perhaps this country's most eminent sociologist, in an autobiographical article published in 1970. He expresses great regret that, at the start of his career, he had read Freud "only very fragmentarily" and had not understood the importance of psychoanalytic thought before publishing his first book, *The Structures of Social Action;* in fact he makes a point, in later introductions to that seminal and frequently reprinted work, of confessing that its most glaring omission was the absence of a section on Freud and the psychoanalytic perspective.[22]

In the autobiographical piece he recalls that, just prior to his "discovery" of Freud, he was studying the American medical profession in general, planning to use it as a paradigm of "rational self-interest" and analyzing the implications of private practice, personal gain, and their impact on the efficacy of medical treatment. He "proposed, in addition to canvassing the literature, to approach it through the methods of participant observation and interview" (p. 835). He had thus chosen a form of experiential learning very rare for an academic study, even if "the semi-public nature of medical practice in the modern hospital" made such experience possible (p. 835). And he did in fact observe hospital rounds, operations, and home visits, while also conducting numerous interviews with M.D.s themselves.

A good deal of his time was spent at Massachusetts General Hospital, where he became aware of a general interest in psychoanalysis; one conversation in particular, with Elton Mayo, persuaded him of the importance of reading Freud "seriously and comprehensively," which in turn led to a broader study of the major movements in psychoanalysis up to that point: this was during the late 1930s and early 1940s, when he was an assistant professor at Harvard. Once he found the time for such extensive reading, it resulted in "one of the few crucial intellectual experiences of [his] life" (p. 835).

He continued his clinical observations of medical practice, but now from a psychoanalytic perspective: "In the context of the social-emotional aspect of medical practice, I came to analyze some of the phenomena which were then commonly called the 'art of medicine' (as contrasted with the 'science') in terms of Freud's conception of the relation between analyst and analysand, notably the phenomenon of transference" (p. 837). He consequently framed medical training and its assumptions within a psychoanalytic context, which clarified for him that the American view of medicine was too restricted, an essentially private enterprise, its most common goal that of "private practice." This understanding made him realize how powerfully the profession had come to be seen—by doctors themselves as well as by their potential clientele (the general public)—as an objectively "scientific" discipline, traditionally respected because it was so insistently portrayed as devoted to the public welfare at the expense of the individual (arduous training, long hours, night calls, etc.). The last way in which the medical profession would want to regard themselves would be to balance the genuine sacrifices they did have to make against this other dimension of "rational self-interest," which had attracted most of them to their profession in the first place and then helped motivate them during their demanding course of training.

Parsons argued that medical practice had traditionally been described in terms of "a relation between cultural systems (scientific knowledge) and organisms, with social agents only implementing the obvious implications of knowledge." By contrast, he now proposed "treating medical relationships, at least in part, as cases of the subtle interplay between unconscious motives at the personality level and particularities of the structure of social systems" (p. 838). Parsons was suggesting that the medical paradigm itself, even where it seemed most "scientific," the doctor a mere "agent" who implemented proven data in the process of treatment or cure, also would have to take into account the significance of a personal and subjective distortion of that data, or its application, or both. To see medicine in this way was not to demean it, but rather to embrace at once its doubly demanding nature—as both a "science" and an "art." Practitioners who discovered themselves "too involved" personally, who were "overly concerned" about particular patients or unresolved problems, or who believed they were reading certain symptoms too "subjectively" should not automatically perceive these qualities as personal failures, deeming themselves inadequate to the supposedly reasonable, purely "scientific" and "objective" standards of their profession. Rather, they would be more effective if they could acknowledge the subjective, as well as the objective, dimensions of the field.

As soon as Parsons had the "crucial intellectual experience" of reading Freud, he assumed, logically enough, that he would proceed to acquire full training in that field: "This, of course, prepared the way for formal psychoanalytic training—*at the level permitted* [my italics]—about a decade later" (p. 835). That training began in 1946 at the Boston Psychoanalytic Institute, where he was carefully restricted from doing any analytic work himself but managed to attend certain ongoing case presentations ("clinical case seminars"), after taking considerable effort just to overcome a bias that had, by then, become a constant irritant—and obstacle—in his pursuit of knowledge:

> I entered into formal psychoanalytic training as a "Class C" candidate. . . . The more general intellectual grounds for my interest are perhaps clear from the above discussion, though I also had some personal reasons for seeking psychotherapeutic help. I count myself exceedingly fortunate in having had as my training analyst Dr. Grete Bibring, who had been a member of the original Freud circle in Vienna until forced into exile by the Nazi takeover of Austria. Of course, without a medical degree I could not have aspired to practice psychoanalysis, and according to the rules in force at that time, I was not permitted to take control of cases; indeed, I was admitted to the clinical seminars only as a special concession. (P. 840)

Parsons's homage to psychoanalysis is tainted throughout by

a gifted scholar's understandable resentment over the various ways in which he was prevented from learning fully an area of such importance to him. He had been trained, and was now working, in an academic community devoted to research, open discussion, and the sharing of knowledge; his credentials had been established with the publication of his first book; and he naturally would have looked forward to mastering this discipline as thoroughly and usefully as he had mastered other fields.

Although his interest in "experiencing" the practice of psychoanalysis may have included a personal motive to obtain therapy, his primary motivation seemed to have been generated by the natural desire for the fullest possible training—practical as well as theoretical—in a field now so crucial to him. And Parsons's conviction of the importance of making psychoanalytic training accessible to any serious scholar was ironically supported, less than a decade later, by the last group one would have imagined reopening the old debate over admitting nonmedical trainees. By the mid-1950s the American Psychoanalytic Association was reconsidering the possibility of training a limited number of lay analysts and determining the criteria for selecting the few who might qualify for such training. These discussions, culminating in an open forum at a national meeting in 1956, led to a consensus that such training, if highly selective, might indeed be appropriate; they then agreed on the necessary requirements for approving a nonmedical applicant. However, almost another decade passed before even the more radical institutes—like the Chicago Psychoanalytic Institute—acted on this resolution. But in the mid-1960s several institutes admitted scholars for full training and successfully proposed candidates for acceptance by the APA: among those who first included such candidates in their programs were the Boston, Chicago, San Francisco, and Southern California psychoanalytic institutes.

In 1966 an assistant professor of history at UCLA, Peter Loewenberg, had applied for full training on his own initiative and was among the first "research psychoanalysts" to be accepted nationally. He was the first such candidate admitted to the Southern California Psychoanalytic Institute, and the faculty observed closely his progress, his impact on his fellow students, his capacity to treat patients. In addition to his positive achievement in these areas, Loewenberg most impressed the institute by his public use of his training: within a short time he was able to speak at national conferences and local forums from a unique perspective, and it was evident that he was representing the institute in a positive way, bringing the academic community and the institute closer (helping the "institute" both as a formal group of analysts and, through his regular inclusion of analysts in his own teaching of history, as individual members of that body). It was, in fact, the combination of his progress and his almost immediate reapplication of his new training in publications and public meetings, along with lucky timing, that enabled me to benefit from the impression he had made. The SCPI decided, in 1970, not simply to continue to admit other candidates, but, recognizing how costly such training would be—effectively excluding virtually anyone who earned a living as a university professor—to create an annual fellowship for training in research psychoanalysis.[23]

But with the successful progress of the first group of accepted scholars, some of whom were close to graduating and applying for membership in the APA, and with the slow but regular increase in the number of such scholars (the SCPI fellowship has resulted in close to fifteen academicians by this point—1985—who have either graduated or are near graduation), all of the old concerns about maintaining the "purity" of the medical status of American analysis, in part deriving from what Parsons had labelled "rational self-interest," resurfaced again. In 1970 a blue-ribbon committee, including such well-known analysts as Margaret Mahler, Otto Kernberg, and George Pollack, reviewed the work of the research candidates, their potential contributions, and any potential damage their affiliation had caused or might cause; they then proposed that such candidates not only continue to receive complete training but, when graduated, maintain equal status with their medical colleagues, thus making them eligible for active membership in the APA. Their recommendation had to be submitted to each individual institute for consideration. These discussions generated powerful emotional reactions, not only within institutes or factions of the APA, but also within many of the analysts themselves. Once it began to resurface again in the 1950s the question of research training was almost constantly reevaluated, debated, and not fully resolved for nearly two more decades, if indeed the recent vote in favor of full acceptance and equal status of qualified nonmedical scholars does constitute a final resolution.

The most immediate cause for reviving this question in the

1950s was the product of a dilemma acknowledged by analysts everywhere, an accepted, if uncomfortable, piece of analytic "folk wisdom" rarely discussed outside that closed community. In a completely unforeseen way the alliance with the AMA had isolated the psychoanalytic institutes; training in the theory and practice of psychoanalysis had been completely separated from the academic community and the new ideas generated there, most significantly in the social sciences and the humanities. At the same time, the exclusive and prestigious nature of the American Psychoanalytic Association's independent training and its alliance solely with the AMA had encouraged in some of its newer candidates the worst side effects of contemporary medical training: a desire to join the medical profession as one joins a well-to-do professional club, its numbers carefully controlled, and conferring, as quickly as possible, a respectable status based on the lucrative practice of a respected medical specialty. This new breed of what might be called a "Babbitt analyst" had neither the time nor the interest to conduct research or to continue the ongoing and essential exploration, expansion, and revision of a field still barely half-a-century old.

Analysts concerned with research were well aware of the many academics who applied psychoanalytic concepts to literature or painting or history, and most analysts who attempted their own "reading" of these same fields recognized, in turn, that any advantages they derived from their own training were inevitably undermined by a parallel set of limitations: a lack of knowledge of the current scholarship and critical methodology of the very fields to which they hoped to apply, or test, psychoanalytic insight. And those who ran the APA, many of them our best-known analysts because of their research and their reformulations of theory and technique, were also those most disturbed by the growing problem of these "Babbitt analysts," who now moved so smoothly from medical school to psychiatric boards, through analytic candidacy to suburban practices. With each new generation of candidates who graduated and joined their respective institutes, the number of such analysts seemed to grow, demonstrating not simply very different goals in becoming analysts but also radically different values.

When the older generation of concerned analytic researchers looked around to see who else *was* advancing, expanding, and challenging analytic theory, they often found that many of the most important contributions from within the field had actually come from "lay analysts" who had been, in that wonderfully ambiguous phrase (simultaneously embracing their wise elders while suggesting in them a certain senility), "grandfathered in." This group was comprised largely of emigrés who had fled the Nazis *after* having established themselves in Europe—analysts like Erik Erikson. Otherwise, most of the innovative reformulations of theory were now occurring entirely outside the institutes, by academics (like Parsons) who found psychoanalysis useful in solving problems in specific fields, ranging from anthropology to art. Cornering the market on what was new and exciting in psychoanalysis (or, more accurately, in psychoanalytic theory isolated from questions of practice or technique), the academic world seemed to have appropriated or "colonized" psychoanalysis proper, generating a series of new critical schools based on their understanding and rereading.

There was substantial conflict, not simply *between* analysts or analytic factions but, most powerfully, *within* many individual analysts, especially among the older generation who now ran the APA and many of the individual institutes—paradoxically, either that group which had emigrated after having shared in the excitement of the Freud circle in Vienna or their immediate "descendants," trained by the emigrés and thus directly affected by their enthusiasm and their sense of excitement, of a nonconformist creativity constantly at the center of debate, of publishing new and often shocking discoveries and concepts. Both the group from Europe and, to a lesser, but still significant, extent, their trainees, were also powerfully afflicted by a cautious, at times reactionary, need for professional (and implicitly, personal) security. The older group had, of course, suddenly lost all they had known and achieved, and in deciding to come to America they were then seeking a country that had not experienced, within its own borders, two successive major wars.

Many famous analysts who spoke for the analytic "establishment" were thus simultaneously committed to seeking the kind of security which had already been provided by affiliation with the AMA while they were also aware that their field was quickly losing its creative originality. Ironically, many of the well-known analysts who fought for the creation of a program for "research analysts" were simultaneously fighting an internal war between their own liberal and conservative tendencies. The final decision of the organization was not really a reversal of their earlier, and seemingly established, policy over lay analysis; rather it was another form of pragmatism, a solution to an otherwise insoluble problem. They were paradoxically "rebelling" with the same "rational self-interest" which had first attracted the founding group of American psychoanalysts to their affiliation with the AMA—that group whose irrational rationality had been so quickly repudiated, with equal pragmatism, by Freud.

The research program was an attempt to bring back into the analytic community established academics who had already proven an interest and skill in applied psychoanalysis and, implicitly, to cautiously initiate a process of slowly "co-opting," reintegrating, and subordinating within their organization much of the creative research that was now being conducted elsewhere and that otherwise threatened to take control over the future of new psychoanalytic thought, of psychoanalysis itself. The institutes acting on the suggestions "from above" also hoped to change their own training "from within," not simply bringing back into their community leading academic scholars, but changing the interests and attitudes of their many medical clinical associates who would now be in training with active researchers and scholars.

In 1977 California passed a bill, currently administered by the state's Board of Medical Quality Assurance, certifying and licensing under the title of "research psychoanalyst" anyone who had graduated from one of the analytic institutes recognized by the state.[24] Few people seem to know about this bill, though it was in many ways the most dramatic action taken in response to the quietest of professional revolutions. It was the first formal, legal recognition and accreditation of lay analysis by any official governing body in American history.

It was assumed that on graduation research psychoanalysts would continue to see a limited number of patients and thus maintain a sense of the clinical application of psychoanalytic theory. Our institutes feared that unless we could continue to practice— an experience which, by then, I knew would continue to deepen and balance my sense of an otherwise overly abstract theory and metapsychology—we could not retain, or maintain, the training we had received. And their primary concerns were still those of finding ways to expand psychoanalysis itself in encouraging greater interest in analytic research among its medical candidates while also training, without limitation, others who might best question, expand, and apply psychoanalysis, with all its current clinical as well as theoretical changes, to other fields. Such scholarship would also test in part the value and validity of current psychoanalysis.

An unexpected but important development has also made this research program—particularly in such fields as language, literature, and history—far more reciprocal than was anticipated. We have begun to use our knowledge to reconsider the nature of analytic discourse itself, to frame the practice of psychoanalysis in the context of our own specialities: in the contexts of narrative, fictional and historical, or of the subjective limits of language. But the initial concern by the SCPI to have such work—anticipated or not—conducted by those who had undergone a full psychoanalytic training remains essential to the nature of that research, as it also remains central to the ways in which I have tried to use my own training.

I soon found myself regularly working with institute colleagues on problems of psychoanalytic and psychiatric writing. They typically asked for help in very specific ways, as in how to improve certain phrases or descriptions in their clinical write-ups and ongoing case reports. Most frequently they seemed to be asking, indirectly, how to bring back to life *their sense* of a profoundly moving, or frustrating, or "empty" session, or the essential qualities, the dynamics and interactions, in any description of a long-term therapy. These were problems they generally assumed to be unrelated to their own field, but rather restricted to gaining, or regaining, more expertise in language, so that their reports could reflect their work more exactly given "just a little help" by someone with expertise in language and writing. They also generally believed that their problems with what they found descriptively wooden or repetitive could easily be refined by a few techniques in sharpening their analytic prose. But the more involved I became with such problems in any form of analytic interview or case report, the more clearly I saw that the various problems they considered disparate and readily resolved were in fact unresolvable in any complete way; rather they were symptomatic of a much deeper—and universal—interdisciplinary problem.

The problem was writing itself. Analysts required more than

a partial "refresher" in freshman composition; they needed instead entirely to reconceptualize the nature of all writing, from "scientific" to "fictional." Bound by an inappropriate model of scientific reporting, wooden or repetitious prose was symptomatic of a host of mistaken and confining assumptions, inculcated by their medical education, about the necessity for describing their work "scientifically." The restricted model they continued to try to implement affected not only their write-ups but their understanding of their own work and its efficacy. It affected their practice and restricted their capacity to hear and understand in ways that were directly related to parallel constraints and problems in their writing.

I tried to persuade them that their writing problem demanded the most extreme solution: the substitution of a fictional aesthetic for a medical one, accepting and making full use of the valuably clarifying nature of fictive "distortions" and of some of the newer ways we now understand the nature of fictional narrative. Otherwise they would be obliged to set for themselves an impossible and constantly frustrating goal: to describe complex human behavior by "objective" and "complete" accounts of personal histories or a series of interpersonal, therapeutic interactions. I tried to persuade them that such a goal was impossible even in their regular write-ups of a single evaluative session with a patient.

I was able to test some of these convictions the year I graduated from the institute and joined their faculty. In 1978 I also joined their curriculum committee, which created an unheard-of series of required courses on writing—a concept so alien to the educational philosophy of any of the other psychoanalytic training programs that we indeed appeared to be reintroducing freshman composition into a postdoctoral program. In the first year, candidates began with a seminar on general problems in writing, and specifically in writing up clinical data focussed on the institute's semiannual progress reports, required for all analytic cases in supervision. This suite of new writing courses, which would continue throughout their training, concluded with an elective for those who had completed course work and were preparing to write their dissertations or papers for publication. Its overall design was to motivate better writing and more research and to encourage associates to think about research and publication far more than they had expected to do. In that first year I taught two of these courses, including one I had designed in order both to shock and to motivate through what I hoped would be an exciting combination—a seminar comparing "Case History and Fiction." Many of the senior analysts were opposed to the entire program, and a few were simply appalled at the premise of the course I had designed, in which I encouraged clinical associates to regard their reports in terms of narrative fiction. But these same senior analysts were also virtually unanimous in wanting to create, as well, some dramatic and innovative change which would reverse the values questioned throughout the APA in so many of their newer medical candidates.

But my immediate problem was not with the administration, who might watch closely and cancel such a course in the future if the outcome were to prove as distorted as they feared: my immediate problem was with the clinical associates themselves. They were closest in time to their medical indoctrination, which made my own perspective seem like lunacy—or heresy. Initially, they felt their writing problems to be at once purely technical and more general, vague, and unresolvable: although excited by their clinical experience, they found it difficult and frustrating to communicate the precise nature of their work, and they failed to convey a feel for the subtleties and unique qualities of a case; they found, instead, that their patients in print tended to merge with one another, to become wooden and stereotyped and look identical, while the subtle dynamics that distinguished cases were lost in the very attempt to describe them. These student-psychoanalysts then either blamed themselves for what they took to be a peculiar inadequacy of their own writing or even their own perceptions: "I thought I knew this patient or case better than I actually do." Or they blamed the medium: "Writing," they insisted, "reduces and distorts." And, of course, it does. But the way in which it reduces and distorts was central to their problem and, I believe, remains central both to psychoanalytic writing and to the development of an interdisciplinary field of study which we loosely label "literature and psychology."

For analysts who write, or even recapitulate a week's work in supervision, there must be condensation, revision, deletion, restatement: to some extent, in formulating the manifest content or text of their analytic activity, they are engaged in the writer's equivalent of "dream work." They need to become more conscious of writing as an independently creative activity that reformulates their experience and therefore must alter that experience. They have no choice but to change experience through language in a way that they can understand and control; otherwise, they will continue to attempt a translation—even a transcription—into print of everything that happens in their daily exchange with patients.

Inevitably such a rendition will read like a bad and literal translation of a subtle poem: at best, we might glimpse some of the power of the original through an awkward and obfuscating text. If we have discovered over the past half century how difficult and misleading it is to attempt to translate between two relatively close disciplines, like novel into film, then our efforts to recreate in print the experience of the couch or the neuropsychiatric ward are yet far more troublesome. The problems thus raised require all the expertise of contemporary literary criticism—an understanding of language, of textual nuance or image, of narrative voice and mood, of narrative complexity and inconsistency, of gaps and of silence. While psychoanalysis may help to "explain" literature or to illuminate some aspect of literary experience, such as reader response, we also need to exploit those ways in which literary studies may explain and improve the psychoanalytic enterprise. This particular interdisciplinary field needs a reciprocity of influence and explanation in order best to perceive common structures and to create significant change in *both* disciplines.

During the years since graduation I have tried to establish, for analysts, the significance of language and narrative in their daily exchange with patients and their occasional attempts to communicate that exchange through supervision or through reports or articles. I have also devised related courses for students of literature at UCLA in which I have tried to find ways, first, to challenge traditional distinctions between fiction and nonfiction and, second, to expose some students (those taking specialized courses in psychoanalytic literary criticism) to clinical psychiatry, however briefly, so that they may "read" the living experience of a psychiatric interview as well as reading *about* it.

The biannual reports required of clinical associates must give others a sense of the personality of the patient, of the analyst, and, in describing their interaction, of the unique ways in which the analyst's technique in working with different patients is differently developed. In a full case history they must also attempt to describe the larger changes within the transference and within the character structure of the patient. These demands are sufficiently Herculean without adding the usual boredom or feelings of inadequacy created by the restricted, "scientific" model, which generates repeated clichés and stale categorizing. In many ways, comparing case histories with the best of fictional narratives should generate a sense of excitement and new possibility in the writing of clinical associates.

We begin the institute course with a form of practical criticism I have already used in university classes, a mixture of unidentified quotations from fiction and case histories. Whenever I present, without explanation, some version of this material to my UCLA students, they naturally assume the quotations are related to their course (on fiction) and hence will be "literary." Any excerpt from a Freud case history is readily taken to be nineteenth-century fiction, usually fairly good fiction, although sometimes they complain of its being too literary—that is, too stylized and stilted. When I quote from *Splitting*, Robert Stoller's clinical study of a multiple personality, a few students may begin to wonder what they are reading: "When I was shooting him, I was excited. When I was actually pulling the trigger, it was . . . it was . . . like eating something good. I felt it in my throat. I felt it in my guts. It was a good feeling. And I hurt him too . . . He was on the floor and he was crying; he was hurt and he was bleeding; and I just closed the door on him. I didn't call an ambulance. The person that called the ambulance was . . . when I was shooting at the car, I missed once, and it went through somebody's bedroom window and missed their head. . . ."[25]

In Stoller's transcriptions of his patient's narrative, some students have sensed the cadence of direct speech and have wondered if they are encountering either a "nonfiction novel," like Truman Capote's *In Cold Blood,* or a novel that is attempting to reproduce "real" conversations, down to pauses and filler words and dialect, as if they were taped, like George V. Higgin's *The Friends of Eddie Coyle.* Most students, however, believe they are reading bad crime fiction. Indeed, this tends to be the one quotation they are confident they recognize: a quotation from a Mickey Spillane novel.

When I present these quotations in a university course, my aim is not simply to persuade my students to question the way they read and use categories—like fiction and scientific reporting and "real speech"—although that is an essential first step. More important, I want them to explore the ways in which their supposed "misreading" or "misidentification" of hackneyed detective story dialogue may in fact help them to understand Stoller's patient: a woman who believes she is a man and who needs to act tough, a woman who borrows not only the physical trappings of "manliness" (she is certain, among other things, that she has a penis) but also the language of "real men" as it is most consistently available to her—in film, in cheap fiction. Not only does life here imitate bad art, but an understanding of art, of literature and of literary criticism, leads directly back to an understanding of this particular case history. What my literature students are learning as they apply their critical skills to the psychological case history overlaps with what should be, and is slowly becoming, part of a psychoanalyst's training.

The psychoanalyst is by necessity both writer and reader—even Stoller's tape recordings are inevitably condensed and ordered as they are transcribed—and, I am convinced, any analyst is a better analyst for being a better writer and a better literary critic. To take the most immediate example, what my students at UCLA are quick to point out once they do realize the nature and context of the speech of Stoller's patient is the significance of her presumably "ungrammatical" mistakes. Thus her apparent misuse of *their* in the final sentence—"it went through somebody's bedroom window and missed their head"—is less significant as a problem of agreement (between "somebody" and "their") and more interesting as a reflection of the speech pattern of someone classified as "multiple personality." The more sensitive analysts are to language, the more they know about fiction and issues in criticism like narrative point of view or symbolism or discontinuous narrative, the more effectively and fully they can hear the *patient's* history. The patient's life story as it is told and retold through analysis is a personal statement derived from models of various origins, including novels and film and the supposedly true stories told to the patient by others, by friends and family, which in turn influence and are incorporated into the patient's "autobiography." The analytic process itself may be seen in part as the unfolding of one narrative, at first significantly flawed and then gradually revised, until it is more consistent with the world of the patient and the patient's changing sense of self. In his study of Freud's "Dora," Steven Marcus writes:

> Freud is implying that a coherent story is in some manner connected with mental health . . . and this in turn implies assumptions of the broadest and deepest kind about both the nature of coherence and the form and structure of human life. On this reading, human life is, ideally, a connected and coherent story, with all the details in explanatory place, and with everything (or as close to everything as is practically possible) accounted for, in its proper causal or other sequence. And inversely illness amounts at least in part to suffering from an incoherent story or an inadequate narrative account of oneself.[26]

Freud himself was quite aware of the way in which his own case histories might read like fiction, and when he was the most conscious of the parallels he repudiated them:

> I am aware that—in this city, at least—there are many physicians who (revolting though it may seem) choose to read a case history of this kind not as a contribution to the psycho-pathology of the neuroses, but as a *roman a clef* designed for their private delectation. I can assure readers of this species that every case history which I may have occasion to publish in the future will be secured against their perspicacity by similar guarantees of secrecy, even though this resolution is bound to put quite extraordinary restrictions upon my choice of materials.[27]

Throughout this case history he recognized the fictional qualities of his medium only to deny them: "I must now turn to consider a further complication to which I should certainly give no space if I were a man of letters engaged upon the creation of a mental state like this for a short story, instead of being a medical man engaged upon its dissection."[28]

However, at other times Freud responded to the exchange of an analytic session as a literary critic might respond to a novel, and everywhere in his reports of patients, in the quality of his writing itself, Freud demonstrated a remarkable literary sensibility. As early as 1895, in *Studies on Hysteria,* he described different versions of the same story told to him by his patient, Frau Emmy Von N., and by contrasting narrative variants he established the nature of the repression and of the material repressed. He thus learned that "an incomplete story under hypnosis produces no therapeutic effect," and he drew an immediate and pragmatic connection between fiction and cure: "I accustomed myself to regarding as incomplete any story that brought about no improvement. . . ."[29]

Every analysis creates at least two sets of stories: one story develops as the patient speaks both to himself or herself and to the analyst; it becomes a set of stories as it is heard, experienced, retold, and reconstructed by both analysand and analyst; in turn, the analyst recounts (understands, interprets, reorganizes as new material and new narratives unfold during the course of his or her experience of hearing the patient); and the analyst will often attempt then to recapture and retell these stories, in a unified form, to supervisors, in reports, or, finally, in print. Fictions, in the broadest and least pejorative use of that term, are being created and reworked constantly, by both parties, throughout the process of analysis. Definitions of success, failure, or analytic impasse may be reformulated in terms of language and narrative, so that what we understand about literary constructs has a direct bearing on clinical problems and their solution.[30]

Such a reciprocity of disciplines is implicit in the way I have structured my writing course for psychoanalysts. After the initial session of practical criticism, we match good psychoanalytic writing with fine short fiction. The fiction is selected to allow us to discuss some common problem of presentation, such as the writer's emotional distance from his or her subject, or different approaches to a similar subject, like aging. We begin with a comparison between Anton Chekhov's "Lady with a Pet Dog" and Freud's "Dora," both written at roughly the same time, both remarkably vivid in tone and subtlety of emotion.[31] I usually follow with pairings like the following: Erikson's "Reflections on Dr. Borg's Life Cycle" and John Cheever's "The World of Apples" (two works about aging and death which use dreaming to achieve reconciliation, if not resolution); Stoller's *Splitting* and stories by Flannery O'Connor and Joyce Carol Oates (each about women and violence and each seeking a form which reflects the fragmented world of madness within their central figures).[32] The final class draws entirely from the students' latest clinical reports and concludes as we began, with a form of practical criticism, but one derived now entirely from the students' work, which by this point should demonstrate a new sense of the case history and its relationship to fictional narrative.

I have also made that relationship the subject of an NEH summer seminar for college teachers ("Case History and Fiction: Reciprocal Influences in Narrative Structure"). Its immediate goal was obviously quite different from teaching psychiatrists; but it, too, developed the parallels between psychiatric and literary stories and studies, in much greater detail, and dealt with the way in which each affects the other. Freud's many statements of indebtedness to creative writers are well documented. But if Freud drew from earlier literary models, he also helped to establish a new approach to psychological analysis which quickly found its way back into fiction, from Italo Svevo's *The Confessions of Zeno* to Philip Roth's *Portnoy's Complaint.*

Psychology and sociology have influenced fictional structures, as in the growing use or simulation of tape-recorded material in fiction; meanwhile, the greater stylistic freedom of twentieth-century creative writers, from Joyce and Proust on, has expanded the repertory of approaches available to creative psychoanalysts, like D. W. Winnicott, who also write creatively and far more effectively because they are able to exploit current fictional innovations. Thus when my UCLA students readily fit unidentified quotations from Freud or Stoller into literary categories—unless I have warned them in advance that these quotations include material from case histories (Freud is then sometimes spotted, although Stoller almost never; rather, Virginia Woolf is much more likely to be mistaken for Freud, and someone like Lenny, in Pinter's *The Homecoming,* is consistently diagnosed as a patient, rather brilliantly described by his therapist, perhaps even the product of a session recorded and transcribed!)—their readiness to transpose these categories should not lead us to doubt their capabilities. It indicates, on the contrary, how closely allied are literature and psychology, how strongly they influence one another in formal ways. Demonstrating their shared structures should help analysts to organize their own material and, as I have suggested, to analyze more effectively; it should also expand the normal range of what a college teacher of fiction will teach and alter the way that teacher perceives his or her subject.

In the NEH course we studied, in detail, novels from the

nineteenth-century *Bildungsroman* through Robbe-Grillet and the French "new novel," along with case histories by Freud, Erikson, Winnicott, Stoller, and others. One of the issues which Stoller explores is that of multiple personality, a psychological problem that has achieved quick translation into popular, quasi-fictional forms, like Corbett Thigpen's *The Three Faces of Eve* or Hervey M. Cleckley's *Sybil*. I believe that multiple personality is of particular interest to us now—indeed is something that we are better able to perceive now and hence to identify and correct—because it reflects a modern preoccupation with fragmentation and simultaneity that is also reflected in a great deal of contemporary fiction.

Exposing the NEH class to current psychiatric work in this area offers immediate and vivid examples of the common ground between the newly emerging studies of multiple personality in psychiatry and its fictional corollaries. Two Los Angeles psychiatrists working to refine the diagnosis and treatment of multiple personality have spoken to this NEH seminar, and one has shown a film of his clinical work with such a patient. This patient, like other multiple personality cases I have seen, had responded to an early trauma by splitting herself into a series of personalities, largely unknown to each other. The personalities have different names, different handwriting, different voices, different levels of education and—most significant for treatment—different histories. It is the psychiatrist's job to do what the reader of a modern novel so frequently has to do: to connect disparate, and at times contradictory, stories and attempt to integrate a series of apparently discontinuous narratives. The analyst tries to help the patient to accept affects, like anger or envy, that have been too threatening in the past to acknowledge. The psychiatrist does this, in part, by listening to the various personal histories offered by this split personality and then restating to a core personality all that has been heard, so that the splitting is overcome in part by the merging of narratives while the patient's personalities may blend and unify through the understanding achieved by the final emergence of a single, unified history.

The NEH class also attended one clinic interview of a patient—not a multiple personality case—at UCLA's Neuropsychiatric Institute. I have introduced such a procedure into all of the advanced courses on psychoanalytic literary theory that I have taught at UCLA. Invariably the result has been both to sharpen the theoretical issues already studied and to involve the students most fully—intellectually and emotionally—with psychoanalysis as a living science as well as an abstract theory. Here, too, literature students learn to see the interview as a process—a monologue or dialogue—which requires from the analyst and encourages in the patient an acute sensitivity to words and to the structures of language and stories.[33]

In 1919 Havelock Ellis published an essay that, according to Freud, tried to show that Freud's writings "should be judged not as a piece of scientific work but an artistic production." Freud went on to comment: "We cannot but regard this view as a fresh turn taken by resistance and as a repudiation of analysis, even though it is disguised in a friendly, indeed in too flattering a manner. We are inclined to meet it with a most decided contradiction."[34] Although I am both an analyst and a supporter of the psychoanalytic method, I have taken Ellis's sweetened attack much further. When I refer to psychoanalysis as a "fiction," I am still likely to offend most analysts, although the idea of fiction and fictionalizing has been greatly expanded over the past twenty years and purged of most of its purely negative associations; and when I expose students or teachers of literature to the clinic, I am still met with a great deal of skepticism by both analysts and English professors. The courses I have described here have been devised with individual and sometimes highly specialized goals in mind, such as helping psychiatrists to write more effectively; but they are also directed toward broader problems in both fields.

Analysts, I believe, must become more aware of what literary studies may contribute—beyond the occasional apt quotation from Shakespeare—to their work, even to their own clinical work. And psychoanalytic literary criticism needs, in turn, a firmer connection between theory and clinical practice. Much of the psychoanalytic literary criticism that we ourselves now label "reductive" is developed from a unidirectional point of view: psychoanalysis *explains* literature. Psychoanalysis, particularly in clinical terms, then becomes a mystery into which few are initiated but the validity of which is demonstrated by its application to other fields. Literature is thus transformed into a testing ground for another discipline, and all theory moves in one direction.

Courses on writing and narrative have a special value in the training of psychoanalysts, and psychoanalysis has a useful place in expanding an English department's approach to narrative fiction. We need to encourage mutual explication and influence between these two fields, even, when appropriate, by exposing our students to the clinical appreciation of psychoanalysis. Such reciprocity is essential if both fields are to grow and benefit from the special perspective each provides.

NOTES

1. More precisely, a fellowship enabling a scholar to acquire full training in psychoanalysis was unique, as it marked a major shift in accepting and even encouraging nonmedical candidates to apply for such training. I was not the first academician in America to undertake such training, but the first to benefit so tangibly from a gradual transformation in attitude toward nonmedical candidates.

2. Sigmund Freud, "Postscript" (1927) to "The Question of Lay Analysis," *The Standard Edition of the Complete Psychological Works of Sigmund Freud,* 24 vols. (hereafter abbreviated as *S.E.*), trans. and ed. James Strachey *et al.* (London: Hogarth Press, 1953–64), 20: 256.

3. Ralph Greenson, *The Technique and Practice of Psychoanalysis* (New York: International Universities Press, 1967), pp. 15, 17.

4. The concept of "applied" psychoanalysis has been employed in two very different ways: within the analytic community it may simply describe any *clinical application* of theory, so that the term is virtually synonymous with studies in psychoanalytic technique; it is also used by analysts to describe the application of their own discipline to explicate some work or aspect of another field ("explanation" is often a pretext for what they may regard as implicit "proof" for an analytic concept "tested" on a nonanalytic subject). This second meaning, psychoanalysis applied *outside* psychoanalysis itself, has now achieved general currency. Beyond a few clinical and highly specialized essays, the second meaning is in fact the *only* meaning of "applied psychoanalysis" for nonanalytic writers, and it has become the most common meaning, as well, within the analytic community.

Freud tended to use it in this broader sense, most definitively it seemed, in his "Autobiographical Study" of 1925, in which he devoted an entire section to the "History of applied analysis" (*S.E.* 20: 62–70). But in 1933, in lecture 34 of his *New Introductory Lectures on Psychoanalysis* (*S.E.* 22: 136–96), entitled "Explanations, *Applications,* and Orientations" [my italics], he reverted to the far more limited, technical use of the term. And again, in his "Postscript" to "The Question of Lay Analysis" (S.E. 20: 257), he comments that "for practical reasons we have been in the habit—and this is true, incidentally, in our publications as well—of distinguishing between medical and applied analysis. But that is not a logical distinction. The true line of division is between *scientific* analysis and its *applications* alike in medical and in non-medical fields." And here he does manage to obfuscate the entire issue!

5. In his 1984 presidential address to the American Psychoanalytic Association, Dr. Arnold M. Cooper estimated an "active membership of roughly 1250" (*Journal of the American Psychoanalytic Association* 32 [1984]: 259). Even if he is using "active" to limit the figure dramatically, analysts comprise no more than 10 percent of licensed psychiatrists, usually less, and the American Psychiatric Association has about 25,000 members; the American Medical Association has a membership in excess of 300,000. And given the full population of this country, the number of analysts, active or otherwise, is miniscule. Similarly, the *Roster of the International Psychoanalytic Association: 1984*, which includes a "list of the regional associations, component & Provisional Societies, study groups and direct members of the International Psychoanalytic Association," and which covers North and South America, Europe, the Middle East, Australia, and the Provisional Society of Hungary, as well as study groups from Cordoba to Peru, lists 115 pages of names, with under sixty names per page. Fewer than 7,000 people even remotely entitled to claim, world-wide, to be students or practitioners of psychoanalysis is infinitesimal—particularly when we consider what seems its comparably infinite capacity to generate interest, reference, general conversation, and theoretical appropriation in every form.

6. Edward Glover, *The Technique of Psychoanalysis* (New York: International Universities Press, 1974 [first published in 1955]), p. 7.

7. The last phrase is from one of the field's more articulate opponents. In *Speak Memory* (Harmondsworth, England: Penguin, 1969), Vladimir Nabokov snarls at his reader straight away: "Let me say at once that I reject completely the vulgar, shabby, fundamentally medieval world of Freud, with its crankish quest for sexual symbols" (p. 18). But "once" is obviously not enough, since Nabokov seems to find Freud continually in his way and requiring perennial dismissal. His memory is still speaking, on page 230 of that same book, knowing "of course . . . what the Viennese Quack thought of the matter." The "of course" is more presumptuously "medieval" and doctrinaire than anything in Freud, who certainly never claimed oracular powers.

8. Freud, "The Question of Lay Analysis," *S.E.* 20: 192.

9. It is difficult to decide whether analysis and its application is more undermined by its enthusiastically uninformed proponents or by

its more articulate enemies. David Bleich's *Subjective Criticism* (Baltimore and London: The John Hopkins University Press, 1978) is a convincing argument in favor of the first premise. Bleich takes on all of western philosophy, enlisting in his corner, usually through misrepresentation, an occasional heavyweight like Einstein, whose theories are summarized simplistically ("The Theory of Relativity" is "evidence" that all is "relative," and hence supports Bleich's claim that all is subjective!). He then does battle with every major thinker in western society before stepping back to act both as referee and judge, not surprisingly declaring himself victorious over all prior contenders, from Plato to Popper. This practice helps to lower the status of one of the most potentially interesting uses of psychoanalysis: approaching a text through the responses of its readers.

On the other hand, Frederick Crews's regular attacks on psychoanalysis—intelligently articulate, well-informed, and remarkably smooth in their often evasive rhetoric—make it impossible to decide who most effectively misrepresents psychoanalysis: its enemies or its "friends."

In his latest renunciation of a former faith, Crews reviews with careful fervor two recent studies, critical in very different ways of the "scientific basis" of psychoanalysis as an independent discipline: Adolf Grünbaum's *Foundations of Psychoanalysis: A Philosophical Critique* (Berkeley: University of California Press, 1984), and Marshall Edelson's *Hypothesis and Evidence in Psychoanalysis* (Chicago: University of Chicago Press, 1984) (Frederick Crews, "The Future of an Illusion," *The New Republic*, 21 January 1985, pp. 28–33). Crews is even-handedly acerbic, describing his colleagues as "literary pundits, who tend to think of themselves as experts in the world-historical vicissitudes of Desire," literary critics who "still feel free to pillage the Freudian system of its most 'powerful' concepts" (p. 28). But Crews cannot see his own brand of pillaging, used in this case only to attack the system, avoiding those aspects of psychoanalysis—or of a more even-handed, scrupulous, and rigorous logic—that might correct some of its misassumptions and help to make it more useful in its potential application.

Whether Crews resorts to the rhetorical trick of putting *powerful* in quotation marks or, by the insinuating question, leaves behind a trail of accusations without supporting evidence ("Did he [Freud] derive a good part of his supposedly original doctrine from misconstrued evolutionism and from his overreaching friend Wilhelm Fliess?" [p. 28]), Crews himself is still referring to "*the* Freudian system" [my italics], as if there were only one. Or at least he does so until he switches strategies in order to use the competing explanatory systems of psychoanalytic theories as yet another form of deflation ("this Babel of analytic voices").

Toward the end of the essay Crews will approvingly declare, on behalf of Grünbaum, the latter's successful demolition of the claims made by those who argue for the necessary combination of clinical and theoretical understanding before using analysis—on the couch or in the classroom. Here Crews sums up a position he has unquestioningly accepted but presented without a detailed examination of evidence. Instead, he resorts to the technique of considering anyone who would take issue with his conclusions as implicitly unreasonable or foolishly optimistic: "Grünbaum shows that neither the supposed data nor the causal constructions they extract from that situation [the correctives of clinical experience] deserve the trust of a reasonably skeptical person." Then let me wonder how Crews is in a position to affirm such a position when he repeatedly fails to understand these same clinical complexities.

In discussing the complex concept of free association, for example, Crews begins by ignoring its clinical functions, treating it as a purely theoretical abstraction. Once more loading his terms *(official, supposedly)*, Crews describes the process inaccurately: "In the official view, data gathered by analysts are considered adequately uncontaminated because they are largely products of 'free association', a process supposedly allowing the patient's unconscious to express itself without the therapist's interference." But as the "official" writings on analytic technique describe in detail, the concept of free association is enacted in a deliberately paradoxical way: repression is made manifest as "the fundamental rule" is (and must be) violated, and the clinical work of the analytic process is initiated by that violation and its interpretation. The concept to which Crews alludes and then quickly dismisses is misunderstood precisely because it is presented as pure theory, denied the clinical dimension that makes it such an essential, if complex, concept in the total psychoanalytic enterprise.

Crews also joins other critics who question the "scientific" validation of analysis, but he contributes nothing new by returning to the premises of Logical Positivism, insisting that we isolate "objective" data—measurable, subject to the kind of experimental proof that characterizes scientific validation in chemistry—in any study of human behavior and social interaction. On the contrary, he repeatedly displays his misunderstandings of the analytic process. Repeating a question first posed by Grünbaum, for example, Crews urges us to suppose for the sake of argument "that an analyst could glean uncontaminated data from the clinical situation—for example, newly unearthed memories of scenes and conflicts from childhood. How would the analyst know, Grünbaum asks, that those scenes and conflicts were causally relevant to the adult patient's neurosis?" But how can Crews—or Grünbaum—seriously suppose that "newly unearthed memories of scenes and conflicts from childhood" would ever be presented by the patient, much less "gleaned" by the analyst, in an "uncontaminated" way?

Such an argument is especially ironic coming from a literary critic like Crews, sensitive to emotional nuance, tone, the power of words and image, all "data" in his own field that he has elsewhere described so effectively, but that neither he nor any literary critic has ever succeeded in measuring, quantifying for experimental validation, or gleaning "in an uncontaminated way" from the literary text. Meanwhile, Crews's standards for scientific objectivity and validation for a field so often referred to by its own practitioners as an art seem needlessly skewed.

And Crews's case against analysis is strikingly selective, particularly when he refers to the above-cited 1982 presidential address by Dr. Arnold Cooper to the American Psychoanalytic Association (Crews calls it "a document that is more eloquent than it was meant to be" [p. 29]). Thus Crews summarizes Cooper's conclusions: "According to him, what psychoanalysis chiefly needs is more research, conducted by analysts themselves, to settle the 'exciting debates' raging within the field" (p. 30). This simply misrepresents Cooper, who finds these debates exciting insofar as they *are* disturbing, insofar as they call into question the most traditional premises of his own field without alienating the newer, critical movements and splintering the discipline as a whole: "As we all know, significant theoretical disagreements in psychoanalysis did not always evolve in this way in the past. This newer way of handling our differences [mutual education and influence during the recent, 'raucous battle' over Kohut's reevaluation of analytic theory and practice] is a sign of our growing up" (Cooper, p. 246).

More important, Cooper insists that change most often comes from *outside* the closed circle of psychoanalytic training and the writings of medical practitioners: "information not psychoanalytically derived . . . will be [increasingly] important" (p. 255); "psychoanalysis is far too important to be left only to psychoanalysts" (p. 264); "some group of our educational institutions must take seriously our scientific and intellectual obligations and assure that psychoanalysis and the multiplicity of scientific and intellectual fields adjacent to it will continue to inform and enrich each other. Applied psychoanalysis has only begun to make its potential contribution, and the number of people able to make such contributions is still far too small" (p. 263).

Cooper spends the final two pages of his address discussing Freud's wish for "a college of psychoanalysis," and reminds us that Freud himself had urged radical shifts in " 'analytic instruction' " that " 'would include branches of knowledge which are remote from medicine . . . the history of civilization, mythology, the psychology of religion and the science of literature' " (p. 264). The final reference strikes home in two ways. It not only demonstrates that, from its origins, psychoanalysis has sought interdisciplinary research in its best sense, but that it has also used 'science' in its broadest meaning, not the science of physics or mathematics but rather science in its earliest definition, a "possession of knowledge, as contrasted with ignorance or misunderstanding" (the first definition of the term from *Webster's New International Dictionary*, 2nd ed., 1949). The "evidence" Crews and others find wanting is not available, nor is it applicable to a field closer to literary or historical study than to physics, where a Newtonian proposition must be subject to such empirical testing and validation. This is a distinction, as it happens, that Cooper himself does not entirely understand.

10. As my comments throughout this article and its notes reflect, I am often annoyed, in much applied Lacanian psychoanalysis, by what I find to be either a deliberately obfuscating prose or a claim to a peculiar Freudian "orthodoxy." But throughout these periodic assaults on "French Freud" my fundamental objection is consistent with the major premise of this article—that clinical experience should correct and moderate an otherwise overstated and reductionistic theory. My quarrel with so much of Lacan, only reinforced with the recent publication in English of one of his case presentations, was neatly put by Richard Wollheim, in a review entitled "The Cabinet of Dr. Lacan": "Lacan totally depreciates the contribution of experience to psychoanalytic explanation, and it becomes clear that the absence from his writing of case histories and clinical illustration is not just an eccentricity of explanation" (*New York Review of Books*, January 25, 1979, p. 44).

11. Greenson, *The Technique and Practice of Psychoanalysis*, p. 26.

12. Glover urges the beginning analyst to pay particular attention to the patient's affect after the requirement for free association has been explained and the patient is trying to abide by it, because affect is so often the only clue to understanding how and why the rule has been broken at any given moment. "We may be sure," adds Glover, "that, however well intentioned, the patient will straight away neglect this recommendation, and . . . will fail consistently to give any indication of his feelings. In short we may as well face that fact that *from the moment the fundamental rule has been expounded to the patient and has ostensibly been accepted by him, a large part of the analyst's work will up to the last moment consist in an endeavour to circumvent its evasion*" (*The Technique and Practice of Psychoanalysis*, p. 27).

13. J. Laplanche and J.-B. Pontalis, *The Language of Psychoanalysis*, trans. Donald Nicholson-Smith (New York: Norton, 1973, first printed in French in 1967), pp. 178–79. Note that the English version is expanded. Based particularly on the experience of Daniel Lagache, who writes in the English introduction of having "read and discussed most of the draft articles together" (p. ix) with Laplanche and Pontalis, many entries are supplemented, sometimes doubled in size. Thus the entry

cited here is exactly as it appears under "Règle Fondamentale" in the original, but the subsequent reference to "Acting Out" adds more than a full page of commentary to the original, one-page "Mise en Acte."

14. Laplanche and Pontalis, *The Language of Psychoanalysis,* pp. 4–6. And here we have to assume that the "conclusion" is made for them, very possibly as they wished, by the much longer entry in the English version from which I quote. Both versions, however, begin in identical ways and use, or do not use, original German terms, as cited.

15. Greenson, *The Technique and Practice of Psychoanalysis,* pp. 68–69.

16. Joseph Sandler, Christopher Dare, and Alex Holder, *The Patient and the Analyst: The Basis of the Psychoanalytic Process* (New York: International Universities Press, 1973), p. 94.

17. Sandler, Dare, and Holder, *The Patient and the Analyst,* pp. 94–96; but their excellent and exhaustive definition occupies an entire chapter, entitled "Acting Out," pp. 94–103, and is well worth reading in its entirety.

18. Laplanche and Pontalis, *The Language of Psychoanalysis,* pp. 4–6. The initial critique of Freud's "confusion" based on their partial translation from the German is identical in both French and English. However, the subsequent conclusion, the argument for what Freud "enshrines," is considerably expanded in the English version.

My italicized reference to *Returning to Freud* is specifically to Stuart Schneiderman's edition and translation, *Returning to Freud: Clinical Psychoanalysis in the School of Lacan* (New Haven and London: Yale University Press, 1980); but it also alludes to a general belief among one group of analysts who regard Lacan, in both his theories and his practice, as truly "orthodox," rediscovering (and sometimes correcting) Freud's original meanings. James David Fisher, writing on "Lacan's Ambiguous Impact on Contemporary French Psychoanalysis" (*Contemporary French Civilization* 7: 1–2 [Fall/Winter, 1981–82]: 89–114), describes Lacan's claim "that contemporary psychoanalytic theory has mistakenly attempted to discipline or unseat the primary process by rendering it in a closed system. He asserts that the unconscious cannot be bottled up, categorized, domesticated, immobilized." As a result, Lacan's "project" is in part "to liberate psychoanalytic discourse from the arbitrary constraints of Freud's followers and codifiers. Returning to Freud means returning to the unconscious at the level of language" (p. 94).

Lacan wants to rescue the "true" Freud from his misguided followers by returning to Freud's original "intent." Yet he rejects any portrayal of himself as a traditionalist: on the contrary, he perceives his work as radical and liberating, taking off from Freud's early view of analysis as a "talking cure" both to recreate this original concept more fully and to create an entirely new version of Freud because of Lacan's own commitment to a linguistic model for all of psychoanalysis. Fisher writes: "His clinical and theoretical stance privileges the realm of speech and language, while de-emphasizing that of affects and drives. For him the analytic situation is incomprehensible unless the analyst becomes aware of the prime determining role of language in all human exchanges. Language is for him everything, the technique and cure nothing" (p. 95).

Lacan is perhaps the most striking example of an analyst who divides theory, or metapsychology, from practice. Unless they are drawn to see him *because* of their particular neuroses, it is hard to imagine patients cheered at the prospect of being treated by someone who considers "cure nothing." In an unpublished paper ("Clinical Aspects of Lacan's Theory: The Contaminated Interview"), discussing the presentation Lacan permits Schneiderman to publish, Fisher claims that "Lacan's theoretical project is designed to provide a therapy for the psychoanalytic profession as a whole; it is not designed for the benefit of his patients." And, again commenting on this presentation of "Monsieur Primeau," Fisher writes that it "suggests . . . that Lacan sees patients as problems, as linguistic puzzles to unravel, as complex systems which express themselves in language." Schneiderman speaks of "the analyst's obligation to recognize his analysand's desire" but never indicates how this might be done. Further, he makes axiomatic claims of dubious value: "The neurotic patient presents himself for an analysis because he does not know what he wants." That has certainly not been my general experience, nor that of most of my colleagues. In Schneiderman's most recent book, *Jacques Lacan: The Death of an Intellectual Hero* (Cambridge, Mass.: Harvard University Press, 1983), he comments that "nothing real happens in a psychoanalysis; the real must always remain outside. Perhaps because Lacan was hysterical and histrionic, he saw analysis as akin to theater" (p. 37). Perhaps. But Lacan does not seem to offer much of anything *except* theatricality to his patients, having "said that psychoanalysis did not have as its goal curing patients, and that if people in analysis did get better it was a welcome side effect" (p. 50). He certainly did not make it any easier for the patient to get better; on the contrary, he seems to have resented his patients, particularly when they were somehow able, in spite of his methods, to find some satisfaction and self-understanding. In the "Primeau" case Lacan systematically interrupts Primeau every time Primeau attempts to explain his feelings, which, quite naturally, begin to include a good deal of frustration and anger.

Lacan's famous "ten-minute session" is justified as healthy for the patient, shocking him into reality and obliging him to recognize that there is *no* setting of reliability, no situation for a relaxation that will allow for free association. "People in analysis," writes Schneiderman, "often yield up a mass of verbiage whose purpose is to confuse the issue and to cloud over the question. Lacan must have felt that talking too much often was used as a resistance to avoiding the issues. Something about the freedom to say anything that comes to mind is simply too satisfying for the analysand, and this intense satisfaction, often experienced as an erotic satisfaction, is a barrier to desire." Yet analysts have understood the defensive functions of free association from the start.

More balanced in her reading of Lacan is Sherry Turkle's *Psychoanalytic Politics: Freud's French Revolution* (Cambridge, Mass.: MIT Press, 1981), in which she has a chapter not on "returning to Freud" but " 'Reinventing' Freud in France." By placing Lacan within a social and political framework and describing in detail his belief in analysis as a personal calling and a platform for anti-institutional attack, she manages to make more sense out of his most questionable "technical innovations," like his "ten-minute session,"

19. "Analysis Terminable and Interminable," *S.E.* 23: 248; see also *S.E.* 19: 243.

20. Janet Malcolm, *Psychoanalysis: The Impossible Profession* (New York: Random House, 1982), p. 37. Freud's use of "impossible" was less dismissive than Malcolm's; in a strangely Teutonic way it was also ironic but not especially amusing:

> Here let us pause for a moment to assure the analyst that he has our sincere sympathy in the very exacting demands he has to fulfil in carrying out his activities. It almost looks as if analysis were the third of those "impossible" professions in which one can be sure beforehand of achieving unsatisfying results. The other two, which have been known much longer, are education and government. Obviously we cannot demand that the prospective analyst be a perfect being before he takes up analysis, in other words that only persons of such high and rare perfection should enter the profession. But where and how is the poor wretch to acquire the ideal qualifications which he will need in his profession? (*S.E.* 23: 248)

He also recognized the impossible demand, for example, made on the analyst to reciprocate the patient's required "free association" by "free-floating attention," a listening uncontaminated either by the outside world or by any internal turmoil: an evenly suspended and (somehow) entirely neutral, intelligent, thoroughly trained *mind-turned-tabula-rasa-every-forty-five-or-fifty-minutes* in the service of the patient. Malcolm retranslates the technical term as "evenly suspended attention" and reappraises its impossible goals from a more amused perspective: "the aimless, Zen-like state of desirelessness in which he [the analyst] listens" (Malcolm, p. 26).

21. *S.E.* 20: 257–58.

22. Talcott Parsons, "On Building Social System Theory: A Personal History," *Daedalus* 99 (1970): 826–81. *The Structures of Social Action*

(New York: Free Press) was first published in 1937, republished in 1949, and it has, in Parsons's own description, "maintained a steady substantial sale for over thirty years," moving at that point into a paperback edition which also "sold well" through his own description of its sales in the autobiographical article (p. 877, n. 22).

23. Given the estimated costs of such training, the fellowship allowed the institute to select from a much larger pool of applicants: young but promising, or more senior, well-established scholars who had written in this field but would obviously benefit from clinical exposure. Without the various supports provided to research candidates—a $10,000 fellowship, waiver of all tuition fees, and usually a reduced fee for the required "training analysis"—the costs of psychoanalytic education would eliminate young academicians and most senior ones, unless they were independently wealthy. And this would of course absurdly restrict the institute's choice.

As the fellowships multiplied and the program worked even more effectively than first anticipated, the once-isolated institute suddenly found itself at the center of a modest version of the renowned, pre-war "Frankfurt School" (which had included, among others, Theodor Adorno and Herbert Marcuse). Exchanges between the institute and surrounding universities (UCLA in particular, which now has some nine graduates or candidates in training at the SCPI) have flourished: analysts regularly help by appearing in university classes to discuss case material or to provide filmed cases of their own, or, where appropriate, classes from the humanities and social sciences that make extensive use of psychoanalysis have been brought to psychiatric clinics and institutes to observe patient interviews, followed by discussion with the interviewing analyst.

Similarly, instead of the disdainful distance usually maintained by both groups over the latest and most revolutionary thinking about psychoanalysis (what the other group would dismiss as a passing "fad"), radical changes now occurring in clinical work and hotly debated on theoretical grounds, like Kohutian "Self-Psychology," have attracted large audiences from both the universities and the institutes, the two usually combining to sponsor major conferences on these subjects. And, somewhat less spectacularly, recent French approaches to psychoanalysis are being presented (in formal evening classes) to clinical associates and senior analysts alike by academicians who have studied, or even worked with, figures like Lacan or Jacques Derrida.

24. Assembly Bill (AB) 246 was passed by the California State Assembly on 9 September 1977, the State Senate on 13 September, and passed into law on 30 September 1977. *Section 1, Chapter 5.1,* begins under the heading "Research Psychoanalysts": "Graduates of the Southern California Psychoanalytic Institute, the Los Angeles Psychoanalytic

Society and Institute, the San Francisco Psychoanalytic Institute, the San Diego Psychoanalytic Institute, or institutes deemed equivalent by the Division of Allied Health Professions who have completed clinical training in psychoanalysis may engage in psychoanalysis as an adjunct to teaching, training, or research and hold themselves out to the public as psychoanalysts. . . ."

25. Robert J. Stoller, *Splitting: A Case of Female Masculinity* (New York: Dell, 1974), p. 329. All ellipses except the last are Stoller's and indicate either pauses or breaks in the narrative flow.

26. Steven Marcus, "Freud and Dora: Story, History, Case History," *Partisan Review* 16 (1974): 92.

27. Freud, *Fragment of an Analysis of a Case of Hysteria* [Dora], *S.E.* 7: 9.

28. [Dora] *S.E.* 7: 59.

29. *Studies in Hysteria* (Frau Emmy von N.), *S.E.* 2: 79.

30. See, for example, Roy Schafer's gradual and significant attempt to create *A New Language for Psychoanalysis* (New Haven: Yale University Press, 1976). Schafer not only recognizes the problems with current analytic jargon and the importance of language as a key to clinical interpretation; he also introduces literary genres (romance, comedy, irony, tragedy) to clarify and evaluate the analytic process. He concedes to his fellow analysts that the introduction of such terms "suggest[s] that it is my subversive intention to undercut the hard-won scientific gains and status of psychoanalysis by an insidious switch to visionary philosophy and literary device" (pp. 24–25). Although he maintains that every original investigation is potentially subversive and hopes further to turn his attention "to the roots of psychoanalysis in the humanities," Schafer is careful in this initial assault on analytic language to qualify the analytic exchange as something created or imagined while he denies its fictional qualities—or, rather, restricts his definition of fiction to its more limiting and pejorative sense as lie or distortion: ". . . the analytically created life history, while not fictive, is also not what one might call the absolute truth" (pp. 49–50).

But with the works that followed, and that carried much further this radical assault on traditional analytic attitudes as well as therapeutic speech and its implications, he discards much of the classic trappings of energy systems and more openly embraces the most positive use of fictional narrative. Thus, in a chapter on "Narration in the Psychoanalytic Dialogue" from *The Analytic Attitude* (New York: Basic Books, 1983), he writes:

> Freud established a tradition within which psychoanalysis is understood as an essentialist and positivist natural science. One need not be bound by this scientific commitment, however; the individual and general accounts and

interpretations Freud gave of his case material can be read in another way. In this reading, psychoanalysis is an interpretive discipline whose practitioners aim to develop a particular kind of systematic account of human action. We can say, then, either Freud was developing a set of principles for participating in, understanding, and explaining the dialogue between psychoanalyst and analysand or that he was establishing a set of codes to generate psychoanalytic meaning, recognizing this meaning in each instance to be only one of a number of kinds of meaning that might be generated. (p. 212)

See also Schafer's *Aspects of Internalization* (New York: International Universities Press, 1968), working very much with the same issues.

31. Ironically, I matched these two works which Malcolm discusses at such length well before her articles first appeared; of particular interest to me is the discussion she has with the fictional composite-analyst, Aaron Green, about the Chekov story. Her comments and agreements, certainly his strangely moralistic and constrained responses, and even the summaries of the story each renders tell us an extraordinary amount about Malcolm and the depressed, prototypical analyst she has created in Green. Their different readings of the same literary work suggest their shared misconceptions, both on the nature of narrative and on the technique of analysis; and nowhere does Malcolm show us as clearly how she has managed to make Green seem at once "real" yet very unrealistic in his sense of self and of work, so that she is able to make the profession as a whole convincingly depressing—rather than impossible.

32. Erik Erickson, "Reflections on Dr. Borg's Life Cycle," *Daedalus* 105 (1976): 1–28; Flannery O'Conner, "A Good Man Is Hard to Find," and Joyce Carol Oates "Upon the Sweeping Flood."

33. Dr. Stephen Marmer has regularly and generously admitted literary groups to certain of his psychiatric interviews, before discussing with us the nature of the interaction following the interview. He has commented to me that often, after he has finished interviewing the patient and asked if any of us have questions, he will discover that many graduate literature students either raise new but important points or rephrase something he has stated, but in a helpfully different way. We are of course always careful to inform the patient in advance of these observations and only to request permission from those patients we feel are appropriate to begin with—not a paranoid patient, for example!—and even one whose sense of self might, if anything, be enhanced by so much concentrated interest; and Marmer has then frequently noted this additional gain in therapeutic insight from the informed but very different perspectives of such groups.

In 1982, at the divisional meeting of the MLA Literature and Psychology Group in Los Angeles, I was also president of that division. I asked Dr. Marmer to present again, using this time one of his videotapes from work with a multiple personality case. Our discussant, Professor Peter Manning of USC, immediately raised difficult, important, and emotionally charged issues. The discussion then generated by this case material ignited the entire audience into one of the most passionate and informative debates I've ever heard at an MLA meeting. It was certainly a dramatic example of the power and immediacy created when issues of analytic theory are grounded in the immediacy of clinical practice. This single example seemed to bring the theory alive and to remind us all that its context involves the life and mental health of another person; it also demonstrated how educationally important and powerful a genuinely interdisciplinary study may be.

Multiple personality itself has grown in interest over the past few years; within the last three months a national conference, entirely devoted to that subject, took place for the first time. Both Dr. Stoller and Dr. Marmer, leading theorists in this field, have spoken to and demonstrated (through videotape) examples of this phenomenon to several of my UCLA classes and to the NEH course. Obviously the unusually positive experience I have enjoyed here—at both UCLA and the SCPI—has been dependent upon the generosity and thoughtfulness of such psychiatrists, who have given an enormous amount of unremunerated time and energy to participating in these programs. I hope it in no way diminishes that generosity to point out that their own motivation derives not so much from doing a favor for a colleague but from the essential and almost contagious curiosity they have, as active researchers and analytic thinkers, in learning from, as well as contributing to, such academic experiments. Obviously the institutes have produced, and continue to produce, more than the stereotypical "Babbitt analyst" I have described, but rather analysts who are, like these two, concerned with "scientific knowledge" in its best and broadest sense.

34. *Beyond the Pleasure Principle, S.E.* 18: 44.

SUSAN WELLS

Jürgen Habermas, Communicative Competence, and the Teaching of Technical Discourse

An enormous body of technical and scientific discourse penetrates and regulates both production and consumption in our culture. Such writing, and the service of the administrative paper world that forms its social context, absorbs the working time and energy of any number of technically trained people. Just how much time and energy, it is not easy to determine: this writing is often ephemeral, and corporations are not anxious to open their proprietary files to researchers. But our best information suggests that the average entry-level technician writes for some eight hours a week and that time spent writing increases with rank and position.[1]

Even as production and administration are represented in a paper world of technical discourse, technical discourse has generated its own educational reflection—the technical writing program. And such programs, especially in the United States, have been growing rapidly. In 1969, publishers of technical writing textbooks sold 25,000 volumes; in 1981, they sold some 250,000. In 1972, the Association of Teachers of Technical Writing was founded with ten members; in 1981, there were nearly a thousand.[2] Grant support for curriculum development and basic research in technical writing has been forthcoming from the Fund for the Improvement of Postsecondary Education and the National Institutes of Education. Major universities grant advanced degrees in technical and professional communications; it has become a recognized academic speciality.

We could dismiss such programs as high-tech academic fads or as shameful collaboration with corporate manipulation of the university, or we could simply find them academically unrespectable. And there is a basis, as I will show, for all these positions. But these criticisms of technical writing and its teaching also have a disturbing mandarin tone of regret for a past when the university was uncontaminated by social life. That tone should give us pause. What is required, I think, is a careful analysis of technical discourse and of the social relations which it forms and within which it is produced. This analysis would begin with a critique of the current theory of technical discourse and the pedagogy it responds to, proceed to a critical examination of technical discourse as it emerges in social situations, and finally sketch out an emancipatory understanding of technical discourse and how it might function in the classroom.

Let me begin by surveying the current theory of technical writing. A body of rhetorical theory informs the pedagogy for technical writing, published in journals such as the *Journal of Technical Writing and Communications* or the *Technical Writing Teacher,* in collections published by the National Council of Teachers of English, and in the materials in the ERIC data base. Put crudely, this is a discipline in which writers know things but have a hard time situating what they know. Technical-writing theorists would readily grant many ideas that are contested within, or simply excluded from, the normal discourse of the humanities. They know, for example, that there is a relationship between discourse and power, so they write advice like this: "No [written set of] directions should permit the luxury of decision; it is fatiguing in itself and holds the possibility of error."[3] They know that in parts of the world quite remote from metropolitan intellectual centers English may well be the vehicle for technical and professional communication. Teaching classes with a high population of foreign students—over 50 percent in some programs[4]—the technical-writing teacher knows that life on the underdeveloped periphery is *different:* "Semiskilled and nonskilled Nigerian staff are far less proficient, and show far less initiative, than their opposite numbers in developed nations. . . . There is a constant temptation to add hastily that they are charming, helpful, and friendly people."[5] And writers in this discipline probably think and study more about what happens to their students after graduation than in any other area of the humanities: "Teachers of technical communication need to learn something about the perceptions and attitudes students bring to their courses in order to know where to begin indoctrinating them to the demands of the professional world."[6] My introductions to the exhibits in this little horror show are not entirely ironic. I am suggesting that, while the aim of a critique is typically to reveal a hidden structure of interest and domination, such a project would be pointless for the rhetoric of technical discourse. The ideology of technical writing explicitly assents to its instrumental subordination to capital; the aim of the discipline as a whole is to become a more responsive tool. Many technical writing teachers see themselves as academic counterparts to the corporate communications officer. Nor is this identification wholly disinterested. Long excluded from lucrative industrial consulting jobs, English teachers can finally hope to share this wealth by developing an expertise in technical or professional communication. Unlike, say, an ordinary language philosopher, a technical writer would not be shaken by a critique that his or her work served domination. A discipline founded on the principle of service is not ashamed to be of use.

There is perhaps no program of study in any of the traditional humanistic departments that is so instrumental, or so closely adapted to the norms of corporate life, as that in technical writing. The technical-writing course is often directed toward specific job functions, as in "writing for engineers" or "writing for nurses." It is a frank attempt to prepare students for a typical white collar job. Yet to develop an effective critique of the theory and practice of technical discourse, we must move further inside the discipline and the discourse that it strives to represent. Making such an analysis is not simply a rhetorical ploy to catch the attention of communications directors. It is also a way of broadening the scope of critical theory. Since critical theorists have moved beyond the analysis of high cultural texts and explicitly political documents, since we have taken popular culture and the discourse of everyday life seriously, it is appropriate to extend still further the range of texts we analyse and to look very concretely at the technical, scientific, and professional discourse whose production and processing takes up so many working days and which, in a variety of ways, penetrates all of our lives. While the quotations I have chosen do not misrepresent the current range of work in technical writing, they are not the most advanced work in the area. Such writers as Elizabeth Harris, Carolyn Miller, and Linda Flower have constructed more sophisticated theories of technical discourse. In some cases, these theories have been marked by the scientistic self-understanding of the discourse they studied; other theorists have adopted the traditional humanist critique of technology, with contradictory results, while some have recreated the critique of science and technology developed by the Frankfurt School. Moreover, all these positions are transformed by their location within the discourse of rhetorical theory; they all mean something a little different from what they say.

Let me examine this theory, moving from it to the canonic Frankfurt School critique of technology, Max Horkheimer and Theodor Adorno's *Dialectic of Enlightenment.*[7] I will then consider Jürgen Habermas's more recent analysis of communicative competence and suggest that it provides a better basis for a critique of technical discourse and its rhetorical theory. I will develop this argument through an account of a technical writing situation and an analysis of the discourse it generated.

Linda Flower is a convenient example of the scientistic self-understanding of technical-writing theory. Working with a group of researchers at Carnegie Mellon University, Flower has undertaken empirical studies of how readers understand texts and how writers produce them.[8] But although Flower began with the modest goal of catching some glimpses of the writing process, she has become more insistent in describing the protocols as a direct revelation of what writers and readers "really do" in the quite different natural situations of producing and decoding text. A descriptive study of how readers and writers act in laboratories becomes a series of prescriptions for what processes writers ought to follow. Thus, "skilled writers" tend to make elaborate plans for their texts, to think about their audience while writing, and to stay "on task" more than unskilled writers. Unskilled writers are prone to reverie, aimless syntactic play, and false starts. Students are urged to emulate skilled writers.[9] In Flower's analysis, the text has been defined in positivist terms—a text is its cognitive content, abstracted from social relations and the subjectivity of reader and writer. All its indeterminate elements are ignored or treated as simple "errors" that better planning would have eliminated. Flower's work recapitulates, in a compressed form, the progress of scientism: she moves from the "natural history" of an object, in this case reading and writing, through sketches of a global model, into attempts to direct intervention and control.

Against the doubled positivism that defines technical writing as a scientific enterprise to be studied scientifically, other writers have proposed a renovation of the traditional rhetorical model for studying discourse. Elizabeth Harris's "In Defense of the Liberal-Arts Approach to Technical Writing" can stand as an example of this trend.[10] Arguing against a proposal that technical writing be taught by schools of engineering rather than departments of English, Harris maintains that a liberal-arts approach to technical discourse is more appropriate to the study of written texts than an engineering approach would be. She would draw on the concepts and methods of "literary theory and history, traditional and modern rhetoric, linguistics, and the philosophy and history of science and technology." Harris's argument might seem to be one more attempt to extend traditional humanism to new subject areas. That conclusion might be supported by reading her analyses of specific forms and texts, which divorce technical and scientific documents from social forms, historical contexts, and concrete relations of power and influence. It is not surprising that she affiliates technical rhetoric with the "mission of literary criticism" as defined by Matthew Arnold: the creation of "current and new ideas."

But to dismiss Harris's work as mere "humanism" would be mistaken; such a criticism reads her work abstractly, matching it against ideological schemata. It would be more appropriate to interpret Harris's position within its specific discursive context, placing Matthew Arnold against the collection of quotations in the first few pages of this article. Arnold then is no longer a pious icon, but an authority invoked to support an unorthodox position—a critique of the theory of technical writing as "language engineering." Harris's most significant move in the dispute over technical writing instruction is her denial that "we already know or can find out casually what to count or otherwise observe in technical-writing texts and in the processes by which they are generated and received." Here, Harris raises the question of what technical discourse is, and raises it in terms that do not permit a simple empirical answer. As long as that question is held open, the possibility of a critical discussion of technical and scientific writing remains. A positivist definition of the field would close any inquiry into questions of meaning, any attempt to raise the possibility of transforming discourse and the social relations it shapes and expresses.

(At this point, any number of readers are probably thinking about moving on to some other essay. Except for the rare technical-writing teacher who has strayed into this volume, who has heard of these people? Who intends to read them? Why this account of a tiny eddy of controversy in an academic backwater? Because technical writing isn't quite respectable. Because a backwater is also an interesting margin. Because this is a very old dispute, a dispute that was already old for Plato. Because what is contested and conceded here will affect students, will flow almost directly into the discourse of production. Because this theory grapples with questions of language in situations where domination is very hard to forget, so that it supplies us with new information about language and domination.)

An attempt to answer Harris's question about the nature of scientific and technical discourse informed Carolyn Miller's earlier essay, "Technology as a Form of Consciousness: A Study of Contemporary Ethos."[11] Writing on the traditional problem of distinguishing science from technology, Miller held that technical discourse is characterized by a belief in objectivity, interest in structures of cause and effect, externalization of the category of purpose, and exclusion of questions of value. In technical discourse, efficiency, conformity, and competition are valued, and the world is seen as a closed system, to be explained algorithmically. Rhetorically, technical discourse devalues invention, equates rhetoric and logic, and constrains a writer to "impersonal, irresponsible, turgid, narrow-minded discourse" (p. 234). Finally, Miller insists that the technological worldview operates silently: "This is the insidious aspect of technological consciousness—it would hold that it itself does not exist" (p. 236). At this point we might conclude that even though Miller is using the term *consciousness,* she is really talking about *ideology,* a term which Miller does employ, albeit somewhat casually.

The central concerns of Miller's essay are also familiar—the global critique of a culture "taken over" by instrumental activity, the forcible bracketing of causality as an explanatory structure, the interest in the distorting effect of technical understanding on subjectivity. These positions characterize the Frankfurt School critique of positivism and scientism, especially Horkheimer and Adorno's *Dialectic of Enlightenment*.[12] And a critical theorist will also be familiar with the dilemma posed by Miller's argument: it offers nowhere to go. The ideology of technology is all-pervasive and dominates every social institution; technology cannot be engaged, except on its own ground. Miller unconvincingly poses science as an alternative to technology, but the optimism of her remedy is mocked by the despair of her analysis.[13]

For writers concerned with the issues of critical theory, two directions for resolving this dilemma have emerged. The first, represented by deconstruction and poststructuralism, broadens the critique of instrumental discourse, refusing to exempt from criticism the categories of reflection and subjectivity. For Horkheimer and Adorno, these were the very categories that initiated the emancipatory activity of critique, however circumscribed the terrain of emancipation had become. For my purposes, the deconstructive and poststructuralist approaches are not useful: they cannot open a passage out of the dilemma posed by the *Dialectic of Enlightenment*. Both methods are so global that the fine structure of technical discourse is invisible to them. For adherents to either approach, an investigation that focussed on such unselfconscious, unmediated texts as design manuals would be anomalous. There is no point in demonstrating that a manual for troubleshooting a power plant expresses a metaphysic of presence.

An alternate way of resolving the dilemma of critical theory is suggested by Jürgen Habermas's theory of communicative competence. Rather than approaching the critique of technical discourse through the topic of interest, such as analysis would focus on questions of objectification and understanding, on what is communicated in technical discourse. What does its objectification of the world reveal and conceal? What relations among readers and writers does this objectification create? What is revealed, and what is hidden, in conventional positivistic studies of such discourse? What other critical and hermeneutic methods can be used to study technical discourse?

Such a project is also an extension of critical theory, addressing one of its central concerns—the differentiation of reason. In the case of technical, scientific, and professional writing, we encounter an internal differentiation of instrumental discourse, its resolution into distinct, local, and mutually incomprehensible forms, forms that nevertheless share certain assumptions and shape similar relations between writers and readers.

A concrete example would be useful at this point. The problem I wish to examine will form the "text" for my analysis, much as a work of literature might form the "text" for a literary critic.[14] Drawn from the work of a writer of manuals for a large Detroit auto-body manufacturer, my "text" has some of the contours of the cases, the realistic writing assignments, that technical-writing students work with. It demonstrates strikingly the contradictions and paradoxes implicit in ordinary technical documents. I will present the case and then analyze it in terms of Jürgen Habermas's notion of communicative competence, arguing that this method allows us both to grasp the specificity of technical discourse and to maintain a critical distance from its derationalization. I will then suggest some problems with Habermas's theory and consider the pedagogical implications of my analysis.

The problem is to write the manuals required for computer-assisted redesign of an auto-body section. Like any good rhetorician, the author in this case begins with an analysis of her audience. She locates four levels of readers. The ranking reader, the project supervisor, is immediately discounted as a significant audience: she imagines him glancing at the graphics and format, but not using the manual or even really examining it closely. The other three kinds of readers will each, the writer feels, require a separate manual; the systems programmer, the application programmer, and the design engineer will all enter the project with competing desires and interests. The systems programmer is concerned with the overall operation of the computer, with the translation of program instructions into specific circuits, and with the simultaneous management of all the programs. The applications programmer will write the program for this specific design task, translating the visual information of the design into logical operations that càn be coded and understood by the computer. The design engineer, or "user," who is significantly nicknamed the "console jockey," does the actual work of redesigning.

This division of labor generates competing orientations toward their work among the three classes of readers: systems programmers want to guard their knowledge of the workings of the computer and so tend to be secretive and possessive. The applications programmer appears as their enemy, ready to "tweak" or "jiggle" the computer to make his or her job easier, jeopardizing the overall performance of the system. If the systems programmer and the application programmer are seen in clear, almost allegorical outlines by the manual writer, the user is presented in quite contradictory terms. On the one hand, he is only interested in the narrowest job-related problems: "The user wants to know—and this is basically all he wants to know—how do I do my job, how do I move that line, how do I rotate that line." On the other hand, the user is a dangerously curious, almost demonic, searcher after knowledge: "Once the user has it [information used in writing the program] the temptation then is to start manipulating and maneuvering and playing around with those programs. It's—well, it's just irresistible." The competing interests of those three audiences generate a rhetorical plan. The manual writer will produce three documents, with three different levels of information. The system programmer's manual will discuss memory and machine performance, and will take into account his tactics for guarding specialized knowledge—giving the program a strange name, making the code difficult to trace. The applications programmer will have a separate manual, telling him how to do a series of specific coding operations. And the user will be taught how to operate the console, but nothing whatever about the computer or its program: "It's an odd kind of thing in this environment because in many ways the user is most ignorant. He knows the least about the computer graphic system, absolutely the least. And yet . . . that's your engineer . . . but yet all he needs, all he should have, ever, is what he needs for that job and not, absolutely not, one word more." The word *deskilling* could have been invented to describe this situation, and this example certainly fits Harry Braverman's prophetic analysis of the mechanized work situation in *Labor and Monopoly Capital.*[15] It supports one of Braverman's key insights: this odd communicative situation is generated, not by the technology of the computer, but by the social relations of the corporation. Not all organizations that use computers develop such a rigid division of labor; in a research and development facility, for example, the computer might be used to widen access to information. But any large industrial organization that uses a computer for production design will face the problem of protecting the overall operation of the system. Given the segmentation of technical work that is the rule in such corporations, the most convenient way of protecting the system is to restrict access to information.

These constraints only sharpen the basic paradox: a very powerful and expensive tool for generating information has produced a system of suppressing and segmenting it, a system that is not enforced by an external supervision or by the authority of management, but by the social relations among its users. While the relations among workers in Braverman's preindustrial workplace enabled them to resist the process of deskilling, the relations among workers in our example lead them to enforce and accelerate this process.

No individual, least of all the supervisor, has direct knowledge or understanding of all phases of the design process. The systems engineer may understand the computer intimately, but he is indifferent to what is being designed. The user understands the product, but not the tool that produced it. Both the applications programmer and the manual writer play limited, facilitating roles, and the overall supervisor, who is responsible for making decisions, may have only the most general understanding of any of the three technical processes under his or her nominal control.

Having outlined the situation, let me begin to apply some concepts from Habermas's early work to an analysis of it. This conjuncture is not so arbitrary as it might at first seem. Before developing a theory of communicative action, Habermas worked with questions of science and technology, and, in *Knowledge and Human Interests,* developed a notion of instrumental discourse as the peculiar discourse of the natural sciences.[16] He was concerned to define the kinds of knowledge and discourse characterizing the natural sciences, hermeneutics, and critical writing. For the natural sciences, he faced two problems: to provide an alternative to the almost entirely pessimistic analysis of "instrumental reason" elaborated by Horkheimer and Adorno in *Dialectic of Enlightenment,* and to counter the positivistic and delusive "self-understanding of the natural sciences" that recognized no claims to truth but those generated by the scientific method as it was traditionally understood. Habermas approached that problem by using C. S. Peirce's consensus theory of truth, modified to take into account the historical and social situation of scientific investigation. Habermas described the instrumental discourse of the natural sciences as "universal judgments having the form of lawlike hypotheses"

(p. 121), a description that fits our case very accurately. Statements about the memory, circuitry, or coding operations of the computer, like statements about materials or stress relations that might be found in the design problem, will in fact be derived from such universal judgments.

The formation of universal judgments in instrumental discourse, Habermas said, acquires its meaning only from the system of reference of possible *feedback-controlled action*. Its goal is the elimination of behavioral uncertainty. And indeed, within the universe of discourse I have described, feedback systems are highly developed: the designer gets information about design performance; the applications programmer and systems programmer monitor computer functions. Feedback is the source of meaning and verification: within the system, the desire to avoid uncertainty is a very powerful control: "Now your systems programmer says, 'Wait a minute. He [the applications programmer] is going to want seventy-five different programs, thousands of lines to code. What's that going to do to my computer?' " The close relation between knowledge and action characteristic of instrumental discourse is probably more apparent in this industrial example than in the pure sciences that Habermas and Peirce were discussing, but Habermas's summary is exact: "The sentence can be understood as the *formulation* of the plan or intention that guides the *operation*" (p. 127).

Habermas was not, of course, primarily interested in recovering a rhetoric of instrumental texts. (*Rhetorical* is a slightly derogatory term to Habermas.) But one of his comments suggests a central rhetorical feature of such discourse—its monologic character. Indeed, writers of directions are urged by their teachers to cultivate a monologic style: they are advised to use the imperative mood, to assert authority in opening sections, to segment information, and to minimize theoretical explanations. Habermas used the monologic character of instrumental discourse to indicate the faulty self-understanding of the physical sciences and to move to the second of his three interests generating knowledge, the interest in understanding. And it is in analyzing this transition that we find gaps between Habermas's theory of interests and the norms of technical discourse. Habermas held that the monologic tone of scientific discourse perpetuates the illusion that the ground of such discourse is the "purposive rational action" toward which it is directed, the sphere of plans and operations that, as we have seen, organizes instrumental discourse. But, as Habermas pointed out, discourse among investigators is actually grounded in "symbolic interaction among societal subjects who reciprocally know and recognize each other as individuals" (p. 137). There may be some forms of scientific writing—a controversy among scientists or a debate about social uses of scientific techniques—which do in fact fit this description; they are symbolic interactions among reciprocally recognized subjects. In these cases, the objective and universal form of discourse conceals an intersubjective relation, a relation directed toward understanding. But in our example, no such relation holds: the goal of the discourse is systematic misunderstanding and concealment; the subjective responses of readers and writers are irrelevant, and the monologic voice conceals, not a dialogic relation, but the total fragmentation and dispersal of knowledge.

Perhaps the problem does not lie in Habermas's typology of interests producing knowledge, but in our employment of it. Almost surely, Habermas and Peirce were both thinking of scientific research, rather than of its technical applications, in their discussion of technical reason. Another, less honorific category in Habermas's thought might be applicable to our example: systematically distorted communication. The notion of systematically distorted communication was implicit in Habermas's discussion of Freud in *Knowledge and Human Interests,* and it was explicitly developed in his later essay "On the Systematic Distortion of Communication."[17] Habermas distinguished systematically distorted communication by three criteria, and those criteria match our example very closely:

1. The discourse deviates from recognized linguistic rules. This criterion, we should note, reflects a naive understanding of linguistic rules and how they are formed. Nevertheless, writers and readers of technical discourse almost obsessively point out its systematic divergence from both colloquial and academic language: it is heavily nominalized, relies on the passive voice, is highly redundant, and is organized to suit the peculiar reading styles of executives and technicians. A technical report, then, is a document intended to meet the needs of several divergent classes of readers, none of whom will read it continuously from beginning to end, some of whom will start it at the middle, and the most socially

important of whom will probably read only its first page. All of these features of technical discourse are quite rule-bound, of course, just as Freud's grammar of dreams was rule-bound, but the rules of technical discourse produce a distinct syntactic and semantic register that is recognized as deviant (even debased), unlike the equally distinct but privileged discourse of, say, sermons.[18]

2. Behaviorally, systematically distorted communication produces rigidity and compulsory repetition. Again, in our case, behaviors such as secrecy and possessiveness ("my computer") have clearly developed their own irrational force, leading to mutual distrust and a total breakdown of what Habermas would call "steering functions." Nonetheless, these relations are reproduced from project to project, year after year. The answer to a question about how a writer learns to decide who gets what information: "The hard way. On the job, you really do."

3. Finally, systematically distorted communication is marked by discrepancies among its levels. And indeed, in our case, the messages conflict very seriously. The ostensible function of a manual, after all, is to convey information, to enable a reader to do something. But these manuals take on the illocutionary force and syntactic form of commands, directives whose force—in this case—depends on the information they withhold. Obviously, any document that functions within a large organization will serve a variety of purposes, not all of them harmoniously related. But in this example, there is a fundamental disparity between the overt purpose of the writing and its concrete function. That disparity leads to other discrepancies among levels of the message. The user, for example, is simultaneously held to be uninterested in information about how the computer functions and to be possessed by an uncontrollable desire to use this knowledge.

There is, however, a crucial difference between Habermas's notion of systematically distorted communication and the discourse in our example: systematically distorted communication is a deformation of some more normal or rectified form of speech. It can be therapeutically interpreted—Habermas's example, of course, is the psychoanalyst's relation to the patient—so that material that has not been adequately symbolized can emerge for consciousness and be expressed in public discourse. But in this instance, no therapeutic rectification of discourse is possible: for these readers, engaged in this production, specific deformations of information and suppressions of knowledge have already been determined by their social relations: this discourse is indeed "the formulation of a plan or intention that guides an operation," so that without renouncing the operation, no normalized version of the discourse can exist. Further, while this discourse is marked by gaps, discontinuities, and silences, its deformed quality is not unconscious; it is an open secret. Habermas's later reservations about the privileged character of the therapist within the analysis of systematically distorted communication, and his remarks on the dangers of extending the psychoanalytic model to social theory both apply to my example from technical discourse.[19] But they must be extended. A therapist of technical discourse could neither restore this discourse to rationality nor illuminate social relationships by exposing the irrational quality of the discourse: there is nothing to restore, and nothing has been hidden. Finally, since there is no one who understands the whole process, there is no possible therapist.[20]

Neither the model of instrumental discourse nor the model of systematically distorted communication, then, does justice to the problematic character of this case in technical writing, although both of these concepts do reveal some of its traits. Perhaps we should consider that the writing we are discussing is not an instance of communication at all. Perhaps it might better be analyzed in terms of Habermas's early distinction between interaction and labor, or his current distinction between the communicative processes of symbolic reproduction and the functional systems of social reproduction, specifically the functional systems organized by the media of money and power.[21] Our example would fall under the category of labor rather than communication, of system-conserving speech rather than symbolic communication. The distinction between interaction and labor, which Habermas first developed in *Toward a Rational Society* and to which, in different terms, he has returned throughout his work, separates purposive rational action from social interaction.[22] Purposive rational action, which includes both material labor and certain kinds of language, has control for its object—control of nature, of individuals, of society. It is rule-governed, oriented toward success, and sanctioned by concrete results. Social interaction can either be strategic—that is, goal-oriented—or communicative—oriented toward understanding. As Thomas McCarthy points out, this typology can also be used analytically: instrumental activity is normally embedded in social interaction.[23] And, indeed, we can distinguish a purposive rational level from a strategic level in our text. The writer wants door mouldings to fit doors, she wants the computer to keep on functioning, and she also recognizes that her work is expected to preserve lines of authority and restrict access to information. She must accomplish a purpose and respond to a strategy. But, as we saw in our earlier analysis, these aspects of communication do not simply sit quietly down together: they are interdependent and contradictory. From a discussion of this interdependence and contradiction, we can arrive at Habermas's notion of communicative competence, at the pedagogical implications of this example, and at the elements of an intersubjective rhetoric.

We can begin crudely, by indentifying the instrumental level of this discourse with what is said, with information conveyed in a series of manuals, and the strategic level with what is unsaid, with information withheld for purposes of social control. The relations between these purposive rational and strategic levels are ideologically justified under the figure of the individual instance and the general rule: maybe it would be all right for him to know the code this time, but what will he do next time? But, in fact, the establishment of a pattern of distorted and interrupted communication is a costly derationalization, although it appeared to be rational to each of the privileged classes among our readers. We might reverse the force of the comparison between the individual and the general: it may be functional for a systems analyst to restrict his knowledge, but what happens to an overall system in which knowledge is generally restricted? Such a system would be (and is) burdened with an elaborate communicative apparatus, one of whose functions is to block communication. Any genuine steering function is dispersed. The strategic aim of maintaining restricted information conflicts with the purposive rational aim of designing a new car. What is absent in the text controls what is present.

By looking more closely at this contradiction, we may be able to move through it to Habermas's notion of communicative competence. Let us first consider the nature of "strategic action." Strategy is a category relevant to warfare and problem-solving. Who, here, is the enemy, and what is the problem to be managed? The answer is somewhat jolting: the enemy is a desire for knowledge, a pleasure in knowing, even in simply being able to manipulate the apparatus. What must be managed, and managed by exclusion, is a kind of discourse—free, goal-oriented, but subversive of social boundaries. The writer imputes this desire to all the participants in the discourse situation. Counterfactually, then, this system recognizes the basic presupposition for Habermas's ideal speech situation: the availability of all discursive roles to all participants. Or putting it more simply, all the participants in this situation structure their discourse as if every other participant wanted access to all possible roles, both in the purposive rational project and in the subjective relations surrounding it. We can speak, therefore, even in this bleak situation, of an aspiration to communicative action.

It is within this context that Habermas's notions of the claims implied in communicative action and of the development of communicative competence become relevant, both to the analysis I have been elaborating and to the problems of pedagogy. If the participants in this situation are seen as desiring communicative action, it is reasonable to ask what such action would look like and how these readers and writers might perform it.

Habermas sees communicative competence as the ability to enter into a dialogue in which statements are assumed to be true, appropriate, sincere, and comprehensible. Any of these assumptions can be questioned by any participant. In such an "ideal speech situation," relations of force and manipulation do not obtain. Obviously, ideal speech situations are not normally realized in social life, as indeed Habermas is aware. The ideal speech situation is to be seen less as an existing structure than as a critical representation of those forms of communicative rationality which we only encounter, Habermas says, as "traces" and partial realizations.[24] It is still useful, however, to consider how those traces and fragments might be composed, to conceive of relations of discourse in which aspirations to communicative action might be fulfilled.

But it may be that Habermas understands the growth of communicative competence too simply. In describing the development of communicative competence, Habermas, following Piaget in a quite problematic way, posits a series of stages of cognitive development, beginning with the child's understanding of the external world and moving to the development of his or her capabilities for symbolic interaction. For Habermas, then, the capability for purposive-rational action is established once and for all as a relatively early developmental task, and further growth of this capability is simply a matter of accumulating knowledge. The ability to solve the problems of social interaction, however, develops more slowly, evolving more rational and universifiable forms and serving (in Habermas's most problematic move) as the "pacemaker of social evolution."[25] What our analysis here suggests, however, is that the two capacities are not so clearly separated and do not develop so simply. It is not simply a matter of these two capacities being interdependent. Rather, just as strategic action is embedded in purposive rational activity, the aspiration for autonomous discourse is embedded in distorted and constrained communication; both kinds of language are deeply affected by this embedding. Purposive rational action is, in this case, compromised by the needs of dominant groups to block communicative action. And communicative action emerges in this situation, not as a well-formed, propositionally differentiated, and institutionally unbound speech act, but as the irresistible desire to tweak a computer. To be sure, the convergence between these categories would probably not disturb Habermas, who has always presented his theory as an analysis of aspects of discourse rather than a description of a concrete situation. But this close relationship also suggests that Habermas's appropriation of Piaget is at odds with the basic impulses of his theory. Not only does that model make the development of symbolic interaction an unproblematic, purely cognitive process, not only is it open to the charge of premature universalization, but it also rests on a segmentation and isolation of the very discourse forms that establish its basic categories.

To see communicative action as embedded in purposive rational discourse, however, opens up some pedagogical possibilities for a teacher of technical writing. For one thing, it offers an alternative to both messianic and therapeutic models of pedagogy—models which propose the teacher as the bearer of the correct ideology or as the liberator of such ideology as it is imputed to students. The technical-writing teacher is seldom tempted to romanticize his or her work: this is, in the language of curriculum planners, simply a service course. But an understanding of technical discourse that saw it as simply the discourse of domination, and messianically attempted to expose it to students, would present serious problems: a teacher who took this strategy seriously could only abstain from teaching technical writing. More seriously, this messianic notion of teaching renders technical discourse itself invisible: such discourse is simply domination, simply disinformation, and so its particular structures and motions remain obscure. Such a model of teaching could imply a virtually prescientific or, as Habermas would say, a "dedifferentiated" vision of the objective world, in which technical discourse is globally condemned. On the other hand, a therapeutic model of pedagogy would search for the rectified text beneath this distorted communication and search for ways to prompt students in producing this text. We have already seen the problems implied in that conception: there is no rectified text, no qualified therapist. Our aim, rather, should be to work with the contradiction between purposive rational and strategic action, using that contradiction to raise the possibility of entering into communicative action. Such a strategy would ask students and teachers to investigate the specificity of technical discourse, especially as that discourse emerges in the network of social relations on the job.

It would be appropriate to close my comments on this case by outlining how such an investigation might be carried out in the instance of writing a set of directions. We might begin by making overt the authority claim implied in a set of directions and locating this claim within the syntax of the text. We can read directions as expansions of the statement, "I am telling you to do something." Authority claims can be located in each of the major syntactic elements of this statement:

I—The directions can claim authority because of the personal or institutional power of the speaker, as with a court order given by a judge.

am telling—The style or format of the directions can be exploited to give them credibility, as with especially clear or technically very sophisticated directions.

you—The directions express a special relationship with a reader and deserve to be followed for that reason, as with spiritual advice.

to do something—The activity to be performed is presented as intrinsically important. Doctors' orders rely on this claim.

Authority claims can also be questioned on each of these grounds:

Who are you to tell me what to do? (questions *I*)
I can't really follow these directions. (questions *am telling*)
You're asking the impossible. (questions *you*, the writer's understanding of the reader.)
I won't do that. (questions *to do something*)

Such an analysis connects questions about rhetoric with those about authority, and a set of topics for making and contesting authority claims can be constructed from it.

The claims I have just catalogued are analogous to those of truth, sincerity, comprehensibility, and appropriateness—claims that are, according to Habermas, implied in communicative actions. Claims based on the credibility of the writer resemble claims of appropriateness or sincerity; claims based on the relationship to the reader resemble those of appropriateness; claims based on style recall the claim to comprehensibility; and claims based on the nature of the action to be performed resemble claims of truth or appropriateness. This analogy suggests a way of superseding the limits of purposive-rational language, since it is by questioning the claims of truth, sincerity, comprehensibility, and appropriateness that we move from communication to discourse. What happens to a speech situation when one of the authority claims implied in a set of directions is questioned?

For Habermas, to question a validity claim implicit in communicative action is to bring communication to an end and to begin discourse, or discussion directed toward reestablishing agreement on basic principles, so that the consensus enabling communicative action can be resumed. When the authority claims implied in purposive rational discourse are questioned, however, the reader and writer do not necessarily redeem that claim in discourse. Instead, they undertake some strategic discussions that will either resolve the matter prudentially or will move their discussion into the realm of communicative action. If a reader disagrees with the goal of a set of directions, for example, and questions the authority of the writer or his agent to enforce that goal, the two would probably not open a general discourse on social legitimation. Rather, both parties would first attempt to direct the agenda of their talk strategically. Only if these negotiations are happily resolved will the impulse toward communicative action be satisfied, and it will be satisfied, not with a discussion of first principles, but with a limited, finite discussion of problems in the design of auto bodies or the wisdom of console jockeys learning something about coding. If Habermas opens a door between communicative action and the "upper story" of discourse, I am proposing that a door can also be opened between communicative action and the "lower story" of strategic and purposive-rational writing. A pedagogy for technical writing would begin, then, by teaching students the conventional structures of purposive-rational discourse, but then go on to identify the rhetoric of strategic claims to authority, to demonstrate the contradictions between these strategic claims and the purposive-rational intention of technical discourse, and to suggest how such claims can be contested. In all of this activity, the teacher's aim is not to teach students how to "write for success," although it would be irresponsible and futile to ignore the problems students face as writers on the job—problems which are deeply rooted in social relations and not open to simple rhetorical solutions. Rather, our aim would be to work with the structures of technical discourse so that students can negotiate their demands but also be aware of the limited but real possibility of moving beyond them. Even in the highly conventional and restricted boundaries of technical discourse, an impulse for communicative action emerges; we can identify the relations of power that block that desire and offer strategies for subverting that power, for betraying it into communicative action.

These are indeed modest goals, and rightly so; the technical-writing teacher figures in no myths of the vanguard. But I think it is significant that Habermas provides a framework within which even the most prosaic kinds of writing can be connected to fundamental impulses toward emancipation. And, if we move from the forbidding territory of technical writing into the more even terrain of general rhetorical studies, then Habermas's work becomes even more significant. I would like to conclude, then, with a few remarks suggesting how an intersubjective rhetoric could be derived from Habermas's work.

Such a rhetoric would begin by asserting, against the linguistic determinism of current literary studies and against the simple subjectivism of professional composition theory, the intersubjective creation of meaning. The controlling paradigm of composition theory holds that meaning is something generated in the heads of writers, imperfectly realized in speech or writing, and simply transmitted to the more or less understanding reader. This paradigm, obviously, draws heavily on general semantic theory. In current literary studies, the tendency is rather to see utterance as realizing the operations or structure of language itself and to define meanings in terms of either finite oppositions or the free play of differences, both of which operate regardless of the intention of individual writers or speakers. The general semantic position, I would hold, naively ignores the force of social structures in establishing the boundaries of discourse; the structuralist and poststructuralist positions seem to exclude those possibilities of criticism and dialogue that we would want to open for our students, including criticism of the material relations of social production and critical dialogue oriented to emancipation. An intersubjective rhetoric would recognize that language, the ground in which intersubjectivity is realized, is no natural or neutral instrument. But it would also see language as a social creation, open to transformation.

Such a rhetoric would refuse to confine itself to the normal topics of a composition course—organization, usage, the conventions of an academic paper. A rhetoric that takes into account Habermas's typology of the validity claims implicit in communicative action will refuse to leave the truth of a text, its claim to represent the objective world and social life adequately, to be determined by the appropriate specialized discipline. Without quarrelling fruitlessly with the post-Enlightenment differentiation of discourses, an intersubjective rhetoric would attempt to transform public discourse so that questions of truth would no longer be reduced to matters of professional judgment. And students of rhetoric could also treat the themes of domination, of reification, of the humane handling of private discourse, under the rubric of the "rightness" of communication. Both of these categories are more powerful than their traditional rhetorical equivalents—the well-formed argument, the appropriate tone.

An intersubjective rhetoric would accept as its paradigmatic situation the communication of equals who attempt to understand each other, not because such communication is "normal" or usual, but because it is normative: it generates the expectations with which we enter speech situations. An intersubjective rhetoric would describe the development of such texts and distinguish the figures and stances that characterize them, just as classical rhetoric paid close attention to the characteristic forms of persuasive oratory. But unlike classical rhetoric, an intersubjective rhetoric will never meet a fully realized text: no ideal communicative situation exists in our society. An intersubjective rhetoric, then, is the rhetoric of the limiting case, or, to use Raymond Williams's term, of the emergent form—an attempt to project forms of communication from their fragmentary and partial realizations.

An intersubjective rhetoric would not be fundamentally oriented to the production of student papers or to training students in the norms of bureaucratic discourse, although teachers and students would analyze such forms of writing and would investigate how they are produced—as with our example from technical writing. The speech communities that produce such texts are deeply contradictory: they recognize the claims of communicative rationality while they actively block communicative action. In the case of the speech community formed through academic discourse, which is the community that students are immediately concerned with, an intersubjective rhetoric would insist that its values and norms are open to critical inquiry, especially by students who are being inducted into them.

An intersubjective rhetoric would also be concerned with the self-development of students and would see itself as fostering their aspiration to communicative action. It would therefore contest both cognitive development theories, which hold that students cannot write because they do not know how to think, because they have not completed their most basic intellectual development, and also contest various "skills" approaches, which see students as behavioral monads who need to practice basic syntactic operations.

Finally, an intersubjective rhetoric would be interested in absolutely unheroic communication. Its privileged text would not be the journal detailing a student's most private thoughts, nor the passionate statement of rebellion, nor the closely argued analysis of U.S. policy in El Salvador, but rather directions for working a printing press, a description of how patients are treated at a community clinic, a lexicon of the words used to refer to women. Such a rhetoric would share the impetus of Habermas's own project: "Ideas of successful interaction, of reciprocity and distance, of separation and manageable yet not failed nearness, of vulnerability and complementary caution. All of these images of protection, openness and compassion, of submission and resistance rise out of a 'horizon of experience,' to use Brecht's words, of 'friendly life together.' This friendliness does not exclude conflicts, rather it focuses on those human forms by way of which one can survive them."[26]

NOTES

1. Lester Faigley and Thomas Miller, "What We Learn from Writing on the Job," *College English* 44: 6 (October 1982): 557–69.

2. Thomas E. Pearsall, "The State of Technical Writing," paper presented at the annual meeting of the Midwest Regional Conference on English in the Two-Year College (Minneapolis, Minn., February 19–21, 1981), p. 1.

3. Donald Cunningham and John Mitchell, "Teaching the Writing of Instructions," from *Courses, Components, and Exercises in Technical Communication,* ed. Dwight Stevenson (Urbana, Ill.: National Council of Teachers of English, 1981), p. 141.

4. Dwight W. Stevenson, "Audience Analysis across Cultures," *Journal of Technical Writing and Communication* 13: 4, (1983): 319–30.

5. Tom Griggs, "Editing in Nigeria—an Informal Study," *Journal of Technical Writing and Communications* 13: 3 (1983): 249.

6. David Covington and Clifford Knowne, "A Survey of Technical Communication Students: Attitudes, Skills, and Aspirations," *Journal of Technical Writing and Communications* 13: 3 (1983): 206.

7. Max Horkheimer and Theodor Adorno, *Dialectic of Enlightenment,* trans. John Cumming (New York: Seabury, 1972).

8. For articles focussed on technical discourse by Flower and her associates, see "Revising Functional Documents: The Scenario Principle," by Linda Flower, John Hayes, and Heidi Swarts, in *New Essays in Technical and Scientific Communication: Research, Theory, Practice,* ed. Paul Anderson et al. (Farmingdale: Baywood, 1983), and Linda Flower, "Communication Strategy in Professional Writing: Teaching a Rhetorical Case," in Stevenson, *Courses, Components, and Exercises in Technical Communication,* pp. 34–46. For articles representative of their general method, see Linda Flower and John Hayes, "Identifying the Organization of Writing Processes," in *Cognitive Processes in Writing,* ed. L. W. Gregg and E. R. Steinberg (Hillsdale, N.J.: Lawrence Erlbaum, 1980), "The Cognition of Discovery: Defining a Rhetorical Problem," *College Composition and Communication* 31 (1980): 21–32, "The Cognitive Process Theory of Writing," *College Composition and Communication* 32

(1981): 365–87, and "Images, Plans, and Prose: The Representation of Meaning in Writing," *Written Communication* 1 (January 1984): 120–60.

9. Flower and Hayes, "The Cognition of Discovery," 30–32.

10. Elizabeth Harris, "In Defense of a Liberal-Arts Approach to Technical Writing," *College English* 44: 6 (October 1982): 628–36. See also Harris's "A Theoretical Perspective on 'How To' Discourse," in Anderson, *New Essays in Technical and Scientific Communication,* pp. 139–56.

11. Carolyn Miller, "Technology as a Form of Consciousness: A Study of Contemporary Ethos," *Central States Speech Journal* 29 (Winter 1978): 227–36.

12. An application of this critique to the problems of teaching writing appears in Stanley Aronowitz, "Mass Culture and the Eclipse of Reason: The Implications for Pedagogy," *College English* 38: 8 (April 1977): 768–74.

13. For the artificiality of the distinction between science and technology, see James P. Zappen, "A Rhetoric for the Sciences and Technologies," in Anderson, *New Essays in Technical and Scientific Communication,* pp. 123–39. Zappen shows that scientific and technical writing are produced by the same writers, share similar forms, and respond to similar concerns.

14. This example was related by Ruth Reed at the February 1983 meeting of the Professional Writing Project at Detroit, Michigan, under the joint sponsorship of Wayne State University and the Fund for the Improvement of Post-Secondary Education. The analysis presented in this paper, while heavily indebted to the work of the Professional Writing Project, does not reflect their views.

15. Harry Braverman, *Labor and Monopoly Capital: The Degradation of Work in the Twentieth Century* (New York: Monthly Review Press, 1974).

16. Jürgen Habermas, *Knowledge and Human Interests,* trans. Jeremy Shapiro (Boston: Beacon Press, 1971), pp. 65–140. Subsequent citations will be given parenthetically.

17. Jürgen Habermas, "On the Systematic Distortion of Communication," *Inquiry* 13 (1971): 205–18.

18. For a critique of the unitary understanding of grammar in Habermas, see Rainer Nägele, "Freud, Habermas, and the Dialectic of Enlightenment: On Real and Ideal Discourses," *New German Critique* 22 (Winter 1981): 41–62.

19. See Habermas's remarks on the "Organization of Enlightenment" in the Introduction to *Theory and Practice* (Boston: Beacon, 1973), pp. 28–32.

20. This stricture includes the writer, whose understanding of the technical processes involved in the problem is necessarily both indirect and incomplete.

21. For the distinction between labor and interaction, see "Remarks on Hegel's Jena *Philosophy of Mind*" in *Theory and Practice,* pp. 142–70. For more current theory, see "A Reply to My Critics," in *Habermas: Critical Debates,* ed. John B. Thompson and David Held (Cambridge, Mass.: MIT Press, 1982), pp. 278–81.

22. Jürgen Habermas, *Toward a Rational Society: Student Protest, Science, and Politics,* trans. Jeremy Shapiro (Boston, Mass.: Beacon Press, 1971).

23. Thomas McCarthy, *The Critical Theory of Jürgen Habermas* (Cambridge, Mass.: MIT Press, 1978; rptd. 1981), pp. 16–40.

24. Jürgen Habermas, "The Entwinement of Myth and Enlightenment: Re-Reading *Dialectic of Enlightenment,*" *New German Critique* 26 (Summer 1982): 30.

25. Jürgen Habermas, "Moral Development and Ego Identity," in *Communication and the Evolution of Society,* trans. Thomas McCarthy (Boston: Beacon Press, 1979), pp. 69–95. See also McCarthy's critique of this theory in "Rationality and Relativism: Habermas' 'Overcoming' of Hermeneutics" in Thompson and Held, eds., *Habermas: Critical Debates,* pp. 57–79.

26. Jürgen Habermas, "The Dialectics of Rationalization: An Interview with Jürgen Habermas," *Telos* 49 (Fall 1978): 28.

Notes on Contributors

LAWRENCE GROSSBERG teaches speech communication and criticism and interpretive theory at the University of Illinois. He is the author of numerous essays in critical theory and the coeditor of *Marxism and the Interpretation of Culture* (forthcoming). He is presently coauthoring a book with Stuart Hall and Jennifer Slack.

ALBERT D. HUTTER teaches English, comparative literature, and critical theory at UCLA. He also holds a Ph.D. in psychoanalysis and maintains a part-time practice in Los Angeles. In addition to articles on psychoanalytic theory, he is the author of short stories and a novel, *The Death Mechanic*. He is presently completing *Dickens and Detective Fiction*.

VINCENT B. LEITCH teaches English at Mercer University and is the author of *Deconstructive Criticism: An Advanced Introduction* and the editor of *The Poetry of Extonia: Essays in Comparative Analysis*. He is presently completing a history of American criticism.

S. P. MOHANTY teaches English at Cornell University, where he is also managing editor of *Diacritics*. He has edited a collection of essays entitled *Marx after Derrida* and is currently completing *Criticism as Politics: The Ways to History*.

CARY NELSON teaches English and criticism and interpretive theory at the University of Illinois, where he was also the founding director of the Unit for Criticism and Interpretive Theory. He is the author of *The Incarnate Word: Literature as Verbal Space* and *Our Last First Poets: Vision and History in Contemporary American Poetry* and the coeditor of *Marxism and the Interpretation of Culture* and *W. S. Merwin: Essays on the Poetry*, both forthcoming. He is presently completing *Reading Criticism: The Literary Status of Critical Discourse*.

CONSTANCE PENLEY teaches English, film, and criticism and interpretive theory at the University of Rochester. She is one of the founding coeditors of *Camera Obscura* and is presently completing a book on the status of the photographic image in film.

WILLIAM SCHROEDER teaches philosophy and criticism and interpretive theory at the University of Illinois. He is the author of *Sartre and His Predecessors: The Self and the Other*. He is presently completing a book on philosophy and film.

PAULA A. TREICHLER teaches medical communication, communication, women's studies, and criticism and interpretive theory at the University of Illinois. She is coauthor of *A Feminist Dictionary* and coeditor of *For Alma Mater: Theory and Practice in Feminist Scholarship*. She is presently coediting the guidelines for nonsexist writing for the Modern Language Association, editing a collection on feminism and language, and completing a book on women's writing.

SUSAN WELLS teaches English at Temple University. She is the author of *The Dialectics of Representation* and is currently completing a book on Habermas.

LB2331 .T44 1986   010101 000

Theory in the classroom / edit

0 2002 0005372 2

YORK COLLEGE OF PENNSYLVANIA 17403

LB 2331 .T44 1986

Theory in the classroom

DISCARDED

YORK COLLEGE
PENNSYLVANIA

Servire est vivere

LIBRARY